Storytelling Industries

"At a time when most scholars seem preoccupied with the fading borders between different media platforms and industries, Anthony Smith's book provides a rich and much-needed reminder about the importance of categorising media in boxes. Smith's book delves into the kinds of unique narrative trends that have emerged in television, comics, videogames and beyond, tracing how particular contexts of production and platform have led to specific opportunities to tell stories."
—Matthew Freeman, *Reader in Transmedia Communication, Bath Spa University, UK*

Anthony N. Smith

Storytelling Industries

Narrative Production in the 21st Century

Anthony N. Smith
University of Salford
Salford, UK

ISBN 978-3-319-70596-5   ISBN 978-3-319-70597-2 (eBook)
https://doi.org/10.1007/978-3-319-70597-2

Library of Congress Control Number: 2018934709

This Palgrave Macmillan imprint is published by the registered company Springer International Publishing AG part of Springer Nature.
The registered company address is: Gewerbestrasse 11, 6330 Cham, Switzerland

ACKNOWLEDGEMENTS

I am keen to acknowledge the help given to me during the lengthy undertaking of this book's creation. Roberta Pearson and Elizabeth Evans provided me with a substantial amount of expert counsel. Jason Mittell and Catherine Johnson supplied valuable feedback on an early version of this work. The following generously offered me advice or encouragement along the way: Paula Blair, Will Brooker, Martin Flanagan, Matthew Freeman, Mark Gallagher, Paul Grainge, Richard Hewett, JP Kelly, Amanda Lotz, Paul McDonald, Daniel New, Sean O'Sullivan, Debra Ramsay, Gianluca Sergi, Iain Smith, Jacob Smith, Julian Stringer and William Uricchio. Current and former members of the Palgrave Macmillan editorial team, including Lina Aboujieb, Karina Jákupsdóttir, Ellie Freedman and Chris Penfold, ably guided me along the road to publication. I am thankful to all of these fine people. I am furthermore forever grateful to Zoë, Lucinda and Aimee for the love and support they gave me throughout this process.

Parts of this book were previously published elsewhere. Parts of Chap. 3 first appeared (in an earlier form) as 'Putting the Premium into Basic: Slow-Burn Narrative and the Loss-Leader Function of AMC's Original Drama Series', *Television and New Media* 14:2 (March 2013), 150–166, and are reproduced here by permission of SAGE Publications. Parts of Chap. 4 first appeared (in an earlier form) as 'History Left Unsaid: Implied Continuity in Batman's Contemporary Comic Book Narratives' in Roberta Pearson, William Uricchio and Will Brooker (eds.) (2015) *Many More Lives of the Batman* (London: BFI), and are reproduced here by permission of Bloomsbury Publishing PLC.

CONTENTS

LIST OF FIGURES

CHAPTER 1

Introduction

Conditions for fictional storytelling in media have altered considerably in recent years. The production, distribution and consumption of narrative across a range of media have become increasingly digitalised and linked to the internet. An accompanying industrial move towards conglomeration has led to large media corporations circulating popular characters and stories across multiple media platforms. Media studies typically refers to these developments as processes of media convergence.[1] For many commentators, media convergence contexts undermine customary distinctions between popular narrative media. In their introduction to *New Narratives*, a collection focused on digital media storytelling, for example, Ruth Page and Bronwen Thomas claim that 'convergence' demonstrates 'the need to move beyond fixed categories and boundaries in attempting to respond to the ever shifting and evolving practices and affordances facilitated by new technologies'.[2]

This book challenges this position, stressing that the unique characteristics of traditionally differentiated media are essential to an understanding of contemporary popular narratives and wider media culture in the twenty-first century. It argues that distinct media are each characterised by unique industrial practices—such as particular approaches to content commissioning and distribution—that continue to preserve their identities and uniquely condition the ways in which their stories are told. Via a focus on popular storytelling forms—including film, television, comic-book and videogame series, it demonstrates how a given medium's production

© The Author(s) 2018
A. N. Smith, *Storytelling Industries*,
https://doi.org/10.1007/978-3-319-70597-2_1

2 A. N. SMITH

conditions influence producers' development and presentation of fictional narratives in the twenty-first century. As part of this process, the book considers the manner in which a medium's contexts:

- shape the characters, settings and storylines that make up fictional storyworlds;
- influence how storylines and character developments are plotted across a narrative;
- determine the techniques of style—such as approaches to mise-en-scène—by which narratives present storyworlds.

By placing a strong emphasis on the continued significance of medium-specific industrial contexts, the book distinguishes itself from various other cross-media studies of popular fictional narrative. Such studies include those focused on transmedia storytelling, an industrial practice whereby content producers coordinate the dissemination of a given storyworld's fragments across multiple media platforms, resulting in the presentation of a single coherent fictional narrative across media.[3] Examples of such works in this field include Henry Jenkins' *Convergence Culture: Where Old and New Media Collide*, Colin Harvey's *Fantastic Transmedia: Narrative, Play and Memory across Science Fiction and Fantasy Storyworlds* and Martin Flanagan, Mike McKenny and Andy Livingstone's *The Marvel Studios Phenomenon: Inside a Transmedia Universe*.[4] While these and other such key works provide useful and illuminating examinations of transmedia storytelling processes, the significance of a given medium's unique industrial culture to narrative creation is typically left under-explored within such analyses. Through a cross-media examination of popular fictional narrative that accounts for the primacy of a given medium's unique set of industrial contexts, this book provides, within media studies, a unique perspective on storytelling across media.

This overriding concern with the role of medium specificity within the narrative creation process ultimately aligns the book with moves in narrative theory to analyse the ways in which a given medium's unique combination of properties shapes storytelling. This field of transmedial narratology stresses the need to distinguish between the narrative capacities of one medium compared to another.[5] Shlomith Rimmon-Kenan, for example, asserts that a given medium's unique combination of properties 'open[s] up possibilities and impose[s] constraints' upon narrative.[6] As Chap. 2 establishes in detail, a medium can do so by affording (or withholding) the use of certain semiotic phenomena.[7] For example, the medium of television enables television producers to use words, images and/or sounds during their construction of a television drama episode. A medium's set of established cultural practices can further influence a narrative's constituent parts.[8] For example, as Chaps. 2 and 3 detail, the practice of inserting commercial breaks within transmissions of television drama episodes can influence producers to craft episode act structures that complement such insertions.

While this focus upon medium specificity within transmedial narratology has considerably influenced this book, a common trait among works from this field is to conceptualise an individual medium as a fixed homogeneous system and/or neglect to account for a medium's variable industrial conditions. An example of this tendency may be found in Helen Fulton's study of narrative and media. Fulton usefully observes the importance to narrative of industrial organisation within a medium. 'The economic structure of media industries determines [narrative] output', she stresses. But, crucially, while she emphasises the variability of industrial configuration *between* media, there is a failure to acknowledge and explore the potential for such variability *within* a single medium.[9] This paradigm whereby a given medium's stability appears taken for granted is a general reflection of the transmedial narratological approach.

Media are not stable entities, but rather protean cultural formations, each with elements that can vary greatly, including the capacity of technologies, the composition of audiences, the configuration of institutional economics and the organisation and regulation of national/regional markets. This book, then, conducts a thorough examination of narrative and media by considering not only the narrative implications of discrepancies in industrial practices *between* media, but also of differences in production conditions *within* a given medium. The book examines the degree to which the specificities of a range of variable industrial factors within a single medium can contribute to multiple contrasting sets of narrative production conditions. Such variable industrial contexts that the book explores include:

- institutionally configured revenue models (i.e. the particular means by which media institutions generate revenue via the dissemination of a narrative text);
- intended target audiences (i.e. the particular demographic groups that media institutions intend to appeal to via the dissemination of a narrative text);

- technologies of production, dissemination and consumption (i.e. the particular technologies that media institutions utilise in the construction and distribution of narrative texts, and the technologies by which media audiences consume them).

To ascertain the complex ways by which medium-specific industrial factors distinctly inform the creation of narratives, the book explores, across various narrative media, the processes by which narrative texts are assembled. Considering each medium on its own terms, it traces the connections between production processes and the particular industrial contexts within which these practices are situated. To this end, the book combines detailed narrative analyses with extensive research into industry practices. David Bordwell labels this approach to research, whereby a narrative's features are considered in relation to their historical, industrial and technological conditions of production, as 'historical poetics'.[10] Recent significant works that have adopted the historical poetics approach in media studies include Jeremy G. Butler's *Television Style*, Trisha Dunleavy's *Television Drama: Form, Agency, Innovation* and Jason Mittell's *Complex TV: The Poetics of Contemporary Television Storytelling*; each of these expertly connects television narratives to their production conditions.[11] Via its distinctive cross-media focus, this book makes a unique contribution to this body of work.

In order to achieve a logical consistency between its narrative case studies across media, the book restricts its focus to a particular narrative category that is universal within media culture: *serial narrative*. A narrative within this category can be broadly defined as one that evokes an ongoing storyworld across a sequence of textual instalments, with the distribution of each new instalment usually separated by an interval from the last. Due to this particular mode of production and distribution, the dissemination and consumption of a single narrative text can potentially span weeks, months, years or even decades. This narrative category has proved a pervasive method by which media institutions have attempted to offset the high degrees of financial risk associated with cultural industrial production.[12] With its ongoing narrative deferral, the serial format's potential to reduce financial risk stems from its capacity to nurture the loyal consumers who purchase and/or engage with a succession of narrative instalments so as to discover 'what happened next' within the storyworld.[13] The format first began being widely implemented in the West from the 1830s onward as part of publishers' efforts to mass circulate literary narrative fiction for the first time. In the twenty-first century, serial narratives remain a constant presence within media landscapes; the format is ubiquitous within television and comics, for example, while—as the book details—many of the most popular narrative properties in film and videogames garner loyalty due in part to their evocation of ongoing storyworlds across multiple instalments.

The book creates further logical consistency between its case studies by restricting its focus to a particular national context: the United States. This decision is an appropriate one due to the nation's powerful cultural relevance in this period. As a primary provider of popular entertainment the world over, the ongoing storyworlds the US disseminates—via such media as film, television, comics, literature and videogames—have a cultural impact that reverberates widely. Using a set of terms applicable across different US media contexts, the book labels as *processes of narrative design* the modes of production activity through which narratives form. Those individuals engaged in these processes, the members of collaborative teams that, say, bring television series to screens or comics panels to pages, are referred to as *narrative designers*. The changeable production conditions that industrial factors combine to establish are referred to as *conditions of narrative design*.

Chapter 2 establishes the book's distinctive theoretical positioning concerning the relationship between narrative and media. Divided into two main sections, the chapter's first section confirms the significance of medium specificity to narrative design conditions and processes within our era of media conglomeration and technological convergence. Situating its study within debates around medium specificity, it explores how a given medium's distinct range of industry practices uniquely influences narrative design processes, thereby preserving that medium's identity. Using The Walt Disney Company's *Star Wars* franchise as a case study, it demonstrates how a given medium's general modes of production, distribution and consumption help to inform medium-specific narrative features within the new Disney-produced *Star Wars* films and the Disney XD animated series *Star Wars Rebels* (2014–2018).

Having established that distinct methods of industrial organisation are central to a given medium's unique identity, Chap. 2's second section introduces the book's *dimensions of specificity* model as a means to account for the high variability of industrial conditions—across time, and within a given moment—that inevitably characterises a given medium. Via this model, the section argues that narrative production is contingent not only upon the dimension of medium specificity but also upon the specificities of a given medium's industrial dimensions, namely *institutional specificity, national specificity, audience specificity, economic specificity* and *technological specificity*. Continuing the book's particular focus on US narrative production, Chaps. 3, 4 and 5 utilise this model further by focusing on the dimensions of economic specificity, audience specificity and technological specificity respectively. Each chapter is predominantly concerned with exploring the significance to narrative production of a particular dimension of specificity within a single given medium, although each chapter also acknowledges the implications of other industrial dimensions within that given medium.

Chapter 3 analyses the dimension of economic specificity within the context of US television. It examines the contrasting economic models of: (1) broadcast networks—which are primarily funded by advertisers; (2) basic cable channels—which are primarily funded by a combination of advertising revenue and fees paid by cable-package providers; and, (3) subscription services—which are primarily funded by paying subscribers. Relying on six institutions from across these three different revenue-model categories as case studies—the NBC and ABC networks, the FX and AMC basic cable channels, and the HBO premium cable service and the Netflix streaming service, the chapter seeks to ascertain the conditions of narrative design that each of these institutional types imposes upon the construction of serialised drama. It charts the particular ways each set of conditions influences narrative practices within a range of twenty-first century series, including: ABC's *Scandal* (2012–2018) and *Once Upon a Time* (2011–2018); NBC's *The Night Shift* (2014–2017) and *Hannibal* (NBC, 2013–2015); FX's *Fargo* (FX, 2014–present) and *The Americans* (2013–2018); AMC's *Mad Men* (2007–2015) and *Better Call Saul* (2015–present); HBO's *The Wire* (HBO, 2002–2008) and *The Leftovers* (2014–2017); and Netflix's *Bloodline* (2015–2017) and *Orange is the New Black* (2013–present).

Chapter 4 considers the dimension of audience specificity within the context of the twenty-first century US comic-book industry, examining the degree to which narrative production processes are linked to the specificities of the particular audience groups for which a given narrative text is conceived. It examines transitions in the industry's audience-targeting priorities in the early 2000s, whereby publishers increasingly widened their attention from a narrow yet highly dedicated consumer base of white male adults to a broader mix of readers, including teens, females and people of colour, as well as more casual readers; it furthermore shows how these altered priorities have impacted upon writing and illustrating techniques, as well as editorial decisions, implemented in the creation of DC and Marvel's superhero comic book narratives.

Chapter 5 focuses on the dimension of technological specificity within the console videogame industry, analysing the ways in which the sector's technological 'upgrade culture', whereby the capacities of home and portable console platforms continually transform, frequently enables new approaches in videogame narrative. The chapter concentrates in particular on the ways in which the developers of three particular US-published large-budget *story-driven videogame series*—namely *Halo*, *Red Faction* and *Grand Theft Auto*—have altered narrative practices in response to economically driven transitions in console hardware—such as increased graphical processing power and the integration of touchscreen user input—during the course of these series' respective runs.

Each of these chapters makes, on its own terms, a unique contribution to a scholarly field. For example, by connecting a broad range of narrative features to the specificities of network, basic cable, premium cable and internet streaming contexts, Chap. 3 represents a uniquely comprehensive study of narrative design conditions and processes within twenty-first century US television drama. Through its examination of the links between techniques of narrative production and the transformations that have taken place within the US comic book industry in the twenty-first century, Chap. 4 breaks new ground within studies of comic-book culture. By establishing the complex relationship between technology and narrative, Chap. 5 challenges a pervasive mindset within games studies whereby changing technological conditions of videogame development are disassociated from, or regarded as an impediment to, narrative innovation. Together, the chapters make an important contribution towards our understanding of media and narrative in the twenty-first century.

Notes

1. See Henry Jenkins, *Convergence Culture: Where Old and New Media Collide* (New York: New York University Press, 2006); Graham Meikle and Sherman Young, *Media Convergence: Networked Digital Media in Everyday Life* (Basingstoke: Palgrave Macmillan, 2012); Michael Latzer, 'Media Convergence', in *Handbook on the Digital Creative Economy*, ed. Ruth Towse and Christian Handke (Cheltenham: Edward Elgar, 2013), 123–133.

2. Ruth Page and Bronwen Thomas, 'Introduction', in *New Narratives: Stories and Storytelling in the Digital Age*, ed. Ruth Page and Bronwen Thomas (Lincoln: University of Nebraska Press, 2011), 7.

3. Henry Jenkins popularised the term 'transmedia storytelling'; for a detailed definition for the term see Henry Jenkins, 'Transmedia 202: Further Reflections', *Confessions of an Aca-Fan*, 1 August 2011, http://henryjenkins.org/2011/08/defining_transmedia_further_re.html.

4. Jenkins, *Convergence Culture*; Colin Harvey, *Fantastic Transmedia: Narrative, Play and Memory Across Science Fiction and Fantasy Storyworlds* (Basingstoke: Palgrave Macmillan, 2015); Martin Flanagan, Mike McKenney and Andy Livingstone, *The Marvel Studios Phenomenon: Inside a Transmedia Universe* (New York: Bloomsbury, 2015).

5. See Shlomith Rimmon-Kenan, 'How the Model Neglects the Medium: Linguistics, Language, and the Crisis for Narratology', *The Journal of Narrative Technique* 19, No. 1 (1989), 157–166; Marie-Laure Ryan, 'Introduction', in *Narrative across Media: The Languages of Storytelling*, ed. Marie-Laure Ryan (Lincoln: University of Nebraska Press, 2004), 1–40; Marie-Laure Ryan, *Avatars of Story* (Minneapolis: University of Minnesota Press, 2006), 3–30; David Herman, 'Towards a Transmedial Narratology', in *Narrative across Media*, ed. Ryan, 47–75; Mark J. P. Wolf, *Building Imaginary Worlds: The Theory and History of Subcreation* (New York: Routledge, 2012), 245–267; Marie-Laure Ryan, 'Story/Worlds/Media: Turning the Instruments of Media-Conscious Narratology', in *Storyworlds Across Media: Towards a Media-Conscious Narratology*, ed. Marie-Laure Ryan and Jan-Noël Thon (Lincoln: University of Nebraska Press, 2014), 25–49; Jan-Noël Thon, *Transmedial Narratology and Contemporary Media Culture* (Lincoln: University of Nebraska Press, 2016).

6. Rimmon-Kenan, 'How the Model Neglects the Medium', 160.

7. See Ryan, *Avatars of Story*, 18–21; Ryan, 'Story/Worlds/Media', 29–30.

8. See Ryan, *Avatars of Story*, 23–25; Ryan, 'Story/Worlds/Media', 30.

9. Helen Fulton, introduction to *Narrative and Media*, by Helen Fulton, with Rosemary Huisman, Julian Murphet and Anne Dunn (Cambridge: Cambridge University Press, 2005), 3–4.

10. David Bordwell, 'Historical Poetics of Cinema', in *The Cinematic Text: Methods and Approaches*, ed. R. Barton Palmer (New York: AMS, 1989), 369–398.

11. Trisha Dunleavy, *Television Drama: Form, Agency, Innovation* (Basingstoke: Palgrave Macmillan, 2009); Jeremy G. Butler, *Television Style* (New York: Routledge, 2010); Jason Mittell, *Complex TV: The Poetics of Contemporary Television Storytelling* (New York: New York University Press, 2015). Earlier examples of books that adhere to this approach include: Barry Salt, *Film Style and Technology: History and Analysis* (London: Starward, 1983);

David Bordwell, Janet Staiger and Kristin Thompson, *The Classical Hollywood Cinema: Film Style and Mode of Production to 1960* (New York: Columbia University Press, 1985).

12. See David Hesmondhalgh, *The Cultural Industries*, second edition (Los Angeles: Sage Publications, 2007), 23.

13. See Roger Hagedorn, 'Technology and Economic Exploitation: The Serial as a Form of Narrative Presentation', *Wide Angle* 10 (1988), 12.

CHAPTER 2

Narratives in the Media Convergence Era: The Industrial Dimensions of Medium Specificity

INTRODUCTION

This chapter provides an overview of the ways in which twenty-first century media inform narrative design conditions and processes, thereby establishing this book's theoretical position concerning the relationship between narrative and media. It argues that, within our age of media convergence, a given medium should chiefly be conceptualised as a distinct range of cultural activities, including particular industrial practices centred on the creation, dissemination and consumption of narratives. It furthermore establishes a theoretical model to account for the many variations in industrial and broader practices that circulate a given medium at a given moment and over time. The chapter ultimately demonstrates why the concept of medium specificity should be central to our understanding of conditions of narrative design within an era of media conglomeration and technological convergence.

As Marie-Laure Ryan demonstrates, there are three distinct approaches one can take when assessing the particular narrative constraints and affordances of a given medium. The first is a 'semiotic approach', which requires consideration of the particular range of semiotic phenomena that a given medium incorporates.[1] So, whereas literature relies upon printed language primarily, comics are traditionally comprised of language and image, while film and television afford language, image and sound/music.[2] The distinct possibilities of each phenomenon hold certain implications for narrative.

© The Author(s) 2018
A. N. Smith, *Storytelling Industries*,
https://doi.org/10.1007/978-3-319-70597-2_2

11

Language, for example, can, as Ryan and Jason Mittell each explain, enable a narrative designer to convey character dialogue and interior thought, and to describe and evaluate elements of a storyworld, whereas images cannot. Or, conversely, images can show what characters and setting look like, whereas language cannot.[3]

For example, when writing the first chapter of *Great Expectations* (1860–1861), in which a young Pip happens upon the escaped convict Magwitch within a graveyard, use of language permitted Charles Dickens to explicitly define (via Pip's autobiographical narration) the environment as a 'bleak place' and Magwitch as a 'fearful man' with a 'terrible voice'. Use of language further permitted Dickens to filter storyworld occurrences via Pip's interior interpretive thought processes. For example, seeing Magwitch limp though the graveyard's nettles and brambles, Pip imagines the escaped convict is 'eluding the hands of the dead people, stretching up cautiously out of the graves, to get a twist upon his ankle and pull him in'.[4] As a point of comparison, the equivalent scene in the David Lean directed film adaptation of Dickens' novel (1946) lacks such internalised thought and explicit/evaluative descriptions. Reflecting the semiotic affordances of film, however, the scene instead utilises image and sound to evoke within viewers evaluations that synchronise with the novel's descriptions. For example, the scene's depictions of the charcoal-grey sky, shrieking winds and bare, spiky trees, which combine to contextualise Pip and Magwitch in the graveyard, imply the bleakness that Pip directly identifies in the novel.

Ryan's second approach to understanding a given medium's distinctive set of narrative powers is a 'technical approach', in which a medium's general technological capacities are considered with regards to how they determine the manifestation of semiotic phenomena.[5] Film technologies, for example, not only afford narrative designers the use of image but more specifically moving image. This technological capability holds implications for narrative design conditions. For instance, via printed language and/or static images, narrative designers are unable to depict, whether through the semiotic phenomena of language or image, a continuous process within a storyworld; instead those working within these media use language and/or images to summarise an event sequence or report discrete instances of it. Via moving image, however, narrative designers within film are enabled to portray a chronological sequence of action within the story world as a continuous temporal process.

The reveal of Magwitch in *Great Expectations* provides an example of this distinction between technological supports in practice. In the novel, Pip informs the reader, 'a man [Magwitch] started up from among the graves' before 'he seized me by the chin'.[6] Pip's narration here indicates the occurring of an event sequence through time (Magwitch's appearance, his subsequent seizing of Pip's chin), but it cannot present this sequence as a continuous process. Neither can the static images of Rick Geary's comic-book adaptation of the novel (1990). Geary's panels capture particular snapshot instances of Magwitch's appearance and subsequent grasping of Pip that together imply—rather than *show*—a continuous process. Lean's film adaptation, in contrast, is able, due to the facility of the moving image, to display, within a single shot, the continuous process of this action in its entirety.

In contrast to the semiotic and technical approaches, Ryan's third means of gauging a given medium's narrative constraints and possibilities does not ultimately assess the medium's technological capabilities. Her 'cultural approach' instead examines the particular ways in which a distinct media culture shapes narrative designers' utilisation of media affordances.[7] This approach to medium specificity complements Noël Carroll's claim that media are defined not merely by the potential of a particular combination of semiotic phenomena and technological support, but rather by the particular cultural practices that develop around these phenomena and technologies.[8] Henry Jenkins takes a similar position in claiming that the term 'media' should encompass not only the technologies that enable the communication of semiotic phenomena but also the distinct 'cultural systems' that have developed in relation to them.[9]

The example of the *Great Expectations* novel demonstrates how cultural systems constrain and afford the possibilities available to narrative designers within a given medium. As part of the wider cultural practices within the Victorian literary fiction industry, *Great Expectations* was initially published serially in the magazine *All the Year Round*. This condition of narrative design imposed particular obligations for Dickens to meet as part of his narrative design process; Dickens was, for example, obliged to anticipate the division of his novel into discrete instalments, each with a predetermined length, and to account for the weekly interval that separated the publication of each new instalment from the last. As many scholars of nineteenth-century literary production demonstrate, the industrial requirements of serial narrative design strongly influenced within this industry the formation of storyworlds and the ways in which they were conveyed.[10]

Processes of technological convergence have in certain cases undermined the semiotic and technical approaches to assessing the distinct narrative possibilities of a given medium; this is because processes of digitalisation appear to have eroded certain prior differences between media. For example, while film could traditionally be distinguished from comics via semiotic and technical approaches, the rise of the digital comics form has undermined the usefulness of these distinctions. For instance, while the medium of film has traditionally differentiated itself from comics via its use of sound (a semiotic distinction) and moving image (a technical distinction), digital comics can afford narrative designers the use of both sound and moving image. In certain cases, therefore, processes whereby media are connected to a digital base have lessened the usefulness of the technical and semiotic approaches to distinguishing between media. As this chapter shows, however, while the adequacy of the semiotic and technical approaches can sometimes be found wanting in the twenty-first century, a cultural approach to distinguishing between media continues to be a highly useful way to account for differing contexts of narrative creation.

In the media convergence age, a given medium's distinct modes of production, circulation and reception, along with economic models, regulatory systems, and broader socio-cultural attitudes and practices underpinning these processes, can clearly set that medium apart in terms of its narrative constraints and affordances. Utilising the *Star Wars* transmedia entertainment franchise as a case study, the following section establishes this point by demonstrating how medium-specific industrial conditions inform *Star Wars* narrative features within films and television. Via its cultural approach, this case study makes an original contribution to an existing field of research concerning the role of medium specificity within transmedia franchises; while scholars have usefully taken semiotic and technical approaches to the study of how a franchise's storyworld is adapted across media, a cultural approach has largely been neglected within this field.[11] The section begins by establishing the transmedia entertainment franchise form and its contexts before showing how a given medium's unique industry practices inform the creation of the *Star Wars* narrative.

A Cultural Approach to the *Star Wars* Narrative: Industrial Specificity in the Transmedia Entertainment Franchise

I use the term 'transmedia entertainment franchise' here to refer to a grouping of media artefacts that all derive from the same core intellectual property, and which are disseminated across a range of media. One example of a transmedia entertainment franchise is the Marvel franchise, which comprises film, comic-book, television and videogame content, among other media and product forms that feature Marvel superhero characters, thereby utilising the Marvel intellectual property. Many other popular transmedia entertainment franchises similarly draw upon fictional characters and their storyworlds, such as the Batman, James Bond, Harry Potter and *Star Wars* franchises. The practice of transmedia franchising has its roots in the media property licensing practices that emerged at the turn of the twentieth century in conjunction with the development of mass media communications, modern advertising practices and a new consumer culture.[12] This practice led to many popular fictional characters, including Tarzan, Superman, Mickey Mouse and the Lone Ranger, being licensed in the first half of the twentieth century to appear across a range of mass media platforms and consumer products.[13]

Related practices of intellectual property licensing have, following these developments, proved pervasive within media culture.[14] Yet the ubiquitous use of transmedia entertainment franchising within twenty-first century media industries also reflects processes of media conglomeration that have occurred in recent decades.[15] Since the 1980s, a trend for business mergers and acquisitions among film studios, broadcasters, publishers and other types of media companies has led to the formation of giant media conglomerates with holdings across a range of traditionally distinct media industries.[16] Conglomerates, such as Time Warner and The Walt Disney Company, have a strong incentive to develop transmedia entertainment franchises across their various conglomerate divisions; doing so enables them to maximise profits from their intellectual properties via a range of different revenue streams.[17] By spreading its *Star Wars* and Marvel characters across its own media platforms, for example, Disney is able to exploit these popular intellectual properties as a means to boost revenue via box office takings (Walt Disney Studios Motion Pictures), home video sales (Walt Disney Studios Home Entertainment), television advertising and basic cable carriage fee income (Disney-ABC

Television Group), comic-book sales (Marvel Comics), soundtrack sales (Hollywood Records) and merchandise (Disney Consumer Products). Disney can supplement this approach, and its income, via the aforementioned practice of media licensing, permitting toy companies, for instance, including LEGO and Hasbro, to develop products featuring narrative elements, such as characters, from the *Star Wars* and Marvel franchises.[18]

As with the case of the *Star Wars* and Marvel franchises, the film industry has served as a dominant factor helping to drive some of the most popular transmedia entertainment franchises in the twenty-first century.[19] This is due to film studios typically serving as central components within the world's leading entertainment media conglomerates.[20] Hollywood's six 'major' studios indeed each operate as a division within a larger media conglomerate structure. For conglomerates it has now become standard practice for their film studios to develop film series based on pre-existing popular fictional characters and worlds that lend themselves to being adapted across a given conglomerate's various divisions, as well as to media licensing opportunities.[21]

As part of the development of a transmedia franchise, a conglomerate typically looks to generate some coherence between the various textual fragments of a franchise so as to present to audiences a consistent media-spanning brand.[22] One means by which conglomerates achieve such coherence is through what Henry Jenkins refers to as 'transmedia storytelling'.[23] Via this storytelling mode, the coordinated dissemination of a given storyworld's elements across multiple media platforms results in the presentation of a single coherent fictional narrative. Distinct media, as part of this production process, typically each make a unique contribution to the formation of a coherent transmedia storyworld.

For instance, each of the Marvel Studios films, including the Iron Man, Captain America and Avengers movies and their sequels, provide material for a single unified storyworld—referred to as the Marvel Cinematic Universe (or MCU). Various Marvel Television series, however, such as the ABC network's *Agents of S.H.I.E.L.D.* (ABC, 2013–present) and *Agent Carter* (2015–2016), and the Netflix series *Daredevil* (Netflix, 2015–present) and *Jessica Jones* (2015–present), expand the MCU; they do so through focusing on characters and storylines that, while not always connecting directly to the MCU film storylines, do share the same fictional world presented in these films. The storylines contained within the Marvel Comics' MCU-branded comic books further expand this single storyworld.[24]

As films are often industrially positioned as 'tent poles' of transmedia entertainment franchises, they frequently serve as 'ur-text' narratives out of which transmedia storytelling extensions develop. As Colin B. Harvey notes of transmedia storytelling within the *Star Wars* franchise, for example, non-film texts typically fill in ellipses of the film series' narrative chronology.[25] The narrative of the Disney XD animated television series *Star Wars Rebels* (2014–2018), for example, takes place in the story time that passes between the films *Star Wars: Episode III—Revenge of the Sith* (2005) and *Star Wars* (1977, henceforth *A New Hope*); in contrast, many titles from the new line of *Star Wars* comic books launched by Marvel Comics in 2015, including *Star Wars* (2015–present), *Princess Leia* (2015) and *Darth Vader* (2015–2016), present storyworld events that occur between *A New Hope* and *The Empire Strikes Back* (1980).

In many cases, franchise-owning corporations aim to centrally coordinate such processes of transmedia storytelling so as to ensure narrative consistency between a franchise's various textual components, a process Harvey refers to as 'directed' transmedia storytelling.[26] Lucasfilm, for example, following Disney's acquisition of the *Star Wars*-owning company, formed its Story Group in 2014 to regulate the dissemination of the *Star Wars* storyworld across film, television, novels, comic books and theme parks, among other media platforms.[27]

While industry logics in recent decades have motivated widespread use of transmedia storytelling, this narrative mode is not the only means by which conglomerates develop coherence across a franchise. Transmedia entertainment franchises are indeed often populated by many distinct storyworlds, resulting in myriad versions of the same character, as Roberta Pearson and William Uricchio observe of Batman within the DC franchise.[28] As Jenkins, then, posits, the transmedia entertainment franchise can simultaneously comprise both the storyworld 'continuity' that transmedia storytelling generates and also a 'multiplicity' of storyworlds stemming from the same source intellectual property.[29] In the case of the Marvel franchise, the MCU storyworld is both preceded and paralleled by Marvel Comics' so-called Marvel Universe (MU) storyworld; this is the storyworld that the bulk of Marvel comic books have contributed to since its inception in the early 1960s when the publisher introduced its new generation of superheroes (including Spider-Man and the Fantastic Four). The MCU and Marvel Comics' MU are joined within the Marvel transmedia entertainment franchise by further storyworlds, including additional distinct storyworlds in comics and television.[30]

So as to ensure cohesiveness across a given transmedia entertainment franchise's multiplicity of storyworlds, a media company typically generates what we might call *intertextual resonances* between such storyworlds. This practice can involve ensuring some harmony between the components of distinct storyworlds. In the case of Marvel, for instance, as Derek Johnson and Martin Flanagan et al. observe, and as Chap. 4 explores further, Marvel Comics has frequently ensured that key MU storyworld elements, such as the composition of superhero teams, share consistency with film adaptations of Marvel characters.[31] Media companies furthermore generate what Matthew Freeman calls 'stylistic synchronicity' across a transmedia franchise's various narrative presentations, thereby supplying a 'visual coherence' between a franchise's distinct storyworlds.[32] This is evident in the case of multiple Marvel Animation produced series, including *Ultimate Spider-Man* (2012–2017) and *Avengers Assemble* (2013–present), which form the Disney XD cable channel's 'Marvel Universe' block. While each of these series presents a distinct storyworld of its own, these series have been designed to achieve some stylistic synchronicity with Marvel Comics' narratives. With *Ultimate Spider-Man*, for instance, Marvel Television Executive Vice President Jeph Loeb employed Marvel comic-book illustrators as character designers so as to inspire the series' animators to capture the 'tonal flavour' of certain Marvel Comics publications.[33]

Taking a macro view of the phenomenon of transmedia entertainment franchises, it is clear, then, that certain industrial pressures, which span the boundaries of individual media, strongly motivate degrees of narrative coherence and consistency across a given franchise. Nevertheless, this chapter argues, the key factor of medium specificity typically ensures the distinctiveness of a given franchise's media texts in one medium compared to those of another. As noted, various scholars have, in their study of transmedia entertainment franchises, usefully identified the contingency of a given franchise narrative text to a given medium's semiotic possibilities and technological capacity. Via a cultural approach, this section's case study, however, demonstrates the relevance of industrial constraints and affordances within a given medium to the formation of *Star Wars* transmedia storytelling.

Before connecting *Star Wars* narrative to industrial contexts, however, it is first necessary, for the case study, and for the book as a whole, to precisely define what a 'narrative' is. Drawing upon narratological precedent, I break the concept of narrative down into three main components. The first of the components, *storyworld*, refers to the spatio-temporal model of story that a given narrative text evokes and which incorporates:

1. Characters; that is, the beings conveyed by a narrative, such as the *Star Wars* storyworld's villainous Kylo Ren, who is introduced in the *Star Wars: The Force Awakens* film. As Rimmon-Kenan observes, a given character forms as a 'network of character-traits' through depictions of their actions and appearances.[34] For example, Kylo Ren's appearance—a black cloak and metal mask—helps to define the character as someone who seeks to intimidate those around him.
2. Objects; by which I mean the inanimate items that populate the storyworld, which might be available for character use, such as Kylo Ren's lightsaber.
3. The events that are presented as occurring or having occurred through time. Character actions are typical types of events. For example, as depicted in *The Force Awakens*, Kylo Ren kills Lor San Takka by striking him down with his lightsaber.
4. The settings that contextualise these events, objects and characters, such as the small village on the planet of Jakku in which Kylo Ren murders Lor San Takka.[35]

While 'storyworld' denotes that which the narrative text presents, the remaining two narrative components of *plot* and *style* refer to the manner by which a storyworld is presented. Of these two, 'plot' concerns how narrative designers order a given storyworld's chronology of events within the text, and also the textual duration (whether running time or page space) that they afford a given depiction of a storyworld. *The Force Awakens* plot is ordered in such a way that, while it begins with a Jakku-set event sequence that includes Kylo Ren's murder of Lor San Takka, prior storyworld events concerning Kylo Ren are referred to and depicted via a flashback later on within the film's running time. In terms of duration, the Jakku-set sequence in which Kylo Ren murders Lor San Takka is afforded approximately seven minutes of screen time.[36]

'Style', in contrast, refers to the particular technical, practical manner by which narrative designers utilise a medium's semiotic affordances so as to present a plot's events, characters, objects and settings.[37] For example, in moving image media, such as film and television, style emerges, in part, through the composition of editing, lighting, set design, sound design, performance, cinematographic techniques and other aspects of mise-en-scène that comprise a scene.[38] The low-angled shot of Kylo Ren exiting his spacecraft on Jakku (before confronting Lor San Takka), which presents the character as a towering presence thereby emphasising his intimidating personality, is a narrative design choice that pertains to style.

To assess the influence of narrative design conditions that a given medium's industrial formations place upon the *Star Wars* narrative design processes, the following case study examines and compares *Star Wars* narratives from two different media: film and television. While the book's following three chapters examine in detail how industrial contexts determine a narrative's style, this study focuses in particular on aspects of storyworld and plot in *Star Wars* narratives across these two media. This comparative study explores, in particular, two *Star Wars* series that have been (a) created subsequent to Disney's acquisition of Lucasfilm in 2012; (b) produced by particular divisions within the Disney organisation; and (c) developed under the scrutiny of the Lucasfilm Story Group.[39] These series are the post-Disney-acquisition *Star Wars* films and the *Star Wars Rebels* television series. Comparing these two series from the same conglomerate context should limit non-medium-related variable factors and make more clearly apparent the narrative differences that emerge as a result of discrepancies in industrial practices between media. Drawing upon Jan Noël Thon's distinction between media and 'media forms', the study furthermore recognises these series as each being representative of a particular medium-specific form (which is not necessarily representative of its medium as a whole);[40] the media forms examined are the feature film and the television series.

Star Wars *in Feature Films*

A given *Star Wars* film, of course, serves as an example of the feature film form. Reflecting the industrial specificities of film, this form was born out of traditional modes of content dissemination and reception within the medium; the term refers to a film with a running time deemed sufficient to enable it to serve as a sole or primary text within a theatrically exhibited film programme (and therefore distinguishable from the shorts that were once typically screened prior to a feature). A given *Star Wars* film can, however, be more specifically understood as an example of a particular industrial subcategory of the feature; that is, the 'blockbuster'.

The term 'blockbuster' defines a Hollywood feature that: (1) typically relies on an extremely high budget; (2) is given a very wide theatre release in the summer or over the Christmas period; (3) lends itself well to promotion by including, for example, spectacular special effects; (4) has strong potential to serve a media conglomerate's various interests, such as publishing divisions, and/or offers strong media licensing opportunities, such as merchandise and fast-food restaurant chain tie-ins.[41] Inspired by the successes of the *Star Wars* 'original' and 'prequel' trilogies, along with the *Lord of the Rings* trilogy, film studios have, in the twenty-first century, increasingly looked to develop long-running and narratively linked blockbuster film series. Such blockbuster film series include the eight-part Harry Potter film series and the four-part *Hunger Games* film series, as well as the MCU. Adhering to this broader practice of blockbuster film series development, Disney, after having acquired Lucasfilm, announced plans in 2013 to produce five new *Star Wars* films to be released from 2015 onwards.[42]

One key way in which production contexts of the Hollywood blockbuster film series help to determine narrative is by influencing the type of storyworld events that are included within a given instalment. Because of their tremendous cost a given Hollywood studio produces only a few blockbusters a year, typically releasing them in the summer and the Thanksgiving/Christmas period so as to more easily attract younger audiences.[43] This now standard practice of blockbuster production and distribution ensures a low volume of film series instalments and large periods of time between the releases of each instalment. Disney, for example, has (at the time of writing) scheduled for release one *Star Wars* film per year from 2015 until 2019. These films include a new trilogy designed to advance the main serial storylines of the 'original' and 'prequel' trilogies; *Star Wars: The Force Awakens* serves as the first of this trilogy. The two remaining films of this planned quintet have been conceived as narrative 'spin-off' features that add storyworld detail to the history of the *Star Wars* universe; *Rogue One: A Star Wars Story* (2016) is the first of this pair. Due to this relative scarcity of instalments, and the relatively low frequency by which they are released, studios are able to devote months to promoting each instalment's release as a significant moment within popular culture. This cycle of marketing and distribution is seen to minimise financial risk as it serves to generate high amounts of media exposure and viewer anticipation for blockbuster releases, therefore potentially helping to increase box-office takings.

These industrial practices establish a context in which audience anticipation for a single blockbuster instalment is typically ratcheted up over many months, placing the onus on filmmakers to deliver memorable and transformative storyworld developments within each instalment so as to meet audiences' heightened expectations. Blockbuster series instalments therefore conform to the broader Hollywood feature film convention of including a significant degree of storyworld change. An example of such events in *The Force Awakens* would be the film's inclusion of an iconic and beloved character's death, which occurs when the film's chief antagonist Kylo Ren slays his father, Han Solo.

A further example of significant change within *Star Wars* films would be the shifts that lead characters undergo. As previously noted, a character is, from a narratological perspective, a set of interlinked attributes; however, as storyworlds are necessarily defined by change due to their incorporation of event sequences, notes Uri Margolin, a given character's network of traits 'is not enduring but time-bound' and thus 'inevitably gets modified over time'.[44] A typical narrative convention within Hollywood feature films (and also plays and novels) is for a lead character's attributes to undergo significant permanent change—a process typically referred to as a 'character arc'. In the case of Rey, *The Force Awakens* clearly adheres to this convention. The character is introduced as a humble scavenger yet goes on to develop powerful Jedi abilities, such as telekinetic and telepathic skills, throughout the course of the film; by the time of the film's climax she is able to best the formidable Kylo Ren in combat. This example of swift character development in *The Force Awakens* is reflective of narrative design conditions in which significant degrees of storyworld change are anticipated.

A further way in which the *Star Wars* storyworld conforms to Hollywood blockbuster conventions is through these films' prevalence of spectacle. This term 'spectacle' refers to instances within a movie where emphasis is placed on visually striking sequences, such as ambitious and impressive chases and battles, which invite viewers' awe. Hollywood film has long depended on visual spectacle. Studios in the 1950s, for example, relied on big-budget epic spectacle as a means to appeal to audiences that had previously been tempted away from theatres by the emergence of television and other new leisure activities in the post-war period.[45] Two more recent industrial processes have further necessitated movies' requirement for moments of spectacle: (1) the absorption of Hollywood studios into media conglomerates has led to films meeting a demand for spectacular elements that are appropriate for remediation within other conglomerate divisions, such as videogame and theme park businesses;[46] (2) the increasing importance of the global box office to Hollywood studios has seen blockbusters privileging spectacle due to such textual elements, which are typically light on cultural specificities, having potential to translate easily around the world.[47]

The original *Star Wars* trilogy, which uses pioneering visual techniques to represent complex spacecraft battles and lightsaber duels, among other spectacular sequences, influenced the prevalent use of special effects within blockbuster movie-making today. *A Force Awakens* and *Rogue One* continue this tradition through their inclusion of numerous large-scale action sequences that make extravagant use of computer-generated imagery. Such sequences within *The Force Awakens* include a thrilling chase scene in which the Rey-helmed Millennium Falcon spaceship speeds dangerously through the ruins of fallen space cruisers, as well as two complex battles in which a fleet of Resistance X-Wing spacecraft do combat with The First Order.

Critics frequently claim that such grand-scale, computer-generated action set pieces sit in opposition to storytelling, marginalising the narrative of Hollywood blockbusters.[48] However, as Bordwell notes, every blockbuster action sequence is a storyworld event, regardless of the degree of spectacle it achieves, with such scenes often serving to further characters' goals, relationships and understanding.[49] The aforementioned Millennium Falcon chase sequence helps to form a bond between the newly acquainted Rey and Finn, the latter serving as the spacecraft's gunner during the chase. To further understand the specificities of blockbuster film it is also important to observe that high budget, complex action sequences do not feature uninterrupted throughout a given narrative. Despite routine claims of special effects' dominance within blockbuster storytelling, a significant portion of a given blockbuster's narrative is, due to the tremendous cost of effects-laden action sequences, without spectacle; instead many scenes of a given narrative typically further the narrative via dialogue exchanges.[50]

The production contexts of the contemporary blockbuster film series do not only influence the type of events included within a given instalment, they furthermore help determine the plotting of event sequences. A long-standing convention of Hollywood feature filmmaking is for the entirety of a given storyworld's event sequences to be contained within a single film.[51] Film sequels, productions of which have increased in Hollywood since the 1970s, certainly break from this convention but in most cases each includes a largely discrete storyline, with a clear beginning and ending.[52] Yet the contemporary blockbuster film series is a more serialised form, with each entry into a given series typically conceived as an instalment within a wider serial narrative framework and so forgoes clear narrative resolution. This is evident in such films' incorporation of cliff-hanger endings, as in the case of *The Force Awakens*, for example, which ends at the moment in which Luke Skywalker, the original trilogy's lead protagonist, first appears on screen. With particular regard to their use of cliff-hangers, many contemporary blockbusters draw on a key storytelling convention of the Hollywood film-serial form that persisted from the 1910s until the 1950s, rather than any narrative norm of the Hollywood feature.

Despite their incorporation of serial storylines, however, contemporary blockbuster film series nevertheless typically rely on long-standing storytelling conventions of Hollywood features so as to ensure that each instalment provides a coherent, largely unified narrative that has the potential to be enjoyed as a standalone experience. Standard blockbuster practices of production and promotion motivate this narrative requirement. Due to their extremely high production and marketing budgets, blockbuster films are designed to appeal to a broad audience. Therefore, filmmakers must ensure that the viewing of a blockbuster film series instalment is not entirely dependent on significant amounts of narrative information from prior instalments, otherwise a given instalment's narrative might deter potential viewers. *The Force Awakens* progresses distinct pre-existing storylines, such as by advancing Han Solo and Leia Organa's relationship, which had previously developed throughout the original *Star Wars* film trilogy. Yet writers mainly introduce and resolve central dramatic conflicts within the confines of *The Force Awakens*. Organa's heroic Resistance, for example, battles in the film against The First Order, chiefly so as to prevent the antagonists' newly introduced and aptly named Starkiller Base from wreaking galactic destruction. The Resistance thwarts this particular threat in the film's closing stages by exploding the planet-sized weapon. The film thereby provides audiences with the introduction and resolution of a significant conflict while also continuing the franchise's broader serialised saga.

In line with filmmaking convention, the central and largely self-contained storylines of *The Force Awakens* and *Rogue One* are each structured as three acts. As Kristin Thompson observes, via this system of plotting, which has prevailed in Hollywood since the studio system era, the developments of new/altered character goals define each act.[53] In the case of *Rogue One*, for example, the over-arching storyline, which (in story time) occurs prior to the events of *A New Hope*, concerns a band of rebels' efforts to find the secret plans to the Empire's new super weapon, the Death Star (a planet-destroying precursor to Starkiller Base). Yet this storyline is broken into three distinct acts. The first act is built around main protagonist Jyn Erso's efforts on the desert moon of Jedha to procure, on behalf of the Rebel Alliance, information about the whereabouts of her father, who has designed the Death Star; the second act concerns Jyn, and the team she has now formed, attempting to locate her father on planet Eadu; the third act concerns the team's efforts to steal the structural plans of the Death Star from a high security Imperial facility on the planet of Scarif. While Hollywood filmmaking culture predominantly relies on this act structure convention, there is variability concerning the way it is applied. For example, in filmmaking more generally, the third act, which contains a plot's climax, is frequently the shortest of a film's acts; yet, in *Rogue One*'s third act, which contains multiple spectacular combat action sequences taking place on and above Scarif, is by far the longest. The act takes up around 50 minutes of the film's two hour and thirteen minutes running time.

This analysis demonstrates how the underpinning of film's industrial contexts, and the implementation of the medium's conventional production practices, have influenced the narrative of recent *Star Wars* films. The following section provides a useful comparison with this analysis, showing how industrial contexts within the medium of television inform narrative creation. The section focuses on the production of the animated television series *Star Wars Rebels*, which concerns a small starship crew of rebels—comprised of Hera, Kanan, Ezra, Zeb and Chopper—and its skirmishes with the Galactic Empire. It ultimately shows how discrepancies between the industrial contexts of film and television have frequently resulted in *Rebels* narrative designers adopting narrative design processes distinct from those implemented within the *Star Wars* films.

Star Wars *as a Television Series*

Despite traditional distinctions in technology (the projection of celluloid, the broadcast of live/taped content), the respective semiotic affordances and technological capacities for storytelling of film and television have proved broadly similar. In our era of technological convergence—in which film and television narratives are increasingly each constructed and circulated via identical digital production, distribution and consumption technologies—material differences between the two media have further evaporated. However, the contrasting ways in which film and television companies condition narrative design processes continue to validate distinctions between the two media.[54]

For example, one distinctive condition of narrative design that typically underpins television series production is the need for narrative designers to conceive of a series' storyworld without a clear idea regarding how long the series will endure. This is a condition that is largely absent in film, and indeed has not been present in the current phase of *Star Wars* film production. As noted, Disney planned and announced, after its acquisition of Lucasfilm, that the studio would produce a new trilogy of films;[55] Lucasfilm President Kathleen Kennedy was therefore in the position of knowing that she was tasked with extending this pre-existing serial narrative across three features. Such knowledge of a predetermined number of instalments gives narrative designers licence to map out a grand design for an entire serial narrative at its conception. Taking advantage of such conditions, Kennedy, together with *Force Awakens* co-writer and director J. J. Abrams, was able to broadly outline a narrative for the entirety of the third trilogy of *Star Wars* films parallel to the production process of its first instalment, *The Force Awakens*.[56]

Star Wars Rebels' producers, however, have not operated under similar conditions. US television series, such as *Rebels*, are typically each commissioned without a total number of required episodes and/or seasons having been determined. Instead, commissioning institutions normally opt to commission new seasons of a given series for as long as the series' continuation is considered to be economically advantageous. Narrative designers operating within such circumstances are therefore usually able to foresee the shape storylines might take only so far in advance; as a result, such narratives are, to borrow a term from Angela Ndalianis, 'potentially infinite', lacking as they do 'an overall narrative target in place'.[57] Signalling this absence of planning for an over-arching serial narrative during the production of *Rebels*, the series co-creator and executive producer Dave Filoni was, during the hiatus between *Rebels* seasons one and two, apparently entirely undecided regarding the ultimate fate of two lead characters.[58] It was only following the third season, when the decision was made to make *Rebels'* fourth season its last, that Filoni and his colleagues had an end point to target their narrative towards.[59] Prior to this, however, they operated within narrative design conditions that, notes Mittell, require producers to 'design narrative worlds that are able to sustain themselves for years rather than closed narrative plans created for a specific run'.[60]

Filoni, together with series co-creators Carrie Beck and Simon Kinberg, served this requirement as part of their initial development of *Rebels*. A guiding aim for the series at the conception stage was to model *Rebels* on

The A-Team (1983–1987), a US television series concerning a close-knit gang of ex commandos on the run from the military that defends the imperilled. As well as being drawn to the concept of the *Rebels* as a band of heroes that, similar to *The A-Team*, operates outside the law while aiding others, the *Rebels*' co-creators, recalls Kinberg, also 'loved the [*A-Team*] structure of the ensemble crew doing missions week to week'.[61] *Rebels* co-creators therefore devised a storyworld foundation suited to the specific industrial conditions of television series production. Rather than focusing on a narrative trajectory for the entire series, their priority was to design a storyworld premise intended to facilitate a potentially infinite number of weekly adventures, in the way *The A-Team* premise had decades previously. The premise of a small band of rebels repeatedly landing small blows against the Empire met this priority that arises from a typical television production context.

The potentially infinite status of the *Rebels* narrative at its conception has not only influenced the storyworld premise of the series but also motivated high degrees of storyworld stability during the series' run. As we have seen, the specific conditions of blockbuster film production encourage storyworlds to consistently undergo significant change, such as in the case of a given lead character traversing an arc within a single given film's narrative. Conversely, however, the requirements of the potentially infinite television series influence narrative designers to adopt conservative approaches to storyworld change, particularly with regards to characters and their relationships. This is partly due to the centrality of core character groups to the narratives of ongoing series, as well to networks, channels and services' promotion of such series. Charged with ensuring a potential long-term future for a given ongoing series, narrative designers typically maintain the stability of core characters' traits, along with the shared relationships that these characters form; in doing so, producers avoid deterring viewers drawn to particular character personalities and the specific dynamics of a given character ensemble.[62] The conditions of the potentially infinite series, then, commonly result in protagonists undergoing less transformation than those of films (or novels and plays). As Roberta Pearson observes of television series narratives, 'The requirement for a certain degree of stability and repetition shapes the narrative arc of the central characters ... denying them life-altering epiphanies that would threaten the series' format.'[63]

On those occasions when narrative designers *do* implement character transformations, this requirement encourages producers to typically veer towards changes that reinforce the storyworld structure of existing character relationships. Instances of character change in *Rebels* serve as examples of this approach to storyworld development, as series producers have so far favoured character transformation designed to maintain stability amongst the titular rebels. *Rebels* narrative designers, for example, draw upon an approach to character change that Mittell refers to as episodic 'character education', whereby a given character gains, within the confines of a single episode, a new perspective and resolves to change their attitude and actions.[64] In service of ensuring the storyworld status quo of a given series, such educations within television fiction are typically either (a) transitory, resulting in characters appearing in subsequent episodes to have forgotten prior life lessons, or (b) character shifts that help to reinforce character relationships established at a series' outset.

This latter type of character change is evident in the *Rebels* episode 'Out of the Darkness' (1:7), in which Sabine appears to undergo some small change in perspective that ultimately strengthens the existing structural hierarchy of the rebel crew. In the episode, Sabine voices her frustration at Hera's decision to preclude Sabine from Hera and Kanan's exchanges with a rebellion spy. Sabine initially demands greater involvement in these dealings, thus asserting pressure upon the group's familial structure within which Kanan and Hera perform quasi-parental roles to the other rebels. By the episode's end, however, Sabine comes to accept and respect the need for Hera and Kanan's secrecy concerning their intelligence gathering, therefore preserving the group's relationship status quo.

The objective within television's narrative design processes to maintain a storyworld's rigidity can furthermore lead to a technique we might refer to as *arc iteration*. Via this technique, a given character will appear to undergo a serialised transformation over multiple episodes, resulting in changed attributes and altered character relationships, only to lapse back into previously established former behaviour and character ensemble dynamics. As Eric Freedman, who identifies the practice, observes, the requirements of serialised television encourage character 'development and regression, a forward and backward trajectory that continuously plays out'.[65]

The character of Ezra repeatedly appears to undergo this process of arc iteration. In the first *Rebels* episode ('Spark of Rebellion'), the young street-wise orphan Ezra, after first meeting the Rebel crew on his home planet of Lothan, reveals Force-related abilities, which he goes on to develop under the mentorship of the Jedi Knight Kanan. At certain points within *Rebels*, it appears that changes Ezra undergoes might jeopardise this master–apprentice relationship that has been a central component of the series. For example, in the season two finale ('Twilight of the Apprentice' [2:21]), Ezra, inspired by former Sith apprentice Darth Maul, begins embracing the dark side of the force so as to gain further power, distancing himself from Kanan, whom Maul blinds in the same episode. Narrative designers further this Ezra character trajectory in the premiere episode of the third season ('Steps in Shadow' [3:1]). During the episode, a magical Sith artefact—the Sith Holocron, which Ezra acquired in the season two finale—guides Ezra in the way of the 'dark side' of the Force, enabling him to develop new powers. Emboldened by his increased power, an angry and arrogant Ezra tells Kanan that he no longer requires his mentorship. At the end of the episode, however, after Kanan has rescued Ezra from a mission that goes bad, Ezra and Kanan reconcile, restoring their relationship status quo. These examples of narrative designers' approach to character in *Rebels* therefore show that, while the conditions of blockbuster film production encourage storyworlds to consistently undergo significant change, television production contexts, in contrast, motivate high degrees of storyworld stability.

Another distinction between film and television production contexts has led to further discrepancies between the *Rebels'* storyworld and that of the film series. This distinction has arisen through media institutions' divergent approaches to the targeting of audiences. Broadcasters, publishers and film studios frequently aim fictional narratives towards particular demographic groups, such as specific age, gender, class, racial and/or ethnic groups, often so as to maximise economic outcomes or, alternatively, to meet public service remits.

While the targeting of specific demographic segments has become ingrained within industries across media, medium-specific uses of this practice are in operation, as a comparison between the *Rebels'* production conditions and those of the *Star Wars* films demonstrates. Film studios typically aim for blockbusters to appeal to a combination of two different demographic groups of cinema-goers: (1) teens and pre-teens, and (2) parents/grandparents with children.[66] The objective to attract this broad coalition of audience groups is intended to maximise viewership, thus offsetting the potential risks associated with blockbusters' high production and marketing budgets. While this approach to audience targeting has become a key component of blockbuster film strategy, across many television industries, the targeting of series towards a similarly broad segment of viewers has become atypical partly due to the popularisation of new television transmission technologies in the latter part of the twentieth century. The growth in the 1970s and 1980s of cable and satellite television, the 1990s advances in cable technology and the emergence in the late 1990s and 2000s of digital television transmission all contributed to a tremendous increase in available channels. This process has underpinned the fragmentation of prior 'mass' audiences, motivating broadcasters and channels to increasingly focus on niche viewer groups.[67] As Amanda D. Lotz observes, television in this period largely transitioned into 'a narrowcast medium—one targeted to distinct and isolated subsections of the audience'.[68]

The emergence of a range of cable channels targeting child demographic segments specifically has been one consequence of this proliferation of channels and resulting viewer fragmentation, with this range including Disney-branded services. Disney XD, which—together with Disney Channel and Disney Junior—forms part of Disney's current child-focused suite of channels, is configured to specifically target young males aged 6–11, an aim that *Rebels* was primarily intended to serve.[69] *Rebels* has indeed proved successful in this respect, with the series' second season finale, for example, coming second place among its competitors in terms of ratings for this particular demographic segment during its timeslot.[70]

The absence within the *Rebels*' storyworld of events that might be too unnerving for young children reflects narrative designers' requirement to prioritise the series' target audience—as opposed to the broader demographic that the film series is intended to attract. The depicted storyworld events within *Rebels* are never as brutal and tragic as some of the *Star Wars* films' most shocking incidents, such as grim events concerning death. *The Force Awakens*, for example, depicts not only cold-blooded murder, such as when Kylo Ren ruthlessly slays his father, but also the trauma that reverberates from such acts, such as when a clearly disturbed Finn witnesses his fellow Stormtroopers massacre helpless villagers. Depictions of these events might be ill-suited for some younger audiences, as the film's US PG-13 rating suggests. However, by including such 'mature' themes as patricide and mass-slaughter, the film is potentially more appealing to the teen and adult components of its broad target audience. In contrast, *Rebels* producers, by largely eschewing such storyworld incidents, ensure that the series does not have the potential to horrify the primary target audience. As Filoni points out, if *Rebels* were made to be 'too dark', the series' target audience might be 'too frightened by it'.[71]

The series does certainly have some moments that might shock young children, such as when, in the season two finale, a lightsaber cuts away part of Darth Vader's mask, revealing the Sith Lord's staring, gleaming, orange eye. Despite the inclusion of such intense incidents, however, *Rebels* producers, at the request of Disney Channels Worldwide, ultimately lean towards broadly comic storyworld events, including many slapstick sequences, thus ensuring the series' compatibility with its target audience.[72] As Filoni observes, he and his producers tend to construct 'situations' that are 'conducive to being funny'.[73] The aforementioned 'Out of the Darkness' episode provides an example of such slapstick and frivolity. As part of a storyline within the episode, Hera tasks Zeb, Ezra and the droid Chopper with a maintenance chore on board the rebels' ship, placing Zeb in charge of the other two. Later within the episode, following a fallout between Ezra and Chopper, the former is shown perched on the latter's head, beating him with a spanner, while the latter wheels circuitously around the ship, as an infuriated Zeb runs after the pair; the result is a form of anarchic physical comedy perhaps more similar to *Tom & Jerry* animated shorts than the current crop of *Star Wars* films.[74]

As this section indicates, in the case of the *Star Wars* franchise, and also other film-centred transmedia entertainment franchises, 'tent pole' movies are typically aimed at large sections of cinema-going audiences, while franchise content is often designed to attract only subsections of that audience. The case of the MCU franchise serves as a further example of this approach. MCU films are targeted towards the same aforementioned broad audience coalition that *Star Wars* films are; yet the Marvel-produced 'Netflix Original' series *Jessica Jones*, which contributes to the MCU, and which explores mature themes such as assault, abuse and trauma, is clearly specifically configured for an adult audience.

When thinking more broadly about the industrial difference between film and television, however, it is important to acknowledge that films other than blockbusters are often intended to appeal to smaller demographic groups. Horrors and thriller films, for example, are, of course, consistently targeted towards teens and/or adults, while 'art films' are typically directed towards educated, affluent urban-dwellers specifically. Despite the presence of such prevalent practices within film culture, however, we are still able to differentiate between twenty-first century film and television on the basis of divergent approaches to audience targeting; at least in the West, television's multitude of channels/services and highly fragmented audience base tend to not only motivate more niche-targeting practices within this medium than in film, but also result in target audiences that are more narrowly defined.

A further way in which television's production conditions have informed the *Rebels* storyworld is by limiting the amount of grand-scale events that result in spectacle. As noted, in the production of blockbuster films, budget limitations ensure that spectacle-laden set pieces must be rationed within a given running time. Yet the consequence of television series production budgets being considerably lower than those of blockbuster films is that there are far fewer big budget set pieces within series. This is even the case with series depicting storyworlds that lend themselves to spectacle, such as those within science fiction and fantasy genres. With a running time of around two hours (omitting credits), *The Force Awakens'* $200 million production budget, which is comparable to the budgets of other contemporary blockbusters, equates to around $100 million per hour of screen time.[75] In comparison, even the most expensive television series fail to rival the per-minute production spend of blockbusters.[76]

Instances of science fiction spectacle may well be cheaper to produce in an animated series such as *Rebels* than they are in live action content; *Rebels* producers nevertheless aim to restrict the type of spectacular grand-scale conflicts synonymous with the *Star Wars* film series, using *Rebels'* compact cast as a means to do so. As Filoni observes, by 'focusing on a small group of people', *Rebels* narrative designers include 'fewer big battles that would cost us a lot of money'.[77] The large-scale space battle sequences that *Rebels* does include, and which are resonant of analogous set pieces in *Star Wars* films, are typically reserved for season premieres and finales. Narrative designers' approaches to the use of spectacle within *Rebels* therefore appear to reflect the standard inferiority of television series production budgets compared to those of blockbuster films.[78]

Rebels narrative design conditions influence medium-specific approaches not only to the construction of *Star Wars* storyworld material but also to the plotting of narrative. As Chap. 3 shows, television episode plot structures adhere to a range of different act structures. *Rebels'* half-hour episodes are typically divided into a pre-title teaser sequence, a long first act and a short second (final) act. This structure is evident in the episode 'The Antillies Extraction' (3:4), for example. The teaser scene depicts the Empire destroying A-Wing fighters, establishing the rebel objective to procure more pilots. The first act sees Sabine go undercover as a TIE pilot cadet, aiming to convince fellow trainees to fight for the rebel cause; the act ends after Sabine's cover is blown, resulting in her imprisonment. The final act sees Sabine escape imprisonment, recruiting a pair of pilots for the cause in the process. While the durations of the *Star Wars* films enable narrative designers to construct epic, planet-hopping adventures, *Rebels*' half-hour running time limit ensures that the missions the rebel crew undertake are often relatively modest and compact, such as Sabine's in this instance.

Rebels' two-act structures, which complement half-hour episode running times, are therefore distinct from the three-act configurations on which the narrative designers of *Star Wars* films rely and which are conventional within that medium. Yet the contingency of *Rebels*' episode structures to the requirements of advertisers further distinguishes the series' narrative design processes from those of film. Each act within an episode structure is configured so as to complement the incorporation of regular commercial breaks as part of Disney XD's transmissions; the placement of commercial breaks therefore determines when those acts begin and end. While, then, it was permissible for *Rogue One* narrative designers to construct an unconventionally long act, such an approach is typically prohibited in advertiser-supported television. As Mittell observes, while 'a film's exact length and story pacing are flexible', commercial television storytelling 'is far more structurally constrained'.[79]

While the above analysis demonstrates that television's industrial conditions lead to certain distinctive plotting practices, *Rebels*' producers do share with the *Star Wars* films' narrative designers the approach of balancing plot resolution and continuation. Episodes of the series each typically comprise a central conflict—typically a standalone mission—that is introduced and resolved by the episode's end along with small subplots that span multiple episodes. This practice, which Chap. 3 explores in greater detail, is indeed far more common to television than it is to film, despite its presence in twenty-first century blockbuster film series.

Underpinned by a cultural approach to medium specificity, this comparative study between *Star Wars* films and *Star Wars Rebels* demonstrates how medium-specific industrial conditions uniquely inform twenty-first century narrative design processes within transmedia entertainment franchises. While media convergence might, then, appear to diminish media boundaries, distinct sets of cultural, and more specifically, industrial conditions work to preserve them. Crucially, however, while a medium's cultural industrial modes of production, circulation and consumption distinguish it from other media, such practices are at the same time highly variable within a single given medium. For example, while—as noted—*Star Wars Rebels* plots are configured to support commercial interruption, not all television series episodes are organised on the same basis, as Chap. 3 shows. It is this perception of media as unfixed combinations of varied cultural patterns and technological facility that leads Dana Polan to regard the medium specificity paradigm as untenable. With regard to film, he argues, the medium is not 'an object to be fixed in its essence, its specificity', but rather an 'unstable intersection of ideology, technology, desire, and so on'.[80] However, as Steven Maras and David Sutton suggest in response, it is still permissible to preserve 'a central insight of medium specificity claims—that there are identifiable differences between one medium and another', while still recognising a medium's high variability.[81] Accepting the concept of a medium's cultural specificity is necessary but not sufficient; we must also account for the contrasting industrial conditions of production, circulation and consumption within a medium. The next section introduces a theoretical approach designed to account for such variability within a given medium's narrative design conditions.

CHARTING INDUSTRY VARIABILITY: DIMENSIONS OF SPECIFICITY WITHIN NARRATIVE DESIGN CONDITIONS

To unravel the complexities within a given medium's network of industrial cultures, I provide here a taxonomical framework that serves to identify and distinguish between a medium's variable industrial forces. This framework, which I refer to as the *dimensions of specificity* model (see Fig. 2.1), posits that narrative design conditions within a given medium are subject not merely to the cultural specificity of a given medium as a whole; while still aligning with a cultural approach, the model instead posits that narrative design conditions are determined by a range of interrelated factors within a given medium's industrial culture, which are each highly variable over time and at a given moment. To account for this variability in the formation of narrative design conditions, the dimensions of specificity model provides a set of industrial dimensions via which a medium can be approached.

As scholars such as Raymond Williams and David Hesmondhalgh observe, media content commissioning institutions have, since the formation of the media industries in the nineteenth century, organised and controlled media production processes, usually in an effort to achieve economic aims.[82] A given commissioning institution frequently therefore directly establishes the constraints and affordances of narrative design conditions. For example, as the above case study shows, Disney XD, as the commissioning institution behind *Star Wars Rebels*, places certain con-

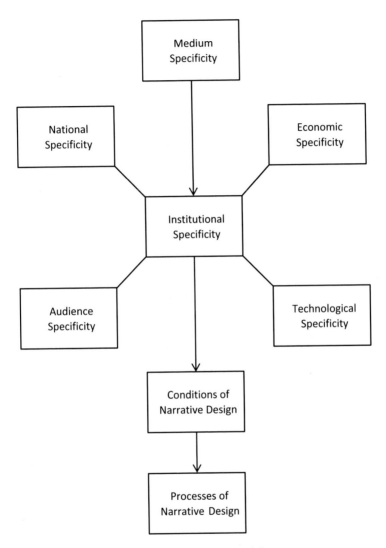

Fig. 2.1   Diagram of dimensions of specificity model

straints on *Rebels* narrative designers; for instance, narratives must appeal to young children so as to ensure institutional audience-targeting aims are met. The contrasting specificities of a range of commissioning institutions should therefore be accounted for in any consideration of the cultural specificities of a given medium; the dimension of institutional specificity accordingly serves as the core of the dimensions of specificity model.

The conditions that institutions impose on narrative design processes are, however, typically informed by key variable cultural factors, which are internal and external to a given institutional structure. These key factors are the perceived requirements of: (1) the particular national industrial context of which a commissioning institution is part; (2) the particular system of revenue that underpins an institution's commissioning of narrative content; (3) the particular media audience groups that an institution hopes to appeal to with a given narrative text; and (4) the particular technological contexts of production, dissemination and consumption in which a commissioning institution operates, as well as the institutional strategies that have formed to utilise a particular technological context. To account for these variable factors, the dimensions of specificity model also incorporates the sub-dimensions of *national specificity, economic specificity, audience specificity* and *technological specificity*. The following sections detail the relevance of each of these industrial sub-dimensions of specificity.

National Specificity

The media convergence age has accelerated the globalisation of media narratives and their production conditions. As Doris Baltruschat observes in her study of 'global media ecologies', 'In the 1990s, changes to media industries in the form of privatization, deregulation and trade liberalization laid the basis for media production ecologies, which network producers, labour and governments into a web of interdependencies that follows the beat of international commerce.'[83] But, while it is important to map the many connections that link media industries around the globe, it is also essential to account for the national and regional conditions that continue to influence how narratives are made. Nationally and regionally imposed policies, such as modes of content regulation, and nationally specific practices of content commissioning, production, dissemination and consumption have the capacity to uniquely inform institutionally imposed conditions of narrative design. As Brett Mills and Erica Horton note with regards to television, 'Despite globalization and complex international circuits of culture the significance of nation remains central to [the medium] in terms of content, production, and purpose.'[84]

Comparisons between different nations' television content-commissioning practices indicate the relevance of the sub-dimension of national specificity to the formation of narrative design conditions. Television institutions in the United States, for example, typically commission primetime television drama seasons ranging from 10 to 24 episodes in length; British television institutions, in contrast, traditionally commission seasons of approximately three, six or eight episodes in length, or, instead, produce primetime soap operas continuously, with no season breaks (similar to US daytime soaps). As Pascal Lefère shows, such discrepancy in institutionally imposed narrative design conditions across nations in a given medium is also present in the differences between comics formats; the combinations of page-length, page-size, paper quality and frequency of publication that each define the typical US comic book, European 'album' and (Japanese) manga magazine, for example, are, as he observes, clearly distinct from one another.[85] As Chaps. 3 and 4 make clear, the particular television season durations and comic-book page lengths that nationally specific industrial cultures establish can have a unique bearing on a storyworld's development and the storytelling means by which it is conveyed. However, while, within a given medium, nationally specific industrial structures and practices have significant impact upon narrative design, so too do the particular economic models that institutions adopt.

Economic Specificity

Within a given medium the features of the economic models that commissioning institutions develop can vary significantly, even within the same national industry. Examples of such variability of revenue models can be found in television and videogames. The production of television narratives can rely on public funding, advertiser payments or subscription fees (or, in the case of transnational productions, potentially a combination of the three), while videogame revenue sources can range from one-off payments for titles to ongoing subscription fees and/or 'microtransactions' for service-based content.

The distinctive elements of a particular economic model can hold important implications for narrative design conditions and processes, as Chap. 3's study of US television drama makes clear; the particular ways in which a commissioning television institution generates revenue can influence, within the production of a drama series, approaches to visual style, episode structure, the plotting of serialised storylines and the conception of story-world material. While it is important, however, when considering narrative design conditions within a medium, to account for the particular configurations of an institution's economic system, it is also vital to account for the specificities of a narrative's intended audience.

Audience Specificity

This sub-dimension pertains to the particular audiences to which a narrative text is to be targeted. Institutions might intend a narrative text to serve the cultural preferences of a particular nation; such an objective might, in turn, have a particular influence on conditions of narrative design. For example, videogame publishers looking to target the lucrative Japanese market specifically will avoid commissioning first-person shooters, as the form is, relative to Western markets, typically lacking in popularity there.[86] Institutions might instead intend a narrative text for, say, a specific class, gender, sexuality, race, ethnicity and/or age group within a given national market or across multiple nations. For example, the ABC television network formed a goal in the mid-2000s of appealing to the growing US Latino population, which resulted in the network encouraging narrative designers to include a greater number of Latino actors within scripted dramas and sitcoms, thereby influencing the identities of characters included in these series' storyworlds.[87]

Due to increased processes of audience segmentation within media cultures in the late twentieth century, which broader patterns of societal fragmentation partly drove, it is especially important to account for the specificities of intended audiences when mapping narrative design conditions over recent decades.[88] As Chaps. 3 and 4 show, for example, the development in the 1970s and 1980s of niche-targeting practices within the US television and comic-book industries strongly influenced narrative design conditions and processes. It is important to acknowledge, however, that, while, in the case of some media, institutions might now differentiate between audiences to a higher degree, instances of audience segmentation have always occurred within media industries. Commissioning institutions' differentiation of audiences has in turn long contributed to variability in conditions of narrative design.

For example, reflecting a low cultural regard for the serial narrative form in US media culture in the first half of the twentieth century, serial narrative texts were generally commissioned specifically for demographic groups perceived as socially subordinate.[89] While, in the 1910s, Hollywood studios appealed to middle-class film audiences with narratively discrete movies, working- and lower-middle classes, along with immigrant audiences, were, notes Ben Singer, targeted via the film serial form.[90] From the mid-1930s, broadcast networks similarly consigned serial narratives to a culturally marginalised group: women. As debates circulated regarding the social role of radio, networks, aiming to gain cultural legitimacy at this time so as to appease regulators and protect a commercial model that was under threat, banished serial narrative forms from their culturally prominent primetime schedules;[91] daytime schedules, which were under less cultural scrutiny, were, in contrast, populated by serialised soap opera narratives explicitly targeted towards female viewers.[92] During this period, therefore, the demographic composition of intended audiences dictated whether or not narrative designers were required to operate within conditions of serial narrative design. However, just as differentiated target audiences, along with contrasting national and economic configurations and practices, can contribute to variable narrative design conditions within a given medium, so too do discrepancies in the technological means of production, dissemination and consumption of screen narratives.

Technological Specificity

Arguing against a paradigm of technological determinism, Williams reminds us that social and industrial practices steer the innovation and utilisation of media technologies.[93] Therefore, rather than perceive, via a technical approach, a given medium as a technology, I regard, through a cultural approach, the developments and implementations of technologies as part of a set of cultural practices that shape narrative design conditions within a given medium.

The cultural development of technological means of production, dissemination and consumption within a given medium can, of course, lead to narrative design conditions altering over time. For example, shifts in television's technological contexts driven by forces of convergence have altered narrative design conditions in significant ways. The rise in use of digital modes of television viewing technologies (e.g. via DVR, DVD and computer), for instance, has enabled audiences to control viewing experiences; these contexts have given rise to what Mittell labels 'forensic fandom' practices whereby viewers carefully scrutinise narrative texts through, for example, repeat viewings and the study of screen captures.[94] Parallel to this trend, the rise of internet culture has provided online venues—in the form of wikis, forums, episode recaps and social media platforms—in which viewers can share insightful findings and theories generated by practices of forensic narrative scrutiny.[95] By enabling audiences to more easily comprehend complex narratives, these cultural contexts shape conditions of narrative design by making complicated and enigmatic storytelling institutionally permissible; these conditions contribute to the institutional viability of, say, the dense and highly convoluted storyworld of the *Game of Thrones* series and the opaque and intentionally misleading storytelling of *Westworld* (by which the first season's non-linear plot structure is carefully concealed). Chapter 3 further considers the influence of twenty-first century television-viewing technologies on narrative design conditions.

However, while noting the variability of technological contexts over time, it is also important to acknowledge that divergent approaches to technology across cultures lead to nations and/or institutions innovating and using technologies in different ways. In the media convergence age, for example, television content is consumed via a range of different screen technologies, ranging from large high-definition screens to mobile devices. These contrasts in consumption contexts can influence variations in narrative design conditions, as different institutions commission narratives intended for different consumption technologies. For example, television institutions have, on occasion, commissioned narratives to be consumed via mobile devices specifically, resulting in narrative designers ensuring that the content they produce complements the specific features of these devices (rather than those of devices with larger screens). As part of their respective studies of *24: Conspiracy* (2005), a transmedia extension of the television drama series *24* (2001–2010) intended for mobile devices, Max Dawson and Elizabeth Evans each analyses the ways in which the webisodes' style is conceived for small displays; the composition consists of a shallow depth of field and a high degree of extreme close-ups, while the split-screen sequences that are characteristic of the television series do not feature.[96] Through its consideration of how the narratives of certain comic books are designed so as to complement their consumption via digital screen devices, Chap. 4 further assesses the significance of the sub-dimension of technological specificity to narrative design conditions within a medium.

Due to the industrial requirement for videogame hardware manufacturers to distinguish their products, the videogame medium incorporates a particularly high degree of differentiation between consumption devices. Variations in hardware graphical processing capacities (which render storyworld activity) and user interface technologies (such as touch screens, motion controls and virtual reality headsets) generate a high contrast in narrative design conditions over time and in a given instance. Via its examination into how a given video game's narrative is tailored to the particular hardware platform(s) for which a commissioning institution intends a game to be released, Chap. 5 demonstrates how a diversity of technological contexts of consumption within the medium influences narrative design processes.

CONCLUSION

This chapter establishes the usefulness of a cultural approach to medium specificity in the twenty-first century. Via its *Star Wars* case study, it demonstrates how medium-specific industrial conditions influence distinct approaches to narrative design. It also confirms the need to account, via a cultural approach to media, for cultural variability within a given medium. Through its introduction of the dimensions of specificity model, the chapter offers a means by which to chart a medium's variations of industrial and broader cultural contexts so as to fully comprehend the complex relationship between media and narrative. The following chapters go on to explore more deeply the relationship between variability in sub-dimensions of specificity and the practices of commissioning institutions, along with the conditions and processes of narrative design that they ultimately shape within a given medium. Due to constraints upon the book's overall size, however, I cannot thoroughly consider the implications of all four sub-dimensions, and therefore I do not explore the significance of national specificity any further.

Instead, each of the following three case-study chapters focuses on a US media context, analysing comprehensively the variability of one of the three remaining sub-dimensions of specificity in relation to a given medium. The first of these chapters concerns the sub-dimension of economic specificity within the twenty-first century US television industry. Tracing connections between the simultaneously variable revenue models of US television institutions and the narrative design conditions and processes of drama series, it demonstrates how differentiation in economic structures influences divergent approaches to storyworld, plot and style.

NOTES

1. Ryan, *Avatars of Story*, 18–21; Ryan, 'Story/Worlds/Media', 29–30.
2. In some cases literary works do incorporate accompanying illustrations, and thereby utilise the semiotic affordances of images.
3. Ryan, *Avatars of Story*, 18–23; Jason Mittell, 'Film and Television Narrative', in *The Cambridge Companion to Narrative*, ed. David Herman (Cambridge: Cambridge University Press, 2007), 156–162.
4. Charles Dickens, *Great Expectations*, Kindle edition (New York: Harper Perennial Classics, 2012 [orig. published 1861]).
5. Ryan, *Avatars of Story*, 21–23; Ryan, 'Story/Worlds/Media', 29–30.
6. Dickens, *Great Expectations*.
7. Ryan, *Avatars of Story*, 23–25; Ryan, 'Story/Worlds/Media', 30.
8. Noël Carroll, 'The Specificity of Media in the Arts' [orig. published 1986], in *Film and Theory: An Anthology*, ed. Toby Miller and Robert Stam (Malden, MA: Blackwell, 2000), 44.
9. Jenkins, *Convergence Culture*, 13–14.
10. See, for example, John Butt and Kathleen Tillotson, *Dickens at Work* (London: Methuen, 1957); John Sutherland, *Victorian Novelists and Publishers* (London: Athlone Press, 1976); Mary Hamer, *Writing by Numbers: Trollope's Serial Fiction* (Cambridge: Cambridge University Press, 1987); Graham Law, *Serializing Fiction in the Victorian Press* (Basingstoke: Palgrave Macmillan, 2000); J. Don Vann, *Victorian Novels in Serial* (New York: Modern Language Association of America, 1985); Deborah Wynne, *The Sensation Novel and the Victorian Family Magazine* (Basingstoke: Palgrave Macmillan, 2001).
11. Examples of semiotic/technical approaches to transmedia narrative include: Wolf, *Building Imaginary Worlds*, 245–267; Harvey, *Fantastic Transmedia*, 155–156; Justin Mack, 'The Dark Knight Levels Up: *Batman: Arkham Asylum* and the Convergent Superhero Franchise', in *Superhero Synergies: Comic Book Characters Go Digital*, ed. James N. Gilmore and Matthias Stork (Lanham, MD: Rowman & Littlefield, 2014), 137–154.
12. See Avi Santo, 'Transmedia Brand Licensing Prior to Conglomeration: George Trendle and the Lone Ranger and Green Hornet Brands', PhD diss., University of Texas at Austin, 2006, 11–20; Matthew Freeman, 'Branding Consumerism: Cross-Media Characters and Story Worlds at the Turn of the Twentieth Century', *International Journal of Cultural Studies* 18, No. 6 (2015), 630.
13. See Matthew Freeman, 'The Wonderful Game of Oz and Tarzan Jigsaws: Commodifying Transmedia in Early Twentieth-Century Consumer Culture', *Intensities: The Journal of Cult Media* 7 (2014), 44–54; Matthew Freeman, 'Up, up and across: Superman, the Second World War and the

Historical Development of Transmedia Storytelling', *Historical Journal of Film, Radio and Television* 35, No. 2 (2015), 215–239; Kristin Thompson, *The Frodo Franchise: The Lord of the Rings and Modern Hollywood* (Berkeley: University of California Press, 2007), 4; Avi Santo, *Selling the Silver Bullet: The Lone Ranger and Transmedia Brand Licensing* (Austin: University of Texas Press, 2015).

14. See Derek Johnson, *Media Franchises: Creative Licensing and Collaboration in the Creative Industries* (New York: New York University Press, 2013).

15. See Angela Ndalianis, *Neo-Baroque Aesthetics and Contemporary Entertainment* (Cambridge, MA: MIT Press, 2004), 25; Jenkins, *Convergence Culture*, 106; Johnson, *Media Franchises*, 4–5.

16. See Tino Balio, *Hollywood in the New Millennium* (London: BFI, 2013).

17. Johnson, *Media Franchises*, 4–5; Freeman, 'Branding Consumerism', 630.

18. For examples of such licensing deals, see LEGO, 'Marvel Entertainment and the LEGO Group Announce Strategic Relationship in Construction Toy Category', LEGO.com, 21 July 2011, https://www.lego.com/en-us/aboutus/news-room/2011/july/marvel-entertainment-and-the-lego-group-announce-strategic-relationship-in-construction-toy-category; Todd Spangler, 'Hasbro Extends Disney Pact for Marvel, *Star Wars* Toys and Games', *Variety*, 22 July 2013, http://variety.com/2013/biz/news/hasbro-extends-disney-pact-for-marvel-star-wars-toys-and-games-1200566115/.

19. With regard to the pivotal role of the film industry concerning the transmedia manifestation of the Marvel franchise, see Flanagan et al., *The Marvel Studios Phenomenon*.

20. See Derek Johnson, 'Cinematic Destiny: Marvel Studios and the Trade Stories of Industrial Convergence', *Cinema Journal* 52, No. 1 (2012), 2.

21. See Thomas Schatz, 'Film Industry Studies and Hollywood History', in *Media Industries: History, Theory, and Method*, ed. Jennifer Holt and Alisa Perren (Malden, MA: Wiley-Blackwell, 2009), 45; Balio, *Hollywood in the New Millennium*, 25–28.

22. Derek Johnson, 'Will the Real Wolverine Stand Up? Marvel's Mutation from Monthlies to Movies', in *Film and Comic Books*, ed. Ian Gordon, Mark Jancovich and Matthew McAllister (Jackson: University Press of Mississippi, 2007), 74–75.

23. Jenkins, *Convergence Culture*, 95–96; Henry Jenkins, 'Transmedia 202: Further Reflections', *Confessions of an Aca-Fan*, 1 August 2011, http://henryjenkins.org/2011/08/defining_transmedia_further_re.html.

24. For detailed analyses of the MCU transmedia narrative, see Harvey, *Fantastic Transmedia*, 79–92; Flanagan et al., *The Marvel Studios Phenomenon*, 177–196.

25. Harvey, *Fantastic Transmedia*, 145.

26. Ibid., 182–202. For more on the authorship of transmedia storytelling, see Elizabeth Evans, *Transmedia Television: Audiences, New Media and Daily Life* (New York: Routledge, 2011), 31–36.
27. See Harvey, *Fantastic Transmedia*, 146.
28. Roberta E. Pearson and William Uricchio, 'I'm Not Fooled By That Cheap Disguise', in *The Many Lives of the Batman: Critical Approaches to a Superhero and His Media*, ed. Roberta E. Pearson and William Uricchio (New York: Routledge, 1991), 164–165.
29. Jenkins, 'Transmedia 202'.
30. For more on the multiplicity of storyworlds in Marvel comics, see Sam Ford and Henry Jenkins, 'Managing Multiplicity in Superhero Comics: An Interview with Henry Jenkins', in *Third Person: Authoring and Exploring Vast Narratives*, ed. Pat Harrigan and Noah Wardrip-Fruin (Cambridge, MA: MIT Press, 2009), 303–311.
31. Johnson, 'Will the Real Wolverine Stand Up?'; Johnson, 'Cinematic Destiny'; Flanagan et al., *The Marvel Studios Phenomenon*.
32. Matthew Freeman, 'Transmediating Tim Burton's Gotham City: Brand Convergence, Child Audiences, and *Batman: The Animated Series*', *Networking Knowledge: Journal of the MeCCSA-PGN 7*, No. 1 (2014), 41–54.
33. Joe Quesada, 'The Birth of Miles Morales', *Comic Book Resources*, 8 May 2011, http://www.cbr.com/the-birth-of-miles-morales/.
34. Shlomith Rimmon-Kenan, *Narrative Fiction: Contemporary Poetics* (London: Methuen, 1983), 60–61.
35. The term and concept of 'storyworld' used here is David Herman's but the model's understanding of story as being more than merely 'the happenings' that a narrative text evokes forms part of a longer tradition within narratology. For example, while some scholars, such as Gérard Genette and Robert Scholes, have traditionally regarded story more narrowly as a mere sequence of events, others, such as Rimmon-Kenan and Seymour Chatman have included characters, objects and environments in their models of story. David Herman, *Story Logic: Problems and Possibilities of Narrative* (Lincoln: University of Nebraska Press, 2002), 13–14; Gérard Genette, 'Frontiers of Narrative', in *Figures of Literary Discourse*, trans. Alan Sheridan, introduced by Marie-Rose Logan (New York: Columbia University Press, 1982), 127; Robert Scholes, 'Language, Narrative and Anti-Narrative', in *On Narrative*, ed. W. J. T. Mitchell (Chicago: University of Chicago Press, 1981), 205; Seymour Chatman, *Story and Discourse: Narrative Structure in Fiction and Film* (Ithaca: Cornell University Press, 1978), 126–145; Rimmon-Kenan, *Narrative Fiction*, 66–67, 69–70.
36. The terms 'order' and 'duration' are Genette's; as Abbott notes, much academic understanding of the term 'plot' stems from Genette's extensive

work on narrative presentation (or 'discourse'). Gérard Genette, *Narrative Discourse: An Essay in Method*, trans. Jane E. Lewin (Ithaca: Cornell University Press, 1980), 33–85; H. Porter Abbott, 'Story, Plot and Narration', in *The Cambridge Companion to Narrative*, ed. Herman, 43–44.

37. Bordwell, Chatman and Meir Sternberg are among those who have previously relied on this distinction between a narrative presentation's structural organisation of storyworld material (plot) and the manner by which a storyworld textually manifests via a medium's semiotic affordances (style). David Bordwell, *Narration in the Fiction Film* (London: Methuen, 1985), 49–50; Chatman, *Story and Discourse*, 10–11, 24; Meir Sternberg, *Expositional Modes and Temporal Ordering in Fiction* (Baltimore: Johns Hopkins University Press, 1978), 34.

38. See Bordwell, *Narration in the Fiction Film*, 50.

39. While not considered here, transmedia extensions to the *Star Wars* films have been produced since the late 1970s across a range of contrasting industrial contexts. Lucasfilm declared in 2014 that much of this transmedia material produced up to that point, which had previously formed what became known as the *Star Wars* 'expanded universe', was no longer 'canon' within the *Star Wars* transmedia fiction established by film and TV series. Anon., 'The Legendary *Star Wars* Universe Turns a New Page', StarWars. com, 25 April 2014, http://www.starwars.com/news/the-legendary-star-wars-expanded-universe-turns-a-new-page.

40. Thon, *Transmedial Narratology*, 19.

41. See David Bordwell, *The Way Hollywood Tells It: Story and Style in Modern Movies* (Berkeley: University of California Press, 2006), 3–4.

42. Ben Child, 'New *Star Wars* Trilogy to Arrive in 2015, 2017 and 2019', *The Guardian*, 18 April 2013, https://www.theguardian.com/film/2013/apr/18/star-wars-episode-vii-trilogy-2015.

43. See Balio, *Hollywood in the New Millennium*, 72–73.

44. Uri Margolin, 'Character', in *The Cambridge Companion to Narrative*, ed. Herman, 73.

45. See Geoff King, *Spectacular Narratives: Hollywood in the Age of the Blockbuster* (London: I. B. Tauris, 2000), 1.

46. See ibid., 2.

47. See Tanner Mirrlees, *Global Entertainment Media: Between Cultural Imperialism and Cultural Globalization* (New York: Routledge, 2013), 188–189.

48. See, for example, Andrew Darley, *Visual Digital Culture: Surface Play and Spectacle in New Media Genres* (London: Routledge, 2000), 103, 106; Michele Pierson, 'CGI Effects in Hollywood Science-Fiction Cinema 1989–1995: The Wonder Years', *Screen* 40, No. 2 (Summer 1999), 158–

176; Scott Bukatman, 'Zooming Out: The End of Off Screen Space', in *The New American Cinema*, ed. Jon Lewis (Durham, NC: Duke University Press, 1998), 248–272.

49. Bordwell, *The Way Hollywood Tells It*, 104–105.
50. Ibid., 107.
51. Mittell, 'Film and Television Narrative', 163.
52. Kristin Thompson, *Storytelling in Film and Television* (Cambridge, MA: Harvard University Press, 2003), 99, 103–104.
53. While the second act of the structure is conventionally longer and more complex than the first and third, Thompson prefers to split this act into two and therefore proposes that we recognise the three-act structure as a four-act structure instead. Kristin Thompson, *Storytelling in the New Hollywood: Understanding Classical Narrative Technique* (Cambridge, MA: Harvard University Press, 1999), 29–35.
54. Writing at the beginning of the 1990s, Michele Hilmes similarly observed that industrial organisation was the key determining factor in the distinction between film and television, and—as this chapter shows—her point is still a valid one. Michele Hilmes, *Hollywood and Broadcasting: From Radio to Cable* (Urbana: University of Illinois Press, 1990), 201.
55. Child, 'New *Star Wars* Trilogy'.
56. Ethan Anderton, 'J. J. Abrams and Kathleen Kennedy Talk About Mapping Out *Star Wars*: Episode 8 and 9', */Film*, 12 August 2015, http://www.slashfilm.com/star-wars-episode-8/2/.
57. Angela Ndalianis, 'Television and the Neo-Baroque', in *The Contemporary Television Series*, ed. Michael Hammond and Lucy Mazdon (Edinburgh: Edinburgh University Press, 2005), 86.
58. Dan Brooks, 'Interview: Simon Kinberg, *Star Wars* Rebels Executive Producer—Part 1', *Star Wars*, 3 October 2014, http://www.starwars.com/news/interview-simon-kinberg-star-wars-rebels-executive-producer-part-1.
59. Andrew Liptak, '*Star Wars Rebels* is Ending with its Fourth Season', *The Verge*, 15 April 2017, https://www.theverge.com/2017/4/15/15313366/star-wars-rebels-ending-fourth-season-trailer-watch.
60. Jason Mittell, 'Previously On: Prime Time Serials and the Mechanics of Memory'. *JustTV*, 3 July 2009, http://justtv.wordpress.com/2009/07/03/previously-on-prime-time-serials-and-the-mechanics-of-memory.
61. Brooks, 'Interview: Simon Kinberg, *Star Wars* Rebels Executive Producer—Part 1'.
62. See Mittell, *Complex TV*, 138.

63. Roberta Pearson, 'Chain of Events: Regimes of Evaluation and *Lost*'s Construction of the Televisual Character', in *Reading Lost: Perspectives on a Hit Television Show*, ed. Roberta Pearson (London: I. B. Tauris, 2009), 154.

64. Mittell, *Complex TV*, 138.

65. Eric Freedman, 'Television, Horror and Everyday Life in *Buffy the Vampire Slayer*', in *The Contemporary Television Series*, ed. Hammond and Mazdon, 171.

66. See Balio, *Hollywood in the New Millennium*, 26.

67. See Dunleavy, *Television Drama*, 133–134; Michele Hilmes, *Only Connect: A Cultural History of Broadcasting in the United States*, second edition (Belmont, CA: Wadsworth, 2007), 299–300; Amanda D. Lotz, *The Television Will Be Revolutionized*, second edition (New York: New York University Press, 2014), 7. The adoption of niche-targeting practices had begun to emerge in US television in the 1970s, after advertiser-supported networks discovered that a demographic group of urban adults aged 18–49 were the primary purchasers of the majority of products featuring in commercial spots. Jane Feuer, 'MTM: Enterprises: An Overview', in *MTM 'Quality Television'*, ed. Jane Feuer, Paul Kerr and Tise Vihmagi (London: BFI, 1984), 3–4.

68. Lotz, *The Television Will Be Revolutionized*, 6.

69. BBC Worldwide, 'BBC's Iconic Drama "Doctor Who" to Premiere on Disney XD Beginning May 9', BBC Press Room, 16 April 2015, http://www.bbcwpressroom.com/sales-and-co-productions/press/bbcs-iconic-drama-doctor-who-to-premiere-on-disney-xd-beginning-may-9/.

70. Rick Kissell, 'Ratings: Disney XD's *Star Wars Rebels* Hits One Year High With Season Finale', *Variety*, 21 April 2016, http://variety.com/2016/tv/news/ratings-disney-xd-star-wars-rebels-finale-1201757980/.

71. Peter Sciretta, 'How Dark Can *Star Wars* Rebels Get? Dave Filoni Responds', */Film*, 5 August 2016, http://www.slashfilm.com/how-dark-can-star-wars-rebels-get/. Filoni appears to be speaking from experience here, having previously noted that *Star Wars: The Clone Wars* (2008–2014), which he developed, 'alienated a good part of younger viewers' after having 'got so dark'. Russ Burlingame, '*Star Wars* Rebels' Dave Filoni Talks Taking Chances, Echoing A New Hope and Not Pleasing Everyone', *Comicbook*, 24 August 2014, http://comicbook.com/blog/2014/08/24/star-wars-rebelss-dave-filoni/.

72. Brooks Barnes, 'Empire Renewed: *Star Wars* Rebels Emulates the Trilogy of Old', *The New York Times*, 25 September 2014, http://www.nytimes.com/2014/09/28/arts/television/star-wars-rebels-emulates-the-trilogy-of-old.html.

73. Dan Brooks, 'Interview: Dave Filoni on *Star Wars Rebels*, Part 2', *Star Wars*, 2 March 2015, http://www.starwars.com/news/interview-dave-filoni-on-star-wars-rebels-part-2.

74. *Star Wars* movies do nevertheless sometimes feature moments of slapstick; such instances are, for example, particularly well evident in *Star Wars: Episode 1—The Phantom Menace* (1999), which—as critics such as Todd McCarthy observed on the film's release—appears tilted towards appealing to children specifically. Todd McCarthy, 'Review: *Star Wars: Episode 1—The Phantom Menace*', *Variety*, 10 May 1999, http://variety.com/1999/film/reviews/star-wars-episode-i-the-phantom-menace-1117499730/.

75. Brent Lang, '*Star Wars: The Force Awakens*: Counting Down the Records It Broke', *Variety*, 20 December 2015, http://variety.com/2015/film/box-office/star-wars-the-force-awakens-records-box-office.

76. The $100 million production budget for the sixth season of HBO fantasy drama *Game of Thrones*, for example, is very much at the high end of television series production budgeting, yet still only amounts to around $10 million per hour of screen time (on average). Hayley C. Cuccinello, '*Game of Thrones* Season 6 Costs $10 Million Per Episode, Has Biggest Battle Scene Ever', *Forbes*, 22 April 2016, http://www.forbes.com/sites/hayley-cuccinello/2016/04/22/game-of-thrones-season-6-costs-10-million-per-episode-has-biggest-battle-scene-ever.

77. Barnes, 'Empire Renewed'.

78. At the time of writing, details regarding the *Rebels*' production budget have not been made publicly available.

79. Mittell, 'Film and Television Narrative', 163–165.

80. Dana Polan, 'Film Theory Reassessed', *Continuum: The Australian Journal of Media and Culture* 1, No. 2 (1988), 15.

81. Steven Maras and David Sutton, 'Medium Specificity: Re-Visited', *Convergence* 6 (2000), 103, 109.

82. Raymond Williams, *Culture* (London: Fontana, 1981), 38–56; David Hesmondhalgh, *The Cultural Industries*, second edition (Los Angeles: Sage Publications, 2007), 53–54.

83. Doris Baltruschat, *Global Media Ecologies: Networked Production in Film and Television*, Kindle edition (London: Routledge, 2010).

84. Brett Mills and Erica Horton, *Creativity in the British Television Comedy History* (New York: Routledge, 2017), 3. Ian Robert Smith, in his study of transnational adaptations also observes the significance of national cultural contexts in the formation of narrative; see Iain Robert Smith, *The Hollywood Meme: Transnational Adaptations in World Cinema* (Edinburgh: Edinburgh University Press, 2016).

85. Pascal Lefère, 'The Importance of Being "Published": A Comparative Study of Different Comics Formats', in *Comics and Culture*, ed. Hans-

Christian Christiansen and Anne Magnussen (Copenhagen: Museum Tusculanum Press, 2000), 100.

86. Chris Kohler, 'In Japan, Gamemakers Struggle to Instill Taste For Western Shooters', *Wired*, 16 September 2010, https://www.wired.com/2010/09/western-games-japan/.

87. Brooks Barnes, 'A Made-for-TV Boss Helps Revive ABC', *The New York Times*, 7 October 2007, http://www.nytimes.com/2007/10/07/business/media/07disney.html.

88. See Hesmondhalgh, *The Cultural Industries*, 388–389; Manuel Castells, *The Rise of the Network Society: The Information Age*, Vol. 1 (Oxford: Blackwell, 1996), 340–341.

89. Cultural aversion towards the serial form can be traced back to the nineteenth century. Despite the prevalence of serial narrative in working- and middle-class targeted publications in the US and Europe, certain upper-class discourses nevertheless exhibited disdain towards the mode. The flavour of such censure is well captured in a *Prospective Review* critique of the two-volume edition of Thackeray's *Pendennis*, which had been published previously in part fiction (1848–1850). The reviewer laments, 'The serial tale ... is probably the lowest artistic form yet invented; that, namely which affords the greatest excuse for unlimited departures from dignity, propriety, consistency, completeness and proportion'. Quoted in Edgar F. Harden, *The Emergence of Thackeray's Serial Fiction* (Athens: University of Georgia Press, 1979), 3.

90. Ben Singer, 'Serial Melodrama and Narrative Gesellschaft', *The Velvet Light Trap* 37 (1996), 72.

91. See Michele Hilmes, *Radio Voices: American Broadcasting, 1922–1952* (Minneapolis: University of Minnesota Press, 1997), 153–154; Robert W. McChesney, *Telecommunications, Mass Media, and Democracy: The Battle for the Control of U.S. Broadcasting, 1928–1935* (New York: Oxford University Press, 1993).

92. Hilmes, *Radio Voices*, 154.

93. Raymond Williams, *Television, Technology and Cultural Form* (London: Fontana, 1974), 14, 124, 130.

94. Mittell, *Complex TV*, 44, 52.

95. Ibid., 261–291.

96. Max Dawson, 'Little Players, Big Shows: Format, Narration, and Style on Television's New Smaller Screens', *Convergence* 13 (2007), 236; Evans, *Transmedia Television*, 124–130.

CHAPTER 3

Economic Specificity in Narrative Design: The Business of Television Drama Storytelling

INTRODUCTION

Narrative design conditions established by television institutions, such as broadcast networks, cable channels and online streaming services, help to preserve television's identity as a distinct narrative medium. As the previous chapter's consideration of television's specificities relative to those of film demonstrates, television institutions (at least those operating outside public service sectors) generally establish such conditions so as to serve their efforts in generating revenue. For example, the requirement for narrative designers to anticipate the inclusion of commercial breaks within episode transmissions is, of course, a consequence of advertisers paying institutions to incorporate commercials within their programming. Institutional economic models within television are, then, responsible for narrative design conditions that distinguish the medium from others; but what are the implications for these conditions—which are so integral to television's identity—of variability between economic models within the medium? This chapter addresses this question, exploring in depth the relevance of economic specificity as a key sub-dimension of specificity in narrative design conditions and processes within a given medium.

The chapter considers in particular the relationships between the contrasting institutional economic models and narrative design conditions and processes of US television drama in the twenty-first century. This combination of period, national market and programming type proves a useful test bed due to the emergence of a contrasting range of economic

© The Author(s) 2018
A. N. Smith, *Storytelling Industries*,
https://doi.org/10.1007/978-3-319-70597-2_3

models driving the commissioning of such programming over the previous two decades. The diversity of economic models engaged in the commissioning of such series can be broken down into three general categories: those of broadcast networks (such as ABC, NBC, CBS and FOX); those of basic cable channels (such as FX, USA, TNT and AMC); and those of cable and online streaming subscription services (such as HBO, Showtime, Netflix and Amazon). The network economic model is primarily dependent on revenue provided by advertisers in exchange for a network's inclusion of advertisements within their programming broadcasts. Basic cable institutions are advertiser supported in the same way as networks, but cable operators (who pay institutions for the right to incorporate their channels in the basic cable packages they sell to viewers) also provide them with a significant supplementary income in 'carriage fees'. The subscription model, in contrast, is based on a direct economic relationship between the institution and its subscribers who pay a fee in exchange for access to programming.

As Amanda D. Lotz argues, it is important to consider the particular implications that each of these three general institutional economic models holds for programming production.[1] But while scholarly comparisons regarding how contrasting economic models within the US television industry influence narrative already exist, they are far from exhaustive. On the one hand, discussion of narrative within such scholarship is often limited, fleetingly focusing only on certain aspects of storytelling (plot, say); on the other hand, these studies typically focus on the distinction between network and subscription service contexts in particular, thus overlooking basic cable's role in the commissioning of drama series.[2] This chapter, through its analysis of connections between three essential narrative elements—namely, plot, style and storyworld, and the full range of economic models underpinning the development of recent US television drama, therefore represents a uniquely comprehensive study of narrative design conditions and processes within the US television industry in the twenty-first century. The chapter primarily explores the significance of the sub-dimension of economic specificity within the same national industry; however, it also acknowledges the implications of variability in target audiences and technological contexts thereby additionally considering the significance of the sub-dimensions of audience and technological specificity.

To ensure a useful comparison between the narrative design processes across these three categories of economic models, I focus in particular on series that conform to a specific plotting system that I refer to here as a *modified soap structure* (MSS). Drawing upon the plotting traditions of US broadcast daytime soap operas, MSS drama series episodes are each organised around a succession of scenes that interweave multiple distinct storylines, with each storyline drawing upon different characters of an ensemble cast, and with at least some of these storylines being multiple episodes in length.

The MSS series, however, does depart from the daytime soap opera plotting blueprint in two key ways concerning storyline pacing and organisation. Firstly, the MSS series will typically incorporate a greater amount of unique dramatic incidents per episode than a soap opera will. One of the narrative characteristics of the daytime soap opera is for a considerable amount of an episode's screen time to be devoted to character discussions concerning a given dramatic event (a car crash, say, or an unexpected pregnancy) from a previous episode.[3] This technique of exhausting the narrative potential of any one dramatic incident complements networks' practice of scheduling episodes of daytime soap operas over five days a week, all year round; the technique thus reduces the amount of original storyworld ideas that producers must develop so as to service a great number of episodes.[4] In contrast to daytime soap opera producers, narrative designers of MSS series, whether working on, say, a 24-episode season for a broadcast network or a ten-episode season for a cable channel, are required to deliver far fewer episodes in a given year. Operating under these different industrial conditions, narrative designers working on MSS series are free to include a greater amount of unique dramatic incidents per episode (as opposed to retellings of prior events), and usually do so. Secondly, because MSS series are, unlike daytime soap operas, segmented into distinct seasons, MSS series are structured to complement the particular season formats that institutions impose; as this chapter goes on to show, the ways in which narrative designers plot storylines across multiple episodes are dependent, for example, upon the number of episodes contained within a season and the scheduling of mid-season breaks.

The MSS concept shares key similarities with the often cited 'flexi-narrative' paradigm that Robin Nelson usefully introduced to account for television drama narrative in the 1980s and 1990s; both terms ultimately refer to drama series plotting systems that evolved from soap opera's storytelling conventions. For the purposes of this discussion I have opted to use the MSS concept, rather than rely on Nelson's, because the flexi-narrative definition cannot account for the range of different soap-influenced plotting techniques that abound in US television today. For example, from the vantage point of 1995, Nelson defined flexi-narrative primetime drama episodes as 'rapidly' cutting between different storylines and including standalone storylines;[5] as this chapter demonstrates, a significant number of twenty-first century multiple-plot ensemble-cast dramas have, due to recent industrial shifts, neglected to adhere to this form.

Since the 1980s, the MSS form has featured within many drama series—from *Hill Street Blues* (NBC, 1981–1987) to *The Shield* (FX, 2002–2008), and from *Dynasty* (ABC, 1981–1989) to *Game of Thrones* (HBO, 2011–present)—that have been introduced across networks, cable channels and online streaming service platforms. This narrative form is furthermore clearly distinguishable from that of the procedural drama series, such as *House* (Fox, 2004–2012) and *Elementary* (CBS, 2012–present), with which MSS dramas have shared primetime schedules in recent decades. Lacking the soap opera system of multiple-storyline plotting, procedural drama episodes are usually organised around a dominant standalone conflict (say, a criminal case or a medical emergency). Serialised sub-storylines concerning longer-arc mysteries or the personal lives of central characters typically augment each episode's primary procedural storyline.[6] While the procedural television drama form has high cultural and industrial significance both in the past and the present, it has been largely confined to network schedules and, to a lesser extent, basic cable channels. Due to its concentration within these institutional sectors, this storytelling form is, compared to the MSS form, of limited value to a comparative study of narrative design across a full range of economic contexts; the procedural form is therefore largely set aside from this chapter's discussions.

In order to consider how contrasting economic models factor into narrative design conditions and processes of MSS series, this case study is broken down into three main sections. Each of these sections focuses on two drama-commissioning institutions that are representative of a distinct economic category within the US television industry. These institutions are the broadcast networks NBC and ABC; the subscription services HBO and Netflix; and the basic cable channels FX and AMC. Each of these institutions represents an appropriate case study subject, as each has played a prominent role in the commissioning of series that adhere to the MSS mode. Each section outlines the industrial shifts that have led to the commissioning of MSS drama series within a given economic category before going on to explore how the specificities of economic models within this given category have informed narrative production.

Economic Specificity in Network Drama Series: ABC and NBC

Reflecting the relevance of the sub-dimension of audience specificity, the US television industry's shift from mass- to niche-targeting served as the key underlying factor behind the sustained presence of the MSS system of plot organisation within networks' primetime schedule from the early 1980s onwards. Prior to this period, notes Hilmes, the 'big three' networks, NBC, ABC and CBS, had established (from the 1960s onwards) an oligarchic system of control over programming production and distribution; as a combined presence, they dominated the nation's audience share throughout the 1960s and 1970s.[7] Each of the networks within this period was largely concerned with addressing the widest possible 'mass' audience so as to consolidate its share of the market. But, as noted in the previous chapter (and indicative of the importance of the sub-dimension of technological specificity), the emergence of cable television technology in the late 1970s diminished the trio's share dominance, thus encouraging a greater shift towards niche targeting (a practice that had steadily grown throughout the 1970s).[8]

This industrial context is reflected in CBS' decision to allow Lorimar Productions to infuse its primetime series *Dallas* with the MSS system of plotting as a means to specifically target the female demographic (towards which daytime soap operas have traditionally been targeted).[9] Prior to this period, hour-long, once a week primetime drama series would centre on casts of continuous characters and settings, with episode storylines rarely transcending the boundaries of the individual hourly format.[10] This is not to suggest that producers and networks did not experiment with the serial form within the series format in the 1960s and 1970s, but rather that the 'episodic series' prevailed as the norm.[11] *Dallas*, however, while not the first 'primetime soap', would influence, notes Hilmes, the 'wholesale importation' of serial narratives to primetime on account of its enviable ratings in the late 1970s and early 1980s.[12] For example, the oil baron saga inspired the popular CBS spin-off *Knots Landing* (1979–1993), plus a string of successful imitators, notably ABC's *Dynasty*.[13]

NBC, the third-rated network at the beginning of the 1980s, was, in contrast to its rivals, without a successful *Dallas*-style primetime soap.[14] *Dallas'* system of plotting nevertheless came to inform the primetime narratives that resulted from the network's own niche targeting strategies, initially with its cop drama series *Hill Street Blues*.[15] NBC intended *Hill Street* for the young, well-educated professionals that advertisers desired, and which accordingly the network now sought.[16] The network thus ensured, together with MTM Production Enterprises, that the series represented an alternative to standard network fare, and could be interpreted as sophisticated by the target upscale demographic. These institutional aims facilitated *Hill Street*'s incorporation of dialogue and storylines that, due to their provocative nature, set the series apart from previous cop dramas, such as *Ironside* (1967–1975) and *Kojak* (1973–1978), the production of those series having been guided so as not to alienate any component of a total audience share.[17] In the wake of *Dallas*' huge cultural impact, however, *Hill Street* further departed from its generic predecessors via its emulation of the MSS system, with its episodes each possessing multiple distinct serialised storylines.[18]

Hill Street Blues sat at the vanguard of the first generation of drama series that would come to attract a 'quality' label within critical discourses, with this programming type ultimately defined by its target upmarket audience and its possession of narrative elements that contrasted with prior network tradition.[19] In the 1980s and 1990s the MSS mode often served as a distinguishing storytelling feature of such series, including ABC's *Thirtysomething* (1987–1991), *NYPD Blue* (1993–2005) and *Murder One* (1995–1997), and NBC's *St. Elsewhere* (1982–1988), *L.A. Law* (1986–1994) and *Homicide: Life on the Street* (1993–1999). While the MSS system of storytelling was certainly utilised (post-*Dallas*) within other types of primetime drama during this period, it become synonymous with drama series targeted towards a high-end demographic, the mode's serial form and the multiple-storyline plot system facilitating the type of complicated narratives that 'quality' audiences have come to revere.[20] Despite, then, the general low cultural status of seriality earlier in the twentieth century that the previous chapter observed, 'quality' drama has, remarks Jane Feuer, predominantly represented 'a peculiar elevation of soap opera narrative structure'.[21]

While the utilisation of the MSS drama formula within network television persisted through the 1980s and 1990s, however, it was hardly a prevailing form within networks' primetime schedules during this period. For example, ABC and NBC's 1996–1997 line-ups included a selection of MSS dramas: *NYPD Blue*, *The Practice* (ABC, 1997–2004), *Nothing Sacred* (ABC, 1997–1998), *ER* (NBC, 1994–2009) and *Homicide: Life on the Street*. But, similar to those of their competitors, these two networks' schedules were dominated by sitcoms and procedural dramas containing little to no serial narrative elements. Networks during this period still demonstrated preference for programming that featured either zero ongoing storylines or only small degrees of serialised narrative for two key reasons. Firstly, while serial storytelling was frequently permitted because it was seen as a way to induce viewer loyalty, it potentially restricted audience sizes, as serialised narrative material within a given episode might deter viewers who failed to catch previous episodes of a given series. Secondly, serialised narratives fail to complement networks' business practice of syndicating programming to be rerun on network affiliate stations and basic cable channels. As Mittell observes, because episodes of a rerun series in syndication might be transmitted in an incorrect order, serialised narratives have traditionally been regarded a poor fit with this ancillary business practice.[22]

However, altered industrial conditions within the twenty-first century have made the presence of serial storytelling more economically attractive to networks, leading to an increased use of the MSS form due to its usefulness as a vessel for serial storytelling. These altered conditions largely concern the emergence from the 2000s to the present of new ways to consume programming away from broadcast schedules and at viewers' convenience. According to Lotz, this period, which she labels the 'post-network era', is characterised by an increase in non-linear viewing practices enabled by digital technologies and online platforms.[23] The influence of these changes therefore again demonstrates the need to take into account the variability of technological conditions of distribution and consumption technologies when assessing narrative design conditions and processes.

These viewing practices include the use of digital video recording devices, which enable viewers to record each episode of a selected series and play back those episodes at their convenience. The penetration of these devices within US television viewing culture is estimated to have grown from 6 per cent of households in 2006 to 50 per cent in 2016, while DVR viewings have formed part of a given episode's cumulative Nielsen ratings since 2006.[24] The widespread use of these devices creates favourable conditions for serial storytelling because, as Jennifer Gillan observes, DVRs make it easier for viewers to 'follow and keep up' with complex ongoing narratives thereby potentially increasing the amount of loyal viewers a series can attract.[25]

Other digital viewing practices that have emerged in the twenty-first century include watching MSS drama series via DVD box sets. As with DVR viewing, this allows viewers to watch every episode of a series and control the pace of their viewing, thereby making it easier for individuals to follow serial storylines. This practice developed into a lucrative ancillary window for networks in the 2000s, as MSS network dramas, such as ABC's *Lost* (2004–2010) and Fox's *24* (2004–2010), often proved to be strong sellers in this format. Network success in this market has in some cases been a factor in the commissioning and renewal of such series. President of Twentieth Century Fox Television Gary Newman, for example, commented that the 'healthy' DVD sales enjoyed by *24* had proved essential to its continuation.[26]

A related and more recent viewing practice that has helped to make conditions more favourable for MSS dramas in the network context is the watching of TV series via on demand streaming services such as Netflix and Amazon. These subscription services' streaming of television series has opened up new lucrative markets of content syndication for networks. While serialised dramas might be a poor complement to networks' traditional syndication practices, this programming type has the potential to perform well in rerun via this syndication route because, as with DVR and DVD viewing, viewers are able to easily view all of a series' given episodes in order when consuming series in this manner.

These changes to distribution and reception practices lessened some of the economic risks associated with seriality in the network context and so increased the feasibility of the MSS series in recent years. These altered conditions have, as a consequence, contributed to the increased presence of MSS series within twenty-first century network schedules. Comparison between ABC and NBC line-ups from the 1990s and those of the 2000s and 2010s demonstrates this increase. For example, ABC and NBC's 1997–1998 schedules together feature only six MSS series; these include ABC's *The Practice* (ABC, 1997–2004) and *NYPD Blue*, and NBC's *ER* and *Homicide: Life of the Street*.[27] The 2007–2008 NBC and ABC line-ups, in contrast, contain a combined total of 18 MSS series, including ABC's *Lost* and *Grey's Anatomy* (2005–present), and NBC's *Heroes* (2006–2010) and *Friday Night Lights* (2006–2011).[28] US network television has continued to commission a high volume of MSS series in the 2010s; a combined total of 17 MSS series populated the ABC and NBC 2016–2017 schedules, including ABC's *Scandal* (2012–2018) and *Once upon a Time* (2011–2018), and NBC's *This Is Us* (2016–present) and *The Night Shift* (2014–2017).[29]

Alongside altered technological conditions of reception, changing practices within cable television have also served to motivate the increased commissioning of network MSS series. As I will go on to cover in detail, from the early 2000s, the cable sector significantly increased its commissioning of

MSS drama series; a handful of these series, such as HBO's *The Sopranos* (1999–2007) and *Game of Thrones*, have dominated discourses around television drama and generated viewing figures that have rivalled those of network series. Cable channels' achievement of cultural prominence via their original drama programming has in turn influenced network practices. As Gary R. Edgerton and Jeffrey P. Jones observe with regard to the influence of HBO's original dramas in the 2000s, these series 'provoked an "after effect"' within the wider industry, informing the narrative features of broadcast network dramas.[30] As part of this wider process of influence, networks have more widely embraced the MSS structure in an effort to diminish the distinctiveness of cable dramas with which their programming competes.

Cable channels' practice of scheduling original MSS series all year round has also proved a factor in the increased number of MSS network dramas. Networks have traditionally scheduled reruns during the periods in which their dramas are on a break, such as during the summer months; however, networks now look to ensure that their schedules contain new episodes of drama programming all year round, so as to offer stronger competition to cable channels, resulting in networks originating more dramas overall. For example, rather than schedule reruns in the *Agents of S.H.I.E.L.D.*'s Tuesday evening timeslot while the series underwent a winter break during the 2014–2015 schedule, ABC instead introduced its debut season of *Agent Carter* in this timeslot; with *Agent Carter*, which forms part of the same Marvel Cinematic Universe as *Agents of S.H.I.E.L.D.*, ABC hoped to retain its *Agents of S.H.I.E.L.D.* viewership during this series' hiatus.[31]

Having outlined the industrial motivation for the increased presence of the MSS drama series in NBC and ABC primetime schedules, I move on here to consider the ways in which the specificities of the network economic model have informed these narratives. This analysis is broken down into multiple sections wherein connections between network narrative design conditions and elements of storyworlds, plots and styles are explored within individual episodes, across multiple episodes and through seasons.

Network: Storyworlds

The storyworld settings of network MSS primetime drama series tend to reflect networks' imperative to continue the production of a given series for as long as that series is economically attractive. As Robert C. Allen observes, narrative designers of such ongoing programming typically conceive of storyworld environments so as to ease the task of introducing new characters and storylines, and to provide endless opportunity for characters of an ensemble cast to interact.[32] Twenty-first century MSS primetime drama series that conform to this logic include workplace environments, such as the Boeing 707's interiors in *Pan Am* (ABC, 2011–2012), *Grey's Anatomy*'s Grey Sloan Memorial Hospital and the offices of Olivia Pope & Associate's consultancy firm in *Scandal*. Also typical are those location types emulative of soap opera's traditions, such as small towns and neighbourhoods, as in *Desperate Housewives* and *Once Upon a Time*, as well as the domestic spaces linked by family connections, as in *Parenthood* (NBC, 2010–2015) and *Brothers & Sisters* (ABC, 2006–2011). As these are sites within which varied combinations of characters are likely to meet, such settings afford great flexibility to the narrative design processes of long-running series. By enabling the recycling of a limited number of settings in successive episodes of a given series, such writing practice also proves extremely cost effective for ongoing productions.

In terms of the characters that populate these types of spaces, the protagonists of twenty-first century network MSS dramas often draw upon the innovations of late 1980s 'quality' series. Prior to the widespread uptake of niche-targeting strategies in the 1980s, networks had, in an effort not to alienate any component of their total audience share, generally been guided by a principle of 'least objectionable programming'.[33] As a consequence of this institutional philosophy, main recurring characters of primetime drama series, such as Joe Friday, John Walton and James T. Kirk, would often be decent, upstanding and inoffensive. Conversely, many of the main recurring characters of network 'quality' series that emerged in the 1980s and 1990s have significant flaws. Characters in such series might routinely exhibit supreme arrogance, such as Dr Peter Benton (*ER*); or possess bigoted views, such as Andy Sipowicz (*NYPD Blue*); or compromise themselves through such acts as heavy drinking, as Detective Mike Kellerman does (*Homicide: Life on the Street*); or pursue morally questionable romantic lives, such as caddish divorce attorney Arnie Becker (*L.A. Law*), who routinely sleeps with his clients, and middle-aged Sergeant Phil Esterhaus (*Hill Street Blues*), who opts to leave his wife so as to date a high school girl. Such imperfect character traits supported the network model during this period due to their potential appeal to a target upscale audience as challenging and unorthodox narrative elements.

Twenty-first century network MSS dramas frequently utilise this model of the 'quality' protagonist, relying on characters who demonstrate mastery at their vocations yet who also have certain failings or imperfections in terms of their personalities. *The Night Shift*'s Dr TC Callahan, for example, is a gifted ER surgeon who suffers from PTSD due to his experiences as an army medic in Afghanistan, which fuels instances of anger and psychological breakdown. *Hannibal*'s (NBC, 2013–2015) Will Graham is similarly brilliant within his professional field and also psychologically damaged. He is a criminal profiler with the unique capacity to understand murderers' ways of thinking, enabling him to help bring killers to justice; yet he is also depressive and socially dysfunctional, while his taxing work method, which requires him to have deep empathy with killers, contributes to a fragile personality that sometimes results in disorientation and hallucinations.

As Matt Zoller Seitz notes, this character type—the exceptionally talented protagonist undermined by personality flaws—has become formulaic across contemporary American television drama.[34] The specificity of the network advertiser-supported context, however, guarantees that there are limits to the extent that network protagonists can depart from the baseline of the conventionally perfect character that typified the 'least objectionable programming' era. As many advertisers might balk at associating their brand with an ongoing character who repeatedly carries out heinous actions, networks usually typically ensure that protagonists' flaws run only so deep. While TC and Will are both psychologically unstable they are typically virtuous, carrying out worthy actions (e.g. saving people, pursuing killers), and are therefore reflective of a norm whereby network drama protagonists are morally decent. As Jill Soloway, creator of the comedy drama *Transparent* (Amazon, 2014–present), observes on the basis of her experiences pitching to networks, the requirement to appease advertisers leads networks to typically 'play it safe' and veer towards protagonists with character traits reflective of social mores.[35]

Recent high-profile exceptions to this norm, however, suggest that advertisers might be more willing to support dramas containing morally dubious protagonists than long-standing conventions dictate. Olivia Pope, the lead protagonist of ABC's *Scandal*, for example, typically appears to operate without any moral compass. This character, whose firm resolves crises so as to protect public reputations, helps to conceal heinous acts and rigs a presidential election. Pope is the product of a writing team that, according to *Scandal* creator Shonda Rhimes, consciously works against 'the very traditional idea' that audiences require characters to be 'good'.[36]

As Mittell observes, morally ambiguous protagonists, such as Pope, have the capacity to appeal to audiences through their encouragement of fascination and intrigue.[37] But, from many advertisers' perspectives, their association with series centred on morally bereft protagonists risks tarnishing their brands, hence the scarcity of this character type within a network context. Yet, speaking to the relevance of audience specificity within the creation of characters, industry perceptions of audience members' preferences can permit exceptions to this norm, as in the case of *Scandal*. Advertisers, for example, currently perceive that convention-breaking drama content has the strong potential to attract affluent 18- to 34-year-olds.[38] This is a demographic group that advertisers especially covet due to its spending habits but find difficult to address due to this group's increasing migration away from traditional forms of television consumption to on demand services.[39] Advertisers therefore appear to have a growing incentive to put aside misgivings concerning the storyworld content of certain series, such as *Scandal*, which do achieve significant success in attracting this particular audience group.[40] Such exceptions aside, however, the specificity of the network economic model still typically motivates networks to develop dramas with protagonists who are, ultimately, underpinned by conventionally sound morals. The following section, which explores plotting and style within individual episodes of network MSS drama series, further ascertains how the dominating determining factor of advertiser support within networks' economic models influences narrative design processes.

Network: Episode Plots and Styles

Approaches to the plotting of episodes within the narrative design processes of network drama series typically lead, observes Michael Z. Newman, to episodes comprised of short scenes (often two minutes or less).[41] The perception within the network environment that a brisk presentation of storyworld is a reliable method with which to hold viewers' attention (and thus deliver them to advertisers) underpins this plotting technique. 'In a fast-paced story a long scene can derail the sense of forward progress', notes Newman; 'given the commercial imperative of keeping the audience interested, most forms of television present a rapid succession of short segments'.[42] The plot device of swiftly cutting from one set of characters to another throughout a given episode of an MSS series also potentially maintains viewer interest. As Nelson observes, 'Any lack of interest … in one story-line is thus not allowed to last long as another story with a different group of characters is swiftly taken up.'[43]

The narrative styles of network drama series scenes often support this perceived economic imperative for fast-moving storylines. Within television, the term narrative style encompasses compositional elements of mise-en-scène, such as framing, lighting, set design, as well as editing, camera movement, sound design, performance, and other textual elements that comprise a scene.[44] In network drama series the styles of shooting, editing and performance, in particular, typically combine to contribute to the presentation of a story that potentially conveys to viewers a continued sense of urgency. For example, just as episodes often represent a sequence of short scenes, these scenes are often comprised of successions of brief shots. Jonathan Lupo's statistical analysis of sample episodes from *Friday Night Lights*, for example, discerns an average shot length (ASL) of between 2.3 and 3.9 seconds per episode.[45] Such cutting pace is consistent with other twenty-first century network series, such as Fox's *24* and CBS' *CSI: Crime Scene Investigation* (2000–2015).[46]

Network series furthermore employ alternative modes of style that, similar to high-tempo editing, have the potential to encourage the impression of narrative velocity that networks mandate. These modes include the significant use of camera movement, such as handheld documentary-style camera movements, which *Hill Street Blues* pioneered in the network sector.[47] Another use of movement in visual style is the highly-kinetic Steadicam-facilitated shooting style whereby the camera is restless and roving as it tracks performers, which the NBC series *ER* and *Homicide: Life on the Street* helped to popularise within television drama.[48] Use of significant, sometimes excessive, amounts of camera movement within scenes has become ubiquitous within twenty-first century network MSS series, and such agile camera work is often complemented by swiftly delivered dialogue potentially contributing to an overall perception of busyness and urgency.

This approach to visual style, performance and, in terms of scene length, plot, is evident in the opening scene of *Scandal's* pilot episode, in which Harrison Wright of Olivia Pope & Associates meets Lindsay Dwyer in a bar to offer her a job at Olivia's firm. In line with Rhimes' mandate for the series, dialogue within the scene, which is two minutes and twelve seconds in duration, is rapidly delivered with little pause between lines.[49] The scene's visual style complements this fast-paced dialogue delivery, alternating between shots offering multiple perspectives of Dwyer observing

Wright and vice versa. With many of these shots, the camera is slowly, gracefully orbiting the performer to the left or right, thereby infusing fluidity into the scene. The scene's 2.2 second ASL ensures a high cutting tempo, further suggesting that events are unfolding at a brisk pace. The scene's visual style ultimately results in an assemblage of brief, gently gliding shots—a sequence of graceful movements. In support of the network economic model, this visual style's balletic quality, coupled with the performers' breathless dialogue delivery, emphasises action.

Not all modern ABC and NBC dramas include the same storytelling features as *Scandal*, of course. They do, however, tend to rely on techniques that encourage within viewers a sense of narrative momentum. As a point of comparison with the *Scandal* pilot, the dialogue delivery in the pilot episode of ABC's FBI drama *Quantico*, for example, is not as hurried, while the episode's shots are typically not as kinetic. To meet the network-specific objective of conveying to viewers a sense of narrative acceleration, however, the episode does include scenes that feature speeded up shots and jump cuts.

In addition to motivating the production of episodes comprised of succinct scenes and styles designed to convey the sense of activities occurring speedily, the network economic model furthermore dictates the plotting of episode act structures. As discussed in Chap. 2, the incorporation of commercials within television transmissions often requires narrative designers to ensure that each act is configured so as to conclude prior to a commercial break. Prior to the 2000s, a network drama episode would typically be divided into a four-act plot structure, with each act similar in length.[50] This template was often superseded within network television in the early 2000s by plot structures incorporating an ever-increasing amount of acts (thus enabling networks to include more commercials), with many series over the previous decade incorporating a five- or six-act structure. Episodes of ABC's *Lost*, *Desperate Housewives* and *Grey's Anatomy*, for example, comply with a network-mandated six-act structure.[51]

Acts within network drama series are defined by their final scenes, which typically provide a mini climax to an episode's storyline (usually via a cliff-hanger event), and which are intended to discourage viewers from channel-hopping mid-episode. A clear example of such a moment would be the *ER* scene (from the episode 'Another Thursday at County' [15:2]), in which an unexpected Ricin threat to County General Hospital's emergency room occurs. Within the scene Dr Tony Gates and three young interns grapple with a patient who has just been hurried into the emergency room. Afflicted with minor burns and a broken leg, the patient responds angrily to medical attention, but Gates nevertheless strives to scissor open the patient's shirt so as to assess his lungs. In so doing, however, the doctor unexpectedly slices open the bag of homemade weaponised Ricin concealed within the patient's clothes. 'I told you not to touch me', the deranged patient barks. 'Now we're all *dead*.' In response, Gates alerts the reception desk to the danger and immediately thereafter the scene halts.

Such scenes are known as 'act-break' scenes, and they are, notes the screenwriter Jane Espenson, the 'tentpoles that support the structure' of an episode.[52] These act-break scenes are traditionally distinguished by a jarring style whereby the edit to commercial occurs a second or two after an act-break event has transpired, and character responses have been conveyed. In the case of the above scene, for example, the final shot frames the worried faces of Gates and the interns, conveying the high tension within the storyworld before the cut to commercial. These scenes are often followed—after commercial interruption—by a scene that carries the storyline on from the previous abrupt cut. This technique often renders the act-joins of episode plots as highly conspicuous, especially if viewed without commercial interruption (via, say, DVD or Netflix). For example, the *ER* scene subsequent to that concerning the Ricin exposure, which in broadcast form follows a commercial break, opens on various medics and administrators updating ER chief Cate Banfield (and viewers also) on the outcome of their calls to various emergency services in response to the bio-toxin exposure. This scene thus suggests that a small amount of story time, comparable to a commercial break's duration, has lapsed.

The spacing of act-break events throughout episodes thus serves commercial interests by potentially restraining viewers from switching channels during breaks. This commercially enforced system of plotting should not, however, be considered a hindrance to the construction of storytelling. The plotting strategy indeed ensures that regular turning points, each altering protagonists' immediate concern, are integrated within a storyline. As Kristin Thompson argues,

> Such divisions of programmes into acts ... are not simply arbitrary. They give an episode a sense of structure ... They provide the spectator with a sense of progress and guarantee the introduction of dramatic new premises or obstacles at intervals. They allow for the rising and falling action that many writers refer to as crucial to good plots.[53]

The example of the aforementioned *ER* episode demonstrates how act breaks become the impetus for the fresh directions that storylines take. One of the first act's multiple storylines concerns the introduction of the new interns and their settling into the emergency room's chaotic environment. But the event of the first act break functions as a clear turning point for this storyline; Tony and the interns, following their exposure to the Ricin, are sealed within a consultation room (so as to limit the bio-toxin's spread), and have to battle within the second act to save the lives of the two patients also sealed in the room. This act-break event thus changes the storyline's trajectory, providing characters with an entirely new conflict with which to engage.

The conditions of narrative design within network contexts therefore demand certain approaches to plotting with regard to episodes (short scenes, act structures that anticipate commercial interruption at designated moments). The following section continues with a focus on narrative designers' methods of plotting within network conditions; but it is concerned not with the organisation of a storyworld's storylines within individual episodes but rather the techniques used in the plotting of storylines over multiple series instalments.

Network: Serialised Plots

As noted, the MSS drama series draws on the daytime soap opera multiple-plot formula that had developed in previous decades. But there is an important distinction between the serial plotting of the traditional soap opera and that of the primetime network MSS series that emerged in the 1980s; whereas, in soap opera narrative, the parallel storylines of a single episode are likely to each be serial in nature, a network's MSS primetime episode often features one or more discrete 'standalone' storylines alongside those that span multiple episodes.[54] Such storylines each typically take the form of a distinct storyworld conflict that is both introduced and resolved within the confines of a single episode. The advent of this approach can be traced back to *Hill Street Blues* and *St. Elsewhere*, and its implementation continues to be commonplace within the network sector.[55]

Following the tradition set by network drama procedurals, standalone storylines within MSS series most frequently involve a lead character carrying out a particular work-based task to its conclusion, with this type of storyline often referred to as a 'case of the week' within television culture. Such cases of the week are evident in the legal drama *How to Get Away*

With Murder, for example, which centres on defence attorney and law professor Annalise Keating, as well as her students and employees. A complex serialised storyline concerning the murder of Annalise's husband threads through the entire first season; yet most episodes within this season also each introduce a storyline concerning Annalise's defence of a client, which is resolved by the episode's end. Many other ABC and NBC MSS series, including *Hannibal*, *Grey's Anatomy* and *Agents of S.H.I.E.L.D.* have also incorporated vocation-based standalone storylines.

Other types of standalone storylines within MSS series include flashback sequences that concern a discrete set of events within the storyworld's past. For example, this type of storyline is present in *Lost*, a series that concerns the travails of a group of air crash survivors marooned on a mysterious tropical island. Episodes of the series' early seasons typically each contain a flashback plot that conveys a sequence of events involving a *Lost* character prior to their time on the island. Each of these plots not only adds to a character's backstory but also operates within a given episode as a self-contained tale.[56] NBC's *This Is Us* adopts a similar approach. Focusing on three adult siblings in the present day, the first season's episodes each incorporates a distinct flashback story that centres on a significant moment in their family's past.[57] One such storyline, in 'The Right Thing to Do' (1:11), concerns their parents' discovery that they are expecting triplets.

The network economic model's reliance on advertiser support underpins the persistence of this 'story of the week' plotting system within networks' MSS drama series. While concern among networks for demographics has replaced concern for total audiences, networks are still required to maximise the greatest number of the particular demographic group that it hopes to attract. This approach to plotting helps networks to meet this aim because, as Jeffrey Sconce observes, it 'allows new and/or sporadic viewers to enjoy the stand-alone story of a particular episode, while also rewarding more dedicated long-term viewers for their sustained interest in the overall series'.[58] By addressing a core, loyal audience while simultaneously satisfying less-committed viewers, plot systems that balance stand-alone storylines with multi-episode storylines increase networks' chances of attracting a larger section of its target audience. Perhaps unsurprisingly, due to its potential for maximising desired audiences, networks have enforced adherence to this method of plotting. For example, screenwriter Jesse Alexander notes that, while working on season four of ABC's espionage thriller *Alias* (2001–2006), the network mandated an increased number of standalone storylines so as to make the series more accessible.[59]

Joss Whedon, creator of *Buffy the Vampire Slayer* (WB/UPN, 1997–2003) and *Angel* (WB, 1999–2004), similarly recalls that the WB network insisted that he incorporate standalone storylines in episodes within both of these series.[60]

While pressure has certainly been applied on narrative designers to incorporate episodic standalone tales alongside serialised storylines, twenty-first century shifts within viewing technologies and business practices have, however, increasingly lessened the industrial necessity for this plotting system. The incorporation of standalone storylines is not required for a given network series to succeed within the DVD box set market or when licensed on streaming service platforms (since, via these means, viewers are able to watch every episode of a given series with ease); the emergence of DVR technology has additionally made it easier for viewers to catch every episode of a broadcast series, thereby potentially lessening casual modes of consumption (and so diminishing the need for standalone storylines). These conditions might account for the fact that networks have permitted narrative designers of certain network series, such as *Scandal*, to drastically reduce their quota of standalone storylines; with *Scandal*'s first season, narrative designers typically balanced crisis management 'cases of the week' against serialised storylines, but with later seasons they constructed episode plots in which standalone storylines are typically absent.

Despite such ongoing shifts, however, the practice of combining episodic tales with serialised storylines has remained dominant within twenty-first century network MSS drama series due to its potential effectiveness in maximising desired audiences on behalf of advertisers. Further prevailing approaches to network drama plot structure have been developed to complement the specifications of network season formats, as the following section details.

Network: Season Plots

Two key features typically define the season formats of MSS series in the twenty-first century. The first of these features is a relatively long season length; network primetime seasons have traditionally included more than 20 episodes, with this tradition commonly adhered to throughout this period. The second of these features is the inclusion of breaks in the weekly frequency with which episodes are transmitted within a season. Both of these features are intended to serve the networks' particular economic model. A lengthy season permits networks to maximise cumulative advertising receipts per season of a given series. A season's disrupted weekly frequency ensures that episode transmissions of popular series coincide with network 'sweeps' periods that occur in November, February and May. Nielsen conducts nationwide audience research during these periods so that local network stations can set advertising rates in accordance with their findings. This method of audience measurement provides networks with an incentive to support their own local stations and affiliates by broadcasting new episodes of popular programmes during these months. The result of this system is that networks usually arrange mid-season breaks for series during December and January, and sometimes in March and April, thereby enabling network affiliates to set high advertising rates on the basis of the ratings that new episodes of a given series receive during sweeps periods in November, February and/or May. Within these narrative design conditions, narrative designers working on a given series typically incorporate distinct storylines of varying lengths, but with relatively few being a season in length. As Newman suggests, due to such methods, a season of a serialised network drama series is 'at best a loose kind of narrative unit'.[61]

Two key factors contribute to this looseness. Firstly, on a practical level, the process of incorporating shorter storylines into a lengthy network season renders narratives more manageable for narrative designers. As *West Wing* (NBC, 1999–2006) executive producer Thomas Schlamme recalls, the series' showrunner Aaron Sorkin regarded the network season format largely incompatible with season-length storylines; 'Aaron just doesn't trust the idea that he's writing a play in 23 acts', he noted.[62] Secondly, as Newman explains, narrative designers often adapt to the breaks between a season's sweeps periods by ensuring that storyworld material intended for each of the sweeps segments achieves its own narrative coherence.[63] These episode groupings function as distinct acts or 'sub-conflicts' in which 'definable problems are introduced and resolved'.[64] One particularly common approach for narrative designers is to divide the season into two main serialised story arcs, placing one arc within a run of episodes broadcast prior to a winter (December and January) hiatus, and the second within the sequence of episodes broadcast after that break. In such instances, seasons are split into two distinct narrative portions.

An example of this approach to plotting and arc creation can be found in season three of ABC's fantasy series *Once Upon a Time*, which follows the lives of the various fairy tale characters who reside in the town of Storybrooke. The first eleven episodes of this 22-episode season, which aired without disruption in weekly frequency prior to a winter hiatus, are structured around a major storyline. This storyline sees Storybrooke resident Emma Swan journey, along with other main characters, to Neverland so as to rescue Emma's son Henry from the clutches of Peter Pan. In the eleventh episode, Henry is saved, and Pan is slain, leading to a resolution to this particular storyline. However, the same episode simultaneously establishes a new storyline, as the curse enacted by Pan prior to his death takes effect, leading to Storybrooke's residents being magically returned to faraway fantasy lands. The storyline contained within the second half of the season, which originally aired following the winter break, concerns the exiled characters' journey back to Storybrooke, which involves their battle with a new foe, the Wicked Witch of the West. Other series that adopt a similar approach of segmenting seasons into two distinct narrative portions in response to networks' scheduling practices include ABC's glamorous thriller *Revenge* and NBC's superhero saga *Heroes*.

Despite the dominance this century of such network season commissioning and scheduling practices, alternative approaches have emerged. In recent years, networks have ordered shorter seasons for certain MSS series, broadcasting these seasons without any interruption to a weekly broadcast schedule. Such series include *Hannibal*, *The Night Shift*, *American Crime* and *Secrets and Lies*, which all possess seasons ranging from eight to thirteen episodes in length. There are a couple of factors driving networks' shift in approach here. Firstly, the aim to provide year-round original programming in response to the increased competition from cable channels has resulted in networks with relatively small gaps in their schedules that previously would have been filled by reruns; compact seasons can plug these schedule gaps.[65] NBC, for example, scheduled thirteen episode seasons of *Hannibal* and *The Night Shift* for the summer months.

Secondly, there has been, within twenty-first century television culture, the development of the idea that shorter seasons benefit serialised narrative. ABC Studios' Executive Vice President Patrick Moran, for example, claims that 'highly serialised' dramas 'creatively lend themselves to a shorter [episode] order'.[66] This received wisdom posits that narrative designers working on such series benefit creatively from having less narrative material to generate and organise. For example, Matthew Weiner, creator and showrunner of *Mad Men* (AMC, 2007–2015), which contains seasons that are 13 episodes in length, observes that, in comparison with working on lengthy network series, it is 'a lot easier creatively to deal with thirteen [episodes]'.[67] The general acceptance of this view is an additional after-effect of the rise in cultural prominence of cable drama in the early 2000s. As this chapter details in subsequent sections a shorter season format became standard for MSS cable dramas in the 2000s, motivating positive discourses around the format, such as those above.

In contrast to the more common lengthy network seasons, the shorter season format, when utilised in the network space, seems to result in a less segmented, more coherent serialised narrative across the season as a whole; as Newman observes, the format permits narrative designers to conceive of a given season as a 'meaningful narrative unit'.[68] *Hannibal* showrunner Bryan Fuller, for example, claims that the series' short seasons enabled him to preclude storyworld events that fail to advance the 'broader story', thereby freeing him to plot more 'focused' storylines across each season.[69]

While it is important to acknowledge this recent emergence of an alternative, shorter network season format, it is equally useful to note that lengthier seasons are still common due to the economic drivers of network television. Compared to the shorter season format, the conventional lengthy season typically enables a successful series to generate a greater amount of advertising revenue, which continues to be networks' primary objective. As Jeff Bader, NBC's president of programme planning, strategy, and research, observes, 'the holy grail is still the 22- to 24-episode show. We're going to do everything we can to keep those going.'[70]

The specific features of the network economic model can be seen to have informed myriad aspects of MSS primetime drama series that networks commission. The networks' primary requirement to deliver viewers to advertisers helps to determine the conception of storyworlds, the evocation of storyworld events via narrative style, and also the plotting of storyworlds across seasons. The following section examines the influence of a different category of economic model on narrative design by exploring the relationship between the subscription-based models of HBO and Netflix, and the MSS drama series that these services commission.

ECONOMIC SPECIFICITY IN SUBSCRIBER-SUPPORTED DRAMA SERIES: HBO AND NETFLIX

Just as historical shifts motivated the networks' moves into the commissioning of MSS primetime drama series in the early 1980s, industrial change proved a crucial factor in HBO's turn to such series in the late 1990s. An increase in the overall numbers of channels in that decade intensified cable competition, adding pressure on the premium cable service's efforts to secure and nurture its subscriber base.[71] HBO's response to this increased competitiveness was to commission its first original ongoing drama series, *Oz* (1997–2003), followed two years later by *The Sopranos*.[72] As former HBO chairman and CEO Chris Albrecht notes, its series were conceived as 'a retention device' to enable a closer, more sustained relationship with its subscribers.[73] 'As the marketplace became more competitive', recalls Albrecht, 'we had to go from being an occasional use medium to something people use on a regular basis in order for people to justify paying for us … original programming became a tool for doing that.'[74] Speaking to the sub-dimension of audience specificity within the commissioning of this new raft of programming, HBO's series were primarily intended for the same upscale audiences that networks had sought to attract with 1980s 'quality' dramas, such as *Hill Street Blues* and *Thirtysomething*. The rationale for HBO targeting this content towards high end demographics was, as Albrecht remarked, that such audiences 'can probably more easily afford to keep our service'.[75]

To justify the subscription fees it solicits, HBO has consistently positioned its original programming as distinct from its network and basic cable rivals, a strategy crystallised by the institution's famously provocative (and now retired) promotional slogan, 'It's Not TV. It's HBO'.[76] In line with this branding strategy, narrative designers of HBO's original drama series have consistently perpetuated discourses that ally their narratives to culturally privileged media, such as film, theatre and literature.[77] Yet, contrary to such rhetorical posturing, HBO drama series nevertheless adhere to the network 'quality' precedent via their reliance on the soap system of plot organisation. *Deadwood* (2004–2006), for example, utilises the MSS mode to pull together diverse storylines emanating from a nineteenth-century Black Hills gold-mining settlement, while *Game of Thrones* adopts this plot system so as to collate the storylines of a range of characters situated across George R. R. Martin's lands of Westeros and beyond. The premium cable service's wide adoption of this storytelling mode, which has been regarded from the 1980s onward as a textual mark of sophistication, strongly reflects HBO's aims to court professional, well-educated viewers who seek 'quality' content.

Economic factors similarly drove Netflix to become a purveyor of subscriber-supported MSS drama series, despite the online streaming service having emerged from a different sector within the media industries. Netflix had built up its name in the late 1990s and early 2000s as an online DVD rental service but, by the late 2000s, it began to transition this core business into one centred on streaming content online. Netflix appealed to potential subscribers in the late 2000s and early 2010s chiefly via an offer of hours of streamed film and television entertainment licensed from rights-owning media companies, including the CBS Corporation and The Walt Disney Company.[78] While this offer proved highly successful, enabling the service to grow its subscriber base from 9.4 million in 2009 to 24.6 million in 2011, Netflix's expansion of its market motivated rights holders to demand higher prices for the streaming rights to their content.[79] In the early 2010s, faced with rising content acquisition costs, Netflix developed an alternative model designed to reduce its reliance on rights owned by rival media corporations; the service began to ramp up expenditure on original content, aiming to lure potential subscribers with not only films and television series that had originated elsewhere but also by an offer of exclusive entertainment.[80]

An integral part of this strategy has been to invest in serialised narrative specifically; this objective has led to Netflix developing a number of drama series that conform to the MSS formula, including *Bloodline* (2015–2017), *House of Cards* (2013–present), *Stranger Things* (2016–present), *Orange is the New Black* (2013–present), and the Marvel Cinematic Universe dramas, *Daredevil* (2015–present), *Luke Cage* (2016–present) and *Jessica Jones* (2015–present). Netflix's accumulated website user data helped to motivate the adoption of television's serialised storytelling mode. The data demonstrated that, while users desire a strong movie selection, they watch TV series more often than they do film. This user preference therefore incentivised significant investment in television-style forms, including drama and sitcoms.[81] The data furthermore indicated to Netflix the popularity among users of 'binge viewing'—the practice of watching multiple episodes of a given television series in one sitting.[82] As Kevin McDonald observes, Netflix aims to encourage this intense form of subscriber engagement though its famed practice of releasing all episodes of a given season simultaneously.[83] Netflix has, however, further served this aim by favouring the development of MSS dramas with high degrees of serialisation, therefore tempting viewers to engage with multiple instalments in quick succession so to discover 'what happens next' within continuing storylines.

While subscription fees are ultimately the source of revenue that drive HBO and Netflix's commissioning of MSS drama series, it is important to acknowledge that HBO and Netflix are different types of services in terms of their respective technological conditions; the former transmits scheduled drama programming via cable television technologies while the latter makes drama series available to viewers via online streaming. As Chuck

Tryon observes, discourses within television culture tend to highlight this difference, claiming that the affordances of its internet-based mode of distribution permit Netflix to develop series that have 'challenged traditional TV storytelling'.[84] Netflix's own discourses, for example, posit that, in comparison to network and cable services' practice of transmitting one episode of a given season a week, Netflix's simultaneous release of a season's episodes results in distinct and enhanced conditions of narrative design. According to these claims, notes Tryon, Netflix's distributional approach, through its facilitation of binge viewing, enables 'innovative storytelling practices because a show's creators can assume that ... viewers will be ... likely to remember subtle details' from recently watched prior episodes.[85]

The specificities of Netflix's technological conditions of distribution and consumption therefore distinguish the institution from subscriber-funded premium cable services such as HBO. While HBO offers, alongside its premium cable service, access to its series via the 'over the top' online streaming service platform HBO Now, it nevertheless only makes one new episode of a given drama available per week via this service so as to support the cable channel's linear schedule. However, as the following sections show, despite discourses distinguishing Netflix from cable (as well as network) institutions, the subscription-based economic model on which Netflix and HBO each rely has influenced the two institutions to adopt many similar approaches to the production of MSS narrative. In the case of both institutions, their subscription models have furthermore enabled the narrative designers in their employ to depart from network drama conventions, as the following section concerning the storyworlds of Netflix and HBO dramas reveals.

Subscriber-Supported Services: Storyworlds

The storyworld settings of subscriber-supported MSS primetime drama series are, if only at an abstract level, broadly similar to those of networks. Primary recurring locations include, for example: domestic spaces, such as the family homes of *Big Love* (HBO, 2006–2011) and *Bloodline*; workplace environments, such as the mortuary in *Six Feet Under* (HBO, 2001–2005) and the glass-walled laboratories of *Westworld* (HBO, 2016–present); and the spaces of a single particular town or city, such as in the New Orleans-set *Treme* (HBO, 2010–2013) or *Stranger Things'* fictional small town of Hawkins.[86] This shared commonality reflects the fact that

HBO and Netflix series are, like those of networks, conceived to be ongoing. While a given network hopes to maximise all possible advertising revenues from a given narrative, subscription-based services typically aim to continue with a series' production and transmission for as long as it contributes to the value proposition that the service offers to subscribers.

Despite this broad similarity in storyworld setting across these two institutional models, HBO and Netflix are nevertheless regularly able to budget for the type of locations and ambitiously assembled sets that are usually well beyond network means in terms of the budgets required. HBO, for example, has permitted *Game of Thrones* producers to employ extensive, and expensive, location shooting in nations including Malta, Croatia, Spain, Iceland, Morocco and Northern Ireland. This approach, which serves the producers' aims to visually represent the source novels' diverse fantasy universe, contributes to the series' large per episode spend, which has increased from $6 million to $10 million over the span of its multiple seasons.[87] As well as facilitating the narrative production of epic, fantasy landscapes, HBO has also invested heavily in period recreations, such as the ancient civilisation of *Rome* (2005–2007; $6 million per episode, on average) and 1970s New York in *Vinyl* (2016; $10 million per episode, on average).[88]

Netflix has made similar significant investments in ambitious period recreations and location shooting, as exemplified by its dramas concerning the early biographies of Marco Polo—*Marco Polo* (2014–2016)—and Queen Elizabeth I—*The Crown* (2016–present). Enabled by an average per episode spend of a $9 million, the former was shot on location in Italy and Kazakhstan, and on extravagant sets, including a replica of Kublai Kahn's large golden throne room.[89] With a $5 million average per episode spend, the latter provided in its first season an ambitious recreation of mid-twentieth-century British royal opulence and pageantry, aided by the production of 20,000 historically accurate costumes.[90] With an average cost of a network drama episode being around $3 million, and per episode budgets rarely exceeding $4 million, networks typically fail to rival the production budgets of such HBO and Netflix programming.[91]

For networks, the particularities of their economic model limit comparable investment in a single given drama. As each hour within primetime schedules is a source of advertiser revenue, networks are pressured to divide their budget on an array of different content so as to ensure diversity across each of their schedules. In contrast, the specificities of the subscription service economic model enable drama production expenditures that surpass those of networks. While HBO, for example, transmits programming as part of a linear schedule, the service is without the imperative to ensure that each primetime hour presents a distinct opportunity for advertisers to address viewers. It is instead able, notes Toby Miller, to load its schedules with a far higher number of repeats than networks could ever sanction (due to their relatively low worth to advertisers).[92] These conditions allow the service to accordingly boost series production values through the funnelling of its commissioning budget into a far smaller volume of original programming. Netflix, of course, has no linear schedule whatsoever to support. Instead, like HBO, it merely needs to develop drama series that appeal to both existing subscribers and potential subscribers; as long as these series succeed in that goal, the quantity of drama series can be limited, enabling Netflix to concentrate their funds on a relatively small amount of drama series, thereby elevating per episode budgets.

Due to their high budgets, subscription services such as HBO and Netflix can countenance uncommon storyworld settings, including an elegant 1920s Atlantic City boardwalk in *Boardwalk Empire* (HBO, 2010–2014); a 1930s Midwest dustbowl environment in *Carnivàle* (HBO, 2003–2005); and a damaged yet culturally vivacious 1970s South Bronx landscape in *The Get Down* (Netflix, 2016–2017). Such extravagant expenditure within the subscription service space also permits resource intensive and logistically demanding storyworld events. *Game of Thrones'* occasional immense battle sequences, including its ambitious depictions of the Battle of Blackwater (in 'Blackwater' [1:9]) and the Battle of the Bastards (in 'Battle of the Bastards' [6:9]), which require scales of production rarely achieved via the industrial practices of US television, serve as examples of such ambitious events.[93] By permitting the realisation of such storyworld material, subscription services support their aims to distinguish their content from network programming, thereby serving to justify the subscription fees they charge.

The specificities of the subscription service model furthermore facilitate characterisations within HBO and Netflix series that mark departures from those developed within network contexts. While, as noted, networks' primary reliance on advertiser support has typically ensured that characters' failings have their limits, the absence of the requirement to appease sponsors permits the presence of all manner of morally dubious traits and actions in HBO series. Lead characters, such as Tony Soprano (in *The Sopranos*), Francis Underwood (in *House of Cards*) and Al Swearingen (in

Deadwood), for example, commit cold blooded murder repeatedly and typically without apparent remorse. Other taboo activities in which recurring characters in HBO series engage include polygamy (*Big Love*'s Henrickson family) and incest (*Game of Thrones*' Jaime and Cersi Lannister, and *Boardwalk Empire*'s Jimmy and Gillian Darmody), two particular lifestyle choices that many advertisers might find deeply problematic.

The US television industry's regulatory contexts further enable subscription services to create storyworld material that is distinguishable from that within network content. Due to the content of streaming and premium cable services being beyond the purview of the Federal Communications Commission, narrative designers working on HBO and Netflix series are also able to incorporate depictions of certain types of provocative storyworld events that would not be permissible on networks. Such events include: dialogue exchanges strewn with profane language—in, for example, *Deadwood* and *Orange is the New Black*; lengthy and detailed sex scenes—in, for example, *True Blood* (HBO, 2008–2014) and *Tell Me You Love Me* (HBO, 2007); and also acute, elaborate violent acts—in, for example, *Boardwalk Empire* and *Game of Thrones*. As with the extreme moral ambiguity of some Netflix and HBO characters, such censurable storyworld actions have come to support institutional aims by further distinguishing these subscription services' narratives.[94] The specificities of the subscription service context thus facilitate clear deviations from network series regarding the type of storyworlds that Netflix and HBO's original series possess. The following section shows how the subscription service model informs the methods by which Netflix and HBO's narrative designers convey these storyworlds via plotting and style within individual drama episodes.

Subscriber-Supported Services: Episode Plots and Styles

Similar to broadcast networks, HBO requires programming that is compatible with a linear schedule, and has therefore generally adhered to the traditional hour-long drama episode format as part of its commissioning policies to ensure that episodes can occupy hour-long schedule slots. Despite Netflix having no linear schedule, the service nevertheless commissions series containing episodes that are typically 50–60 minutes in duration. There is a key determining factor driving Netflix drama series' adherence to the traditional hour-long format. Despite discourses positioning Netflix content as a radical alternative to conventional television forms, the online service has strong economic incentive to develop dramas that have some general likeness to series emanating from broadcast and cable sectors. As previously noted, a core part of Netflix's offer to subscribers is drama content initially produced for networks and cable channels, which 'Netflix Originals' are intended to complement. As Netflix's chief content officer Ted Sarandos acknowledges, the service will 'always have a place … for catch up programming that originates on other networks. What we really want is to be perceived to be the best of broadcasting … plus our own original programming.'[95] Presenting its original drama content as analogous to network and cable series, its online platform interface categorises and labels series such as *House of Cards, Orange is the New Black* and *13 Reasons Why* (2017–present) as 'TV Dramas'.[96] Netflix's adherence to the hour-long drama episode format therefore reflects the company's goal to develop content that has some basic resemblance to traditional television forms.

A further factor motivating this adherence of Netflix drama series to the conventional hour-long drama model has been the economic aims of those production companies who make 'Netflix Originals'. These series can have the potential, license agreements with Netflix permitting, to be additionally acquired by more traditional channels and services. For example, in 2017, the UK Sony Channel acquired the rights to transmit the Lionsgate-produced *Orange is the New Black* as part of its linear schedule.[97] It is therefore sensible for those production companies making series commissioned by Netflix to rely on episode run times that have the potential to meet the standard requirements of linear schedules.

Despite much rhetoric to the contrary, therefore, the conditions within which narrative designers operate in the construction of HBO and Netflix episodes are not always fundamentally distinct from those that networks impose. However, because HBO and Netflix generate revenues via subscriptions, the 'hour-long' format parameters that these services require narrative designers to operate within are still distinguishable from those of network contexts in two fundamental respects. Firstly, while typically utilising the conventional hour-long drama episode as a unit of storytelling, narrative designers at subscription services typically have more episode time to convey their storyworlds than do those working within a network context. Due to the requirement for network programming to include commercial interruptions, episodes of 'hour-long' network series typically last for little over forty minutes. Netflix and HBO narrative designers therefore are typically operating with around a quarter of an hour more episode time than they would have if working within network conditions. Secondly, and perhaps more importantly, the lack of commercial load within a given hour leads to narrative designers being under no obligation to ensure that their scripts anticipate interruptions at predetermined junctures.

With the framework of longer episode durations, and without the commercial requirement to deploy a set of succinct scenes, narrative designers within subscription service contexts sometimes take an unconventional approach to episode plot structure. For example, narrative designers commissioned by HBO and Netflix sometimes take the opportunity to include uncommonly long scenes within episode plots, disrupting the typical network rhythm of plotting. This is evident in the *Sopranos* episode 'Whitecaps' (4.13), for example, in which Tony and Carmela Soprano's marriage break-up serves as a central storyline. Narrative designers have incorporated two extended scenes within the episode—each featuring a prolonged angry dispute between the couple, and each approximately five minutes in length.

Narrative designers of Netflix's *Daredevil* have taken the opportunity to include lengthy scenes to depict a different kind of extended altercation. The drama, which concentrates on the super heroics of the series' titular Marvel character, includes, in each of its first two seasons, a gruelling and elaborately planned martial arts combat scene, which is presented as occurring in real time and endures for more than five minutes; within these scenes Daredevil battles a multitude of foes, within a corridor in the episode 'Cut Man' (1:2), and on a stairwell in 'New York's Finest' (2:3).

In the case of *Game of Thrones*, HBO's utilisation of lengthy scene durations has, as Mittell's statistical analysis shows, led to episode plot structures that mark major departures from network convention due to their incorporation of relatively low overall numbers of scenes. Whereas the *Lost* episode 'Walkabout' (1.4), for example, contains 48 scenes, the *Game of Thrones* episode 'Valar Morghulis' (2:10) includes a mere 16 scenes (within its longer overall episode duration).[98] Due to the tendency within the *Thrones* narrative design process to combine a succession of long scenes with a large number of characters (ensuring that many serialised storylines are allotted only one or two scenes per episode, if they feature at all), Mittell suggests that the series lacks the 'propulsive' plotting rhythm conventional to television storytelling.[99]

The absence of a commercial obligation to relay the impression of storyworld activity unfolding at a hurtling pace has not only permitted narrative designers within the subscription service space to incorporate lengthy scenes within episode plots; it has also allowed them to develop a combination of unhurried plotting and narrative style within scenes, leading to a further departure from network convention. David Chase, creator and showrunner of *The Sopranos*, speaking about his experience working for HBO, emphasises this particular distinction between network and subscriber service contexts:

> The major difference [between doing a show for HBO as opposed to networks] is the pace at which you're allowed to let the story roll out. [At HBO] you could do a slower pace, a slower release of information, longer silences. Nothing is really happening. It's a different style of editing, not bang-bang-bang-bang all the time.[100]

This slower pace of presentation is not necessarily typified by a decrease in cutting speed, but rather by a mode of plotting and styles of shooting, performance and editing that, as Chase indicates, privileges storyworld *inaction*—that is, instances of story time in which storyworld events are not obviously occurring.

Such inaction within scenes usually falls into two general categories. The first involves scenes that place some emphasis on characters neither talking nor engaged in obvious physical activity but instead undergoing reflection or another form of interior process. Such scenes include dialogue exchanges during which the flow of talk is interrupted by prolonged close-up shots of performers conveying, via facial expressions, non-verbal responses to discussion, such as contemplation or the experiencing of a particular emotion. Such moments of pause, silence and interior process punctuate *The Sopranos'* trademark psychiatry sessions that take place in the office of Dr Melfi (Tony's therapist). These scenes regularly alternate between wordless, static reverse shots between Melfi and Tony, as each waits the other out. 'It was very important to me to let the silences play like they really happen in a psychiatrist's office', notes Chase. 'People don't say anything, they don't get you talking, they let you hang yourself.'[101] A prime example of these protracted silences can be found in 'Irregular Around the Margins' (5:6) in which a scene situated in Melfi's office begins with 53 continuous seconds of silence between doctor and patient. As Polan suggests, such scenes between the two are noteworthy for their 'sheer distinction' from television convention.[102]

For the narrative designers of HBO's *The Leftovers*, the practice of privileging character inaction and of visually emphasising characters' interiority became central to the series' storytelling. The series narrative revolves around the aftermath of an inexplicable global event: the simultaneous disappearance of 2 per cent of the Earth's population. Focusing on those who remain, the series depicts characters struggling to verbally communicate their states of mind in a society in which most have lost friends and loved ones due to this rapture-like event. Characters' feelings of grief, loss, confusion and frustration are often principally conveyed via shots in which performers non-verbally express their characters' emotions.

This approach to characterisation is evident in the depiction of Nora Durst, whose husband and two young children are among the 'departed'. In the episode 'Guest' (1:6), as part of her interactions with other characters, Nora typically appears reserved, regulating her emotions; her dialogue tends to be precise, and usually delivered by the performer Carrie Coon with firm, unfaltering speech. Yet, a subtle, largely dialogue-free opening sequence visually expresses the deep grief that Nora typically opts not to articulate verbally; one prolonged shot within the sequence frames Nora as she stares despondently while sat at the kitchen table at which her family has previously disappeared (see Fig. 3.1). Taking advantage of HBO's economic contexts, *The Leftovers* narrative designers were able to develop an approach to plotting and visual style that ultimately decompresses the narrative, privileging shots of character stillness within the edit so as to provide insights into characters' interior states.

Fig. 3.1 Nora Durst stares despondently in *The Leftovers*. Episode: 'The Guest' (1:6, 2014)

The second category of inaction within scenes concerns the emphasis placed upon storyworld setting. This approach is clearly evident in HBO's *The Wire* (2002–2008), for example. According to the series' showrunner David Simon, a guiding principle for the series' visual style was to stay 'in the wide … Show the world', thereby foregrounding the narrative's Baltimore landscape.[103] Crucially, however, to 'show the world'—to luxuriate in the wide shot—requires the devotion of screen-time. This is evidenced within a scene from 'A New Day' (4:11) in which detective Lester Freamon looks upon rows of Baltimore's boarded-up homes (as it slowly dawns on him that the empty buildings are being used to deposit murder victims). The scene, which contains only 23 words of dialogue, endures for almost three minutes, and is awarded to slow tracking, wide-angle shots surveying a dilapidated urban environment. Such emphasis on setting carried over into Simon's subsequent HBO series *Treme*, within which scenes often accentuate the eroded structures of New Orleans' post-Katrina landscape.

This approach to plotting and style is also standard for many other HBO series. In *Carnivàle*, for example, meditative wide-shots situate the titular travelling carnival's structures (trailers, carousel and Ferris wheel) within CGI-enhanced dust bowl and desert settings, while, in *Boardwalk Empire*, slow, sweeping crane and tracking shots scan Atlantic City's 1920s boardwalk. HBO's distinctive budgeting strategies have proved an important factor in making feasible such focus on setting via its provision for expensive sets and location shooting; but it is the absence of an economic requirement to deliver hurried storytelling that allows editors to dwell on environments in this manner.

A similar emphasis is placed on location in Netflix's Florida Keys-set *Bloodline*, a tense family saga, which revolves around three adult siblings—John, Meg and Kevin Rayburn—whose lives unravel due to the return of their black sheep elder brother, Danny. According to *Bloodline* co-creator Todd A. Kessler, the beautiful, idyllic Keys is as an important ingredient of the narrative. The 'paradise' setting serves as a stark contrast to the storyworld's dark 'underbelly', which incorporates the crimes of drug smuggling and human trafficking carried out around the islands, as well as shameful, deeply-buried family secrets and betrayals.[104]

Taking advantage of the narrative design conditions of subscriber-supported drama series, *Bloodline*'s narrative designers have created a visual style that emphasises this contrast. This approach to composition is evident in a scene, from 'Part 12' (1:12), in which John meets Danny on a secluded beach. The scene, which is over nine minutes in duration, centres on a bitter and increasingly fraught dialogue exchange between the pair, as John, disturbed by the considerable threat that Danny poses to his family, urges Danny to leave home. The visual style situates the brothers firmly within the exquisite and tranquil setting; for example, in one lingering wide shot, a combination of glistening sands, glowing green vegetation and white light reflecting off the sea surrounds the brothers as they sit in the middle distance of the frame (see Fig. 3.2). This approach to mise-en-scène within the series contributes to a distinctive and ironic visual style, the emphasis placed on setting within these types of scenes engineering a stark contrast between the series' graceful and alluring locations and the characters' bleak and desperate moods.

Such lingering and artistically composed wide shots, as well as other approaches to visual style that emphasise costly sets and locations, partly reflect the technological specificity of television's narrative design conditions in the twenty-first century. As Lotz observes, the introduction of high-definition television (HDTV) in the 1990s, and the growing popularity of its use, has motivated subscription services to achieve 'aesthetic excellence and originality'.[105] Compared to the lower definition broadcasts that characterise much twentieth-century television, HDTV trans-

Fig. 3.2 *Bloodline*'s John and Danny Rayburn contextualised within a tranquil setting. Episode: 'Part 12' (1:12, 2015)

missions permit viewers to more fully appreciate detailed sets, striking locations and elegant composition, thereby enabling Netflix and HBO to more clearly differentiate their services from network provision and so justify the fees they charge.[106] However, while these altered technological conditions increase Netflix and HBO's motivation to achieve high production values and styles that showcase large investment, it is, as noted, the economic specificities of the subscription model that facilitate this level of spending.

The traits of style and plotting that characterise scenes within various HBO and Netflix series—the pauses, the silences, the lingering wide shots—contrast with practices that have been developed within network television so as to sustain perceptions of fast-moving narrative.[107] These distinctions in scene construction thus demonstrate the ways in which narrative designers, working outside of the creative conditions specific to networks, have subverted network television's storytelling traditions.

The absence of an obligation to ensure that episodes include commercial breaks at predetermined junctures not only permits narrative designers to decompress their storytelling, it also frees them from an institutionally imposed act structure. It would be wrong to presume, however, that narrative designers granted this freedom abandon all television conventions of act structuring. Reflecting widespread aesthetic presumptions that plots should be punctuated by regular turning points so as to be compelling, narrative designers working on subscriber-supported MSS dramas indeed develop episodes as sequences of acts, with each capped by an act-break storyworld incident. As US television drama editor David Helfland observes, 'you still have act-breaks in terms of story structure [within the subscriber-supported context]—building towards peak moments and climaxes' despite being under no advertiser-supported mandate to do so.[108]

Narrative designers operating in the conditions of subscriber-supported drama series do, however, decide, on the basis of their personal preference, how many acts an episode will be divided into. These circumstances therefore result in contrasting approaches to act structure within this context. The writer-producer Stephen S. DeKnight, for example, regards act durations of networks' five-act and six-act structures to be restrictive; 'it's very difficult to get any momentum between act breaks because [the acts] are short', he claims.[109] Working in a subscriber-supported context on *Daredevil* and *Spartacus* (Starz, 2010–2013), DeKnight has accordingly developed a three-act episode structure, drawing upon conventions of Hollywood filmmaking (discussed in Chap. 2) as opposed to those of network television.[110] In contrast, David Chase and his *Sopranos* writing staff often adhered to a four-act episode structure traditional to twentieth-century network drama series.[111] Narrative designers working on subscriber-supported drama also have the flexibility to adjust their self-imposed act structures should they deem it beneficial to an episode's narrative. *Game of Thrones* co-showrunner D. B. Weiss, for example, appreciates not having to end an act earlier that he might otherwise prefer.[112] As *Orange is the New Black*'s showrunner Jenji Kohan similarly observes, the absence of a requirement to 'hit marks' when in the process of constructing an episode's acts affords her more 'breathing room'.[113]

The absence of commercial interruption furthermore enables narrative designers working on subscriber-supported drama series to forgo the abrupt halting of scenes once an act-break storyworld incident has occurred. Instead act-end scenes are permitted to linger, then settle after a turning-point event has taken place, thereby enabling a smooth transition to the subsequent act. An act-ending scene in the aforementioned *Sopranos* episode 'Irregular Around the Margins' provides an example of this approach. At the mid-point of the episode, Tony Soprano and Adrianna La Cerva, fiancée to Tony's nephew, are involved in a car crash that serves as a major turning point for these two characters' storylines in the episode. The first half of the episode sees sexual tension emerge between Tony and Adrianna. The plot, however, pivots when Tony, driving his SUV, with Adrianna as a passenger, rolls the vehicle to avoid a racoon; following this incident, Tony's violently erratic nephew, who is highly suspicious of the fact his fiancée and Tony were driving together at night, propels the narrative forward. In a network context, an analogous turning-point scene would likely be positioned prior to a commercial break, with the scene concluding immediately after the vehicle's crash. Within the HBO context, however, *Sopranos*' narrative designers were permitted to invest 20 seconds of post-crash scene-time depicting steam spewing from the vehicle and providing a close-up of a spinning wheel on the upturned car. As screenwriter Jill Golick observes of the HBO gangster series, the absence of jarring 'crescendos' at the conclusion of act-break scenes 'brings a subtlety to episodes'.[114]

An example of an act-end scene in the *Bloodline* episode 'Part 10' (1:10) provides a further demonstration of narrative designers taking advantage of subscription service conditions by implementing subtle transitions between acts. As with the previous *Bloodline* example, the scene concerns a tense exchange between John and Danny Rayburn. Within a cold store space of the Rayburn family-owned hotel, John, a police detective, confronts Danny over his involvement in a drug smuggling ring. John informs Danny of the human trafficking operation that his drug-dealer bosses have previously operated; the human trafficking activities resulted in murder, stresses John, leaving Danny with photos of the victims. After offering to help his brother arrange a deal with the Drug Enforcement Agency, which is close to bringing down the drug-dealer bosses, John exits the cold store. The scene's final shot shows the door closing on Danny, the door's window framing the character's severe expression; this mise-en-scène serves as a metaphor for Danny's circumstances by visually boxing the character in. Rather than abruptly concluding the scene at this instant, as network convention would dictate, *Bloodline*'s narrative designers let the shot persist for a further 26 seconds after this point. During this time some of the scene's tension is relieved as Danny looks to the ceiling and appears to exhale. The scene concludes as Danny studies the photos, perhaps reflecting on his next course of action. Through relieving some of the scene's tension, the conclusion to the scene enables a smooth transition to the episode's subsequent act.

The specificities of subscription service revenue models thus permit certain departures from network conventions in the narrative production of individual drama series episodes, with particular regard to scene lengths, act structure and the visual style of scenes. Further examining the importance of HBO and Netflix's revenue model to narrative design processes, the following section focuses on narrative designers' approaches to serialisation in MSS drama series within this industrial context.

Subscriber-Supported Services: Serialised Plots

A dominant feature of HBO drama series over the past two decades has been the absence of standalone storylines within individual episodes. Episodes of *Rome*, *Treme*, *The Wire*, *Deadwood*, *True Blood*, *Boardwalk Empire*, *True Detective*, *John from Cincinnati* and *Game of Thrones*, for example, typically neglect to include self-contained conflicts and are instead usually comprised exclusively of multiple serialised storylines. While there are some HBO series that do consistently incorporate standalone storylines, such as *The Sopranos* and *Six Feet Under*, they are exceptions to the pervasive narrative trend at the institution.[115] As the television critic Ryan McGee puts it, 'HBO isn't in the business of producing episodes in the traditional manner. Rather, it airs equal slices of an overall story over a fixed series of weeks.'[116]

Insight into the narrative design process from season three of *The Wire* provides an example of this approach to plotting in practice. While individual episodes are each credited to individual writers, members of the writing staff were, according to *Wire* writer-producer George Pelecanos, each focused primarily on their own particular serial storylines. 'We sort of drifted towards our interests and what happened was that you naturally picked up the scenes from other episodes', he recalls.[117] This practice ensured that a range of writers contributed towards any single episode, with each writer chiefly concerned with what transpires on their particular storyline rather than in the episode as a whole. As Simon observed, 'You don't have people being protective of the single episode ... you have people being protective of the whole story.'[118] Thus for *Wire* writers, episodes were often little more than vehicles for the delivery of multi-episode narratives.[119]

The storytelling preferences of narrative designers have in part driven the absence of standalone storylines within many HBO drama series. In the case of *The Wire*, for example, Simon wanted to construct a complex serialised narrative that required loyalty and commitment from audiences. Simon's sensibility is evident in an interview in which broadcaster Lauren Laverne suggested that the series' narrative design process displays 'contempt' for viewers who might be unwilling to commit to long-running multi-episode storylines. 'What about the casual viewer, people who want to dip in and out?' Laverne asked Simon.

'Fuck the casual viewer', Simon replied. 'Seriously, who wants the casual viewer? If you're a writer, do you want a casual reader? I don't want those people.'[120]

While their creative ideals no doubt factor into the narrative design processes, Simon and other narrative designers have been able to take this storytelling approach at HBO because the subscription service context permits it. HBO's subscription-based economics indeed encourages the creation of complex serial narratives that reward committed viewers but which casual viewers might find lacking in accessibility.

While networks value both loyal and casual viewers (hence the incorporation of standalone storylines alongside those that are multiple episode in length), HBO, in contrast, as its CEO Richard Plepler acknowledges, prioritises the cultivation of an 'unbelievably loyal' audience through its programming.[121] The institution prizes viewers who are steadfastly committed to its narratives, and who will commit to every episode of a given series. The institution anticipates that such viewers will more likely find value for money in paying a subscription fee than will an audience made up of casual viewers.

HBO, then, commissions narratives with a high degree of serialisation as a means to attract such loyalty. Serial narrative is potentially a powerful tool in nurturing a deep relationship with a core customer base because a series predominantly comprised of multiple-episode storylines will compel subscribers (at least the viewers who enjoy the series) to watch every episode, and thus not 'dip in and out' (in the manner of a casual viewer).

This narrative strategy might limit the size of an audience because it will almost certainly deter casual viewers, but HBO is dedicated only to satisfying a series' committed core viewership. Audience sizes for HBO dramas can sometimes be very modest but as long as their audiences are passionate enough about a series to continue parting with a subscription fee, then the series can be deemed by HBO to be serving its purpose. For example, viewing figures for *The Leftovers*, which developed a fervent fandom around its ambiguous and sprawling serial narrative, were far below those achieved by its HBO drama contemporary *Game of Thrones*.[122] Yet former HBO programming president Michael Lombardo, acknowledging the significance of *The Leftovers'* 'passionate following', nevertheless commissioned second and third seasons of the series despite its limited audience size.[123] Similar to Simon, the HBO business model therefore places a low priority on the servicing of casual viewers' needs.

HBO further enhances its prospects of nurturing loyal audiences by giving subscribers ample opportunity to watch every episode of a given series and thus avoid having to miss instalments of densely serialised narratives. The aforementioned high rotation of programming ensures that a new episode of an original series will be broadcast in multiple timeslots throughout the week as part of linear schedules, while, as Mark C. Rogers, Michael Epstein and Jimmie L. Reeves observe, HBO's multiplexing strategy has allowed the institution to repeat episodes on various channels.[124] Alongside its linear scheduling of episodes HBO in addition offers viewers access to new episodes of a given series via HBO on Demand, a video on demand service offered to digital cable subscribers that the institution introduced in 2001. HBO has, since 2010, made new episodes available to subscribers on internet-enabled devices via its HBO Go internet streaming service. Since 2015 HBO has furthermore offered access to its series via its aforementioned 'over the top' service HBO Now.

HBO's subscribers have certainly taken advantage of the many different opportunities to 'catch up' on new episodes that are made available to them. For example, the average cumulative ratings for the second season of *Big Love* and fourth season of *The Wire*, which both aired in 2007, were, respectively, 5.8 million and 4.4 million, but only 40 per cent of these figures were comprised of viewings of their respective Sunday-night premiere transmissions. The remaining 60 per cent was made up of HBO on Demand viewings, DVR viewings and repeat showings transmitted throughout the week.[125] More recently, *Westworld*'s premiere episode attracted 1.96 million viewers to its debut cable transmission but close to 10 million more viewers sampled the episode via repeat transmissions, HBO on Demand, HBO Go and HBO Now over the subsequent two weeks.[126]

Crucially, the specificities of its economic model make HBO's ample provision of viewing opportunities uniquely advantageous. For networks, the optimum outcome is for viewers to watch the premiere broadcast of a given episode—when advertising rates for commercial load are at a premium. The network economic model therefore influences networks to—in certain ways—restrict viewings of a given episode by other means thereby driving viewers to the premiere network broadcast of that episode. For example, during the airing of *Scandal*'s sixth season (in 2016 and 2017), ABC provided viewers with the chance to catch up with previously broadcast episodes via its ABC.go.com streaming platform and cable operators' video on demand services. But ABC nevertheless regulated viewers' access to the series by withholding new episodes from these non-linear platforms for one week after those episodes' premiere broadcasts. Via this approach, ABC incentivised viewers to catch premiere broadcasts. HBO, in contrast, does not care *how* subscribers watch its content, just as long as they watch it, because HBO requires the episode alone to have an audience, as opposed to a commercial load included within a particular transmission. The subscription service therefore has no economic reason to regulate subscribers' access to new episodes and instead has strong motivation to invest in making new episodes of its dramas easily available to subscribers so as to engender subscriber loyalty through engagement with intensely serialised dramas.

As a subscriber service, Netflix, too, values customer loyalty extremely highly. In contrast to HBO, however, because Netflix does not transmit a linear schedule, the service has no need to weigh up the requirements of the committed viewers versus those of the casual viewer. By making the self-scheduling of episodes the viewers' only mode of consumption, Netflix eliminates 'casual' forms of drama series viewing experienced in network and cable television. The Netflix interface is indeed designed to encourage viewers of a given drama series to view each and every episode of that series in the order that narrative designers intended.

Due to these particular conditions, narrative designers working on an episode of a Netflix-commissioned drama series can be confident that the episode's viewers will have seen all preceding episodes. As Glenn Kessler, co-showrunner of *Bloodline* points out, viewers are not going to begin 'tun[ing] into week seven because there *is* no week seven ... as a storyteller you know that [viewers have] seen everything that you wanted them to see at that point in the story'.[127] Within these conditions, narrative designers can construct episodes comprised entirely of serialised storylines and be secure in the knowledge that the episodes' viewers will have been following the storylines from previous episodes. This Netflix context enabled *House of Cards* showrunner Beau Willimon to conceive of what he refers to as a 'hyper-serialized' narrative whereby 'every little moment and arc plays into a larger whole'.[128] Similar to the narrative production on *The Wire*, little effort is made on *House of Cards* to craft episodes as self-contained units; 'we don't make episodes that have a beginning, middle, and end and exist in and of themselves'. It is this perception of *House of Cards* episodes merely serving as fragments of a whole that led Willimon to label episodes as 'chapters' rather than provide each episode with a distinctive title.[129]

The mode of binge viewing that Netflix facilitates due to its distinctive practice of making self-scheduling central to the subscriber experience also informs narrative designers' approaches to serial plotting. Within these conditions, certain narrative designers presume that, because Netflix enables binge viewing, many of their series' viewers will engage in this consumption mode, and so these narrative designers shape narratives accordingly. For example, working under the assumption that viewers watch *Orange is the New Black* episodes 'all at once', Kohan 'can take [her] time with some storylines'.[130]

Kohan's understanding concerning how *Orange is the New Black* is viewed appears to have informed the serial plot structure of the series' fifth season. The season's thirteen episodes concern a mere three days of story-world duration within which a prison riot takes place at Litchfield Penitentiary. This approach to plotting suggests that Kohan and her team have taken the opportunity that the context provides to fully explore a particular storyline and decompress its telling. Writing with regard to Victorian literary serials, which were typically published over many months, Michael Lund and Victoria K. Hughes suggest, 'A work's extended duration meant that serials could become entwined with readers' own sense of lived experience and passing time.'[131] Network and cable MSS dramas, ranging from *ER* to *Game of Thrones*, have tended to manufacture a similar illusory synchronicity between fiction and life. Just as many viewers experience a seven-day gap between the viewing of one episode and the next, many drama episodes imply that an unspecified number of days within a storyworld has passed since the events of the previous episode. In so doing, television's narrative designers potentially fortify the process that Lund and Hughes identify.[132] In contrast, by suggesting that events are taking place, not over a number of weeks, but rather over three days, *Orange is the New Black*'s fifth season serial narrative potentially synchronises with the presumed lived experience of those Netflix subscribers who binge the season in a short period of time.

The approach of Kohan and her writing staff to serial storytelling, as well as their perceptions concerning how Netflix MSS series are consumed, does not appear more broadly representative of narrative design processes at Netflix. In the case of *House of Cards*, for example, its serial narrative is, claims showrunner Bill Willimon, designed to complement not only a binge viewing mode of consumption, but also the more traditional pace of viewing that some *House of Cards* viewers adopt.[133] Nevertheless, the example does give an insight into how Netflix's technologically enabled practices of simultaneously releasing a season's episodes can alter attitudes within narrative design processes.

There is, then, a clear variance in technological contexts of consumption between premium cable services, such as HBO, and online streaming services, such as Netflix, which operate independently of network and cable's linear schedules. While narrative designers working on a Netflix MSS series can be very confident that their viewers will watch every episode of that series from the first episode onwards, those working on HBO drama series must operate without that degree of confidence. As we have seen in the case of Kohan and *Orange is the New Black*, narrative designers working on Netflix drama series are, unlike those operating within the HBO context, furthermore able to operate under the assumption that their seasons are primarily consumed via binge viewing practices.

It would, however, be unwise to overemphasise the significance of this variance in narrative design contexts. Reflecting the specificities and considerable influence of the subscription model on which HBO and Netflix each rely, both services encourage the crafting of intensely serialised narratives so as to support their shared economic aim of engendering subscriber loyalty. In contrast to Netflix's self-scheduling consumption mode, HBO's linear scheduling practice might result in some casual viewers being unable to 'keep up' with its MSS dramas; however, as previously noted, the premium cable service regards these viewers as expendable. It appears, therefore, that the economic model that HBO and Netflix share bears greater influence upon narrative design conditions and processes than the specific features of either institution's technologically enabled episode dissemination practices. Applying therefore the dimensions of the specificity model as a means to account for the differences and similarities between HBO and Netflix's industrial contexts, it appears that, while there is clear variability between Netflix and HBO within the technological sub-dimension, non-variability within the economic sub-dimension ensures that narrative design conditions and processes are not significantly dissimilar.

The specificities of the subscription model have, as this section as demonstrated, informed a strong preference at both companies for serial storylines within Netflix and HBO's MSS drama series, reducing single-episode storylines to mere exceptions to the prevailing norm. The approaches to serialisation that have dominated these narrative design processes thus serve as a point of contrast to those traditional within network contexts. To consider further the ways in which the specificities of the subscription service model have influenced narrative designers' approaches to plot, I move on here to examine the crafting of overall seasons within subscriber-supported institutions.

Subscriber-Supported Services: Season Plots

While we have seen, over the last ten years or so, networks sometimes break from their conventional season format of 22 episodes or more by commissioning far shorter seasons of MSS drama series, for subscriber-supported services the shorter season has been the norm. HBO's commissioning policy has been largely responsible for establishing this format as the convention in this sector. With *The Sopranos*, HBO settled on a thirteen-episode season model that became largely uniform for its dramas in the 2000s, although, in the 2010s, the shorter ten-episode season has become standard for the premium cable service's MSS drama series. According to industry insiders, the move within premium cable to ten episodes or fewer has been economically motivated by a desire to increase the number of different series within a given service's year-round schedule. Through increasing the number of series they commission, premium cable services potentially raise the number of distinct audiences a service can attract, thereby expanding their subscription bases.[134]

HBO's practice of commissioning seasons ten-to-thirteen episodes in length reflects a general policy of commissioning a low quantity of original programming so as to maximise production values on the handful of series the service does commission, and thus helps distinguish its narratives from those of its competitors. As Jaramillo observes, 'Fewer episodes ordered means more money to spend.'[135] As Dean J. DeFino notes, however, fewer episodes ordered per year also provides narrative designers 'the luxury of slowing down production'.[136] Afforded more filming time than is typically available in the network context, episode directors and directors of photography have more opportunity to consider how best to compose shots. Within an extravagantly budgeted series, such as *Game of Thrones*, for example, this luxury of time ensures that costly sets, locations and costumes can be artistically and meticulously presented. Driven by the same objective to maximise a given series' production values rather than its episode numbers, Netflix has adopted the shorter season model, with many of its original series adhering to the thirteen-episode season format that HBO established in the early 2000s.

The shorter season model is, as previously explained, more likely to result in a season achieving a greater degree of narrative coherence. The particular practices through which episodes of HBO and Netflix seasons are made available to viewers further encourage narrative unity within a season. While the broadcast of a traditional lengthy network season is typically interrupted by a mid-season hiatus, the weekly frequency with which episodes of an HBO season are transmitted is unbroken. Just as the absence of advertiser support within HBO's economic model facilitates the policy of ordering a low quantity of episodes per season, the removal of the requirement to maximise ratings during sweeps weeks makes HBO seasons' unbroken weekly frequency viable. In the case of Netflix, of course, there is no weekly frequency of transmission to interrupt, as all of a given season's episodes are made simultaneously available.

Due to these conditions, HBO and Netflix's narrative designers are not obliged, as network-based narrative designers often are, to break down seasons into coherent sub-conflicts. Narrative designers working on Netflix and HBO series instead often take the opportunity to implement season-spanning storylines (often referred to as 'season arcs') that accumulate slow gradual build-ups throughout the duration of a season. A season's relative shortness and continuous frequency of transmission (or simultaneous release of episodes) raises the chances of viewers 'keeping up with' intricate season-length storylines, as the format lessens the demand placed on viewers to keep track of what has occurred previously in the narrative.

This method of plotting is strongly evident in *The Wire*. As Brian G. Rose notes, 'The basic structural unit [of *The Wire*] would be the series as a whole, permitting vast twelve-or-thirteen-part story arcs.'[137] An example of such an arc is that of Major Bunny Colvin in season three. This storyline centres on Colvin's efforts to reduce crime within the Western District via the legalisation of narcotics within designated areas. Each episode of the season reveals, incrementally and in minute detail, the development, fruition and ruination of his unorthodox project. According to Simon, the showrunner's own literary aspirations inspire the measured pacing of plot that characterises this arc and many others like it within *The Wire*, whereby each episode furthers storylines by only small degrees. Simon draws parallels, for example, between the gradual pace of the first few episodes of *The Wire*'s first season and the similarly non-urgent beginnings of *Moby Dick* (1851).[138] But, while the approach to plotting surely reflects Simon's creative inclinations and motivations, the particular narrative design conditions HBO imposes (via its season format) make it permissible.

Operating in analogous conditions to Simon, many narrative designers working on Netflix MSS drama series similarly conceive of the season, rather than the episode, as a primary narrative unit. For example, according to the narrative designers responsible, the first seasons of *Daredevil*, *Bloodline* and *House of Cards* were each plotted as a 'a very large movie', rather than as a sequence of distinct episodes.[139] These comparisons made to film and literature can, in part, be seen as narrative designers' efforts to attain increased cultural credibility through the forging of associations between their series and culturally legitimate media. These claims do, nevertheless, speak to the approaches to the plotting of seasons that Netflix and HBO's narrative production conditions enable.

For HBO, these approaches to narrative design whereby the season as a unit represents a set of related and unfragmented season-length storylines not only complement its season lengths and uninterrupted frequency of transmission; they also heighten the potential for the series to perform successfully in DVD and Blu-ray markets.[140] Via the binge viewing mode of consumption that DVD and Blu-ray box sets enable, viewers can take in complex season-length storylines, such as those within *The Wire* and *Game of Thrones*, over the course of, say, a single week or even a weekend. Consuming a season in such a way can, argues Mittell, enable viewers to more easily keep track of storyworld connections and details in such intricately plotted seasons.[141] By providing season plots that are appropriate to this popular viewing mode of watching a given season's episodes in brisk succession, such narrative design practices support the institution's goal of capitalising on DVD and Blu-ray sales—a goal it frequently achieves. For example, the largest selling television box sets of 2014 and 2015 in the US were those of *Game of Thrones*.[142]

A key aim guiding HBO and Netflix's commissioning of original drama series has been to generate narratives clearly distinct from network output. As we have seen, the specificities of the institutions' subscription models have permitted narrative design processes to meet that aim in a variety of ways. The resultant narratives have proved highly beneficial to the subscription services in terms of subscriber numbers.[143] HBO and Netflix original series, by garnering awards and critical acclaim, have also been instrumental in elevating these institutions' profiles, thus serving as what Rogers et al. refer to as 'brand equity'.[144] This strategy of brand equity programming, whereby signature content is commissioned so as to not only generate income directly (whether via subscription fees or through the sale of air-time) but also to boost an institution's brand identity, has become widespread among cable and streaming service institutions in the increasingly competitive twenty-first century US television marketplace. In the basic cable sector, FX and AMC are two channels that have strongly pursued this strategy, commissioning many original MSS primetime drama series as a means to enhance their respective profiles. The following section begins by outlining further the development of these channels' drama series commissioning policies, which emerged in the 2000s, before exploring in detail the relationship between these channels' series and the specificities of basic cable's economic system.

Economic Specificity in Basic Cable Drama Series: FX and AMC

FX and AMC's favouring of the MSS drama series form specifically is reflective of the inspiration that HBO original programming had on both channels' commissioning policies and branding strategies in the 2000s. As part of the Fox Entertainment Group, FX had struggled in the late 1990s and early 2000s to attract audiences via repeats of 20th Century Fox Television network drama series, which served as schedule staples.[145] Aiming to make a stronger appeal to audiences and cable operators, the channel began to develop original drama content, such as *The Shield* and *Nip/Tuck* (2003–2010), as a means to form a more distinctive brand identity.[146] To enable the channel to stand out from the basic cable crowd, Kevin Reilly (then FX president for entertainment) and Peter Liguori (FX Networks president-CEO and former HBO executive) resolved to develop dramas that would position the channel as 'the HBO of basic cable'.[147]

Later in the same decade, AMC, which was formerly branded as American Movie Classics and originated as a dedicated movie channel, similarly modelled its approach to original programming on HBO's so as to elevate its profile. This strategy resulted in AMC's commissioning of *Mad Men* and *Breaking Bad* (2008–2013). As AMC's president and general manager Charlie Collier notes, the two series were conceived as 'brand builders and calling cards' for the channel.[148] Due to HBO having ably demonstrated the potential of 'quality' drama series to attract valuable, upscale demographics within the crowded cable space, the emulation of 'quality' narrative became central to AMC's brand-building exercise. 'The network was looking for distinction in launching its first original series', recalls AMC president Ed Carroll regarding the commissioning of *Mad Men*, 'and we took a bet that quality would win out over formulaic mass appeal.'[149] As HBO's original series had become, as noted by Janet McCabe and Kim Akass, the model for 'quality' by the 2000s (as NBC's had been in the 1980s), AMC not surprisingly aspired to the commissioning of narratives redolent of HBO's in particular.[150] The channel's decision to opt for a *Sopranos* executive-producer's proposed series (Weiner's *Mad Men*) as its first high-profile original commission emphasises this institutional intent to commission series similar to those of HBO. As Weiner makes clear, the channel's guiding principle in the commissioning of its original programming, 'was trying to produce shows like HBO'.[151]

Given that the objective of developing narratives that were HBO in type has underpinned FX and AMC's commissioning policies, how have these institutions reconciled this goal with the specificities of basic cable revenue models? As we have seen, the absence of advertiser support facilitates many of the ways in which HBO narratives depart from network convention. In contrast to the premium cable category, the source of advertiser revenues remains an important component of the basic cable model; FX and AMC have nevertheless aspired to approaches to narrative that are generally considered antithetical to advertiser-supported programming. Through studying the narrative design processes of FX and AMC's original series, I go on to ascertain the degree to which the specificities of basic cable economics have facilitated institutionally devised departures from the storytelling conventions of advertiser-supported contexts.

Basic Cable: Storyworlds

At a fundamental level the storyworld environments in FX and AMC's MSS primetime drama series are broadly analogous to ongoing television drama series more generally, with settings comprised chiefly of recurring domestic and workplace environments. For example, key dialogue exchanges in FX's *The Americans* (2013–2018) involving the series' central protagonists, the Russian spy husband-and-wife team Philip and Elizabeth Jennings, occur in their suburban home, while storyworld activity in *Mad Men* often takes place in an advertising firm's offices. But the behaviours of the characters that populate such settings often mark a clear distinction from network narratives, bringing FX and AMC's storyworlds more in line with those of HBO and Netflix fare. The corrupt and brutally violent Vic Mackey is a core presence within *The Shield*'s cast, for example, while the actions of *Breaking Bad*'s most central character, Walter White, include remorseless murder and drug manufacture/distribution.

Similar to those of subscriber service dramas, FX and AMC storyworlds typically offer novel and challenging takes on genres well established in the network drama tradition. For example, while US television has a long tradition of exciting and/or humorous spy dramas, *The Americans* storyworld includes distinctive events that strongly emphasise the harrowing aspects of espionage. These include the disturbing process of Phillip disposing of the corpse of a naïve asset whom he had put in harm's way (in 'Baggage' [3:2]). Furthermore, while the horror genre has manifested in various forms throughout the history of network television, the storyworld instances of gruesome graphic horror that characterise AMC's *Preacher* (2016–present) and *The Walking Dead* (2010–present) differentiate these series from prior network television engagement with the genre.[152]

Through their construction of morally dubious characters and challenging storylines, these narrative design processes align with an institutional aim to generate the types of distinctive and provocative storyworld characters and events that initially became synonymous with HBO. There are still, however, two key distinctions between the storyworld material of FX and AMC series and those of subscriber services. Firstly, while HBO and Netflix are required to signal to viewers that their service is worth a subscription fee in addition to their existing basic cable package costs, FX and AMC have no such requirement. The basic cable channels do not therefore have the same motivation to outlay huge expenditures so as to achieve the superlative production values that Netflix and HBO do. In line with this industrial logic, FX and AMC drama series budgets, while at the high end of basic cable outlays, are not typically able to permit grand-scale sets and epic event sequences, such as those contained within *Game of Thrones* and *Boardwalk Empire*.[153]

Secondly, whereas HBO frequently incorporates nudity, profane dialogue and graphic sex scenes, FX and AMC do not. This is primarily a consequence of FX and AMC ensuring the marketability of its programming to advertisers, and is thus reflective of the discrepancy between the basic and premium cable models. There are apparently limits, then, to the degree by which FX and AMC will allow its content to test sponsors' nerves.

Nevertheless the amoral characters and provocative events concerning sex, violence and other adult themes that typify FX and AMC series storyworlds still represent a difficult proposition for advertisers (despite the absence of nudity and profanities). The frustration that AMC initially experienced as part of its attempts to procure advertisers for *Mad Men*'s first season, with many potential advertisers finding the series' narrative themes disconcerting, illustrates this point.[154] FX's struggle to retain advertisers for *The Shield* after outraged advocacy groups threatened boycotts of advertisers' products and services further demonstrates the tensions that have existed between basic cable channels' aim to differentiate their series from network dramas and the economic requirement to meet advertisers' needs.[155]

So how, then, have FX and AMC been able to permit these types of storyworlds while simultaneously operating within the (part advertiser-supported) basic cable context? As Lotz and Tony Kelso each observe as part of discussions regarding FX's own foray into original series commissioning, basic cable channels are able to overcome certain advertiser skittishness towards potentially offensive story material in 'quality' series due to the lucrative and hard-to-reach demographics that such series engage.[156] This is evident with the case of *Mad Men*, for example; with an audience of high earners, the series attracted exclusive sponsorship deals with such high-end marketers as BMW.[157] The car manufacturer also advertised its 1 Series during *Breaking Bad* transmissions due to the show's ability to attract difficult-to-reach, wealthy young males.[158] As Stella Gaynor points out, the provocative horror-themed storyworlds of *The Walking Dead* and FX's *American Horror Story* (2011–present) have proved similarly successful at luring demographic groups that advertisers find desirable.[159]

As Lotz observes, the guaranteed income provided by a revenue stream of carriage fees additionally permits basic cable channels to be patient in their pursuit of advertisers, which is a luxury that is usually unavailable to networks due to the specificities of their economic model.[160] The following section, which examines plot and style within episodes of FX and AMC drama series, explores deeper this relationship between, on the one hand, narratives that have been conceived to be distinctive within an advertiser-supported context, and on the other, an economic model that depends in part on serving advertisers' needs.

Basic Cable: Episode Plots and Styles

The plotting of FX and AMC series instalments sometimes results in episodes with scene durations lengthier than is standard within an advertiser-supported context. The *Mad Men* episode 'The Suitcase' (4.7), for example, contains only 27 scenes, while the *Breaking Bad* episode 'Grilled' (2.2), contains a mere 15.[161] These types of episodes slow the economically driven rhythm of episode plotting that is conventional to network MSS dramas, whereby distinct storylines are briskly alternated. Taken to its extreme, this type of approach results in plot structures that fully break from the norms of MSS plotting conventions and the narrative principle of television drama series storytelling more generally. The *Fargo* (FX, 2014–present) episode 'Who Rules the Land of Denial?' (3:8) serves as an example of such an approach. While *Fargo* episodes typically adhere to the MSS plot structure formula, the first half of this episode (which equates to around 25 minutes of screen time) is exclusively comprised of a sequence in which ex-con Nikki Swango is pursued across the snow-covered Minnesota wilderness by a trio of murderous thugs. The resulting plot structure is more akin to that underpinning a film thriller than a serialised ensemble-cast television drama.[162]

Just as such plotting techniques serve to distinguish AMC and FX programming from network content, so too do the styles that these series adopt. AMC, for example, has, over the last ten years, formed a catalogue of series that embrace a form of unhurried storytelling, similar to that found in such subscriber service series as *The Sopranos* and *Bloodline*, which creates an impression of decelerated narrative momentum. This is apparent within actors' performances, for example, which are often subtly and unconventionally drawn out in certain AMC series. As part of the narrative design process of *Mad Men*, for instance, Weiner (apparently sharing various aesthetic sensibilities with his mentor, Chase) mandated that dialogue delivery be unhurried, allowing time for pause and for performers' subtle physical reactions to manifest within the edits. As Tim Hunter, a regular director for the series, observes, 'One of Matt's initial dictums was that he didn't want the dialogue rushed ... with snappy, overlapping dialogue.'[163]

AMC's *The Killing* (2011–2014), the first season of which follows a single police investigation into the murder of a teenage girl, possesses similarly measured performances. This is particularly evident in scenes featuring the victim's grieving parents, Mitch and Stan Larsen, whose numbed reactions and torpid movements are often prominent within edits.[164] As actor Brent Sexton (who portrays Stan) suggests, whereas performers would likely be unable to 'show certain transitions of emotions ... on a network show', *The Killing*'s 'kind of slow-burn storytelling' allows him to provide 'an emotional ... response to what's going on in the moment'.[165] Such 'slow-burn' performances are also evident in AMC's *Rubicon* (2010), *Breaking Bad* and *Better Call Saul* (2015–present). *Rubicon*'s narrative, for example, often indulges brooding silence in scenes shared between intelligence agent Will Travers and his superiors while *Breaking Bad* episodes frequently incorporate awkward, hesitant interactions between Walter White and his wife, Skyler.

Similar to those practices also instituted within the subscriber service space, narrative designers' unhurried style manifests within AMC series not only via the unfolding of complex character interactions, but also through the emphasis placed on storyworld setting. *The Killing*, for example, frequently includes lingering wide shots of characters within a gloomy, rain-sodden Seattle, while *Rubicon* often incorporates similar shots of performers set against Lower Manhattan's cityscape. This attention to location has prompted TV reviewers to suggest that the respective environments of these two series each function as characters in their own right.[166] *Rubicon* director of photography (DP) Michael Slovis relied upon analogous techniques in his work on *Breaking Bad*, providing rich depictions of New Mexico's urban, suburban and desert settings. As Slovis explains:

> Directors will say, 'Let's do the *Breaking Bad* wide shot', which in television is not something that you very often see. Vince [Gilligan, *Breaking Bad*'s creator and showrunner] really likes holding things in wider shots and I happen to really like it also—it puts your character into a place or a locale.[167]

But, as Slovis acknowledged during *Breaking Bad*'s run, he depended upon the production culture that AMC affords so as to contextualise characters within their settings. Comparing his experience on *Breaking Bad* to a previous stint as DP on *CSI*, Slovis observed, 'There is no need to rush anything in *Breaking Bad* ... so we have time to actually let people move through spaces, down halls, into homes ... In broadcast network television you sometimes have to advance the story [much quicker].'[168]

AMC's *Breaking Bad* spinoff series, *Better Call Saul*, which Vince Gilligan and *Breaking Bad* producer Peter Gould created, furthers this commitment to emphasising contexts in which storyworld events occur, resulting in the series' signature reserved pace. This approach is clearly evident in a courtroom scene from the series' first episode ('Uno'), which features defence attorney (and series' protagonist) Jimmy McGill. The first minute of the six-minute scene is taken up by a dialogue-free sequence that shows the court waiting for McGill to arrive. The camera dwells on a judge sitting patiently; jury members are slumped, bored; a stenographer idly slurps a soft drink; a councillor sketches on a yellow legal pad; a court bailiff lumbers lethargically through the court (see Fig. 3.3). The visual style of the scene contrasts with the storytelling of slick, fast-paced network legal dramas due to its focus on minor courtroom characters and the more prosaic aspects of the legal profession.

Performance and direction are integral to the non-urgent nature of many of the scenes within AMC series, but so too, of course, are the edit-

Fig. 3.3 A bored stenographer and slumped jury members await Jimmy McGill's entrance in *Better Call Saul*. Episode: 'Uno' (1:1, 2015)

ing processes that privilege moments of inaction (such as pauses within dialogue exchanges and the accentuating of narrative setting). In the case of *Rubicon*, a deliberate editing pace serves as a separate example of style contributing to a slower pace of storytelling than is usual for advertiser-supported contexts. As the series' showrunner Henry Bromell observed, 'There's not a whole lot of cutting' in *Rubicon*, contrasting the series' editing style with the 'very quick cutting pace of ... network television'.[169] My statistical analysis concurs with this claim; looking at three sample *Rubicon* episodes, I observed a median ASL of 6.4.[170] The series thus operates at what Butler determines as the very high end of ASLs within primetime drama series.[171]

Camera techniques prove a further element of AMC series' style that generally serves to complement gradual pacing. *Mad Men*, *The Killing*, *Rubicon* and *Better Call Saul*, for example, are each typically bereft of dynamic camera gestures such as fleeting Steadicam manoeuvres or aggressively jerky hand-held techniques that are commonly found in network contexts. These series instead usually rely on a careful shooting style comprised of static, slow-panning or slow-tracking shots. *Breaking Bad*, in contrast does incorporate a nervy Steadicam style, but its shots do usually maintain a fixed perspective. The opening of the *Breaking Bad* episode 'Better Call Saul' (2:8) exemplifies such restraint. The scene features a four-minute dialogue exchange, between the drug-dealer Badger and a prospective customer, shot in wide with a single stationary camera. By routinely adopting this reserved shooting style, those responsible for *Breaking Bad*'s photography generate dissonance by implementing highly agitated camera movements in the presentations of brutal violence that punctuate the series. In general, however, the subtle camera techniques that characterise the scenes of these five drama series usually do little to convey urgency. AMC, by permitting narrative designers to construct down-tempo styles and plots, shows disregard for the conventional practice within advertiser-supported television of retaining viewership for commercial breaks via the implementation of fast-paced storytelling.

This 'slow-burn' visual style should not, however, be considered representative of AMC's MSS drama output as a whole. The visual styles of *Preacher* and *The Walking Dead* do not place a similar emphasis on storyworld stillness within their narratives, for example. Neither should this particular style be seen as typical of basic cable visual style more broadly. Many basic cable series in the twenty-first century, such as TNT's *The Closer* (2005–2012) and USA's *White Collar* (2009–2014), adopt slick and fluid visual styles that are largely indistinguishable from those that originate in a network context. The 'slow-burn' style found within such basic cable series as *Mad Men* and *Better Call Saul* can instead be seen as part of a range of distinctive styles that the basic cable context has given rise to, with some of these styles departing from the conventions of advertiser-supported visual storytelling. A separate example of norm-challenging style within a basic cable context is contained within FX's idiosyncratic superhero drama *Legion* (2017–present). Labelled 'aesthetically decadent' by *The Guardian*, the series' visual style routinely incorporates expressionistic visual flourishes that strongly emphasise subjective sensory perceptions at the expense of clearly conveying the occurrence of story-world activity.[172]

Examples of this approach can be found in the series' pilot episode, which introduces series protagonist David Heller as a diagnosed schizophrenic being held at Clockworks Psychiatric Hospital. In the episode, David, who is eventually revealed as a mutant with immense psychic powers (rather than a schizophrenic), is immediately attracted to a new resident at the hospital, Sydney Barrett. Soon after meeting her, David is depicted sitting opposite Sydney during a psychiatry session as part of a scene that employs a highly unconventional lighting set-up. Shot from David's perspective, with Sydney's back to the window, bright white light forms around Sydney, blurring her contours, shrouding her features in shadow. The lighting makes it difficult for either David or the *Legion* audience to visually discern Sydney. Later within the episode, after Sydney has agreed to be David's 'girlfriend', a further shot characterised by a peculiar lighting scheme frames the pair; bathed in red, David and Sydney are encircled by blurs and blotches of reflected scarlet light. As with the prior shot, the visual style is arresting yet it conveys the details of the story-world's reality in an indistinct manner.

Legion cinematographer Craig Wrobleski notes that this visual style is designed 'to keep the audience guessing' concerning the authenticity of the storyworld reality that is presented to them via the perspective of a mental patient protagonist conceived by producers as an 'unreliable narrator'.[173] To contribute to this aim, Wrobleski selected camera lenses that do not provide the 'crisp contemporary look' of most modern television series, but instead contribute to unpredictable, albeit 'amazing', visual results, such as those described above.[174] *Legion*'s opaque visual style can therefore be regarded as analogous to some modes of complex plotting, often cleverly designed to obfuscate, which Mittell identifies within twenty-first century US television dramas, and which are evident in such series as *Lost* and *Westworld*.[175] While *Legion*'s visuals have been developed to support the series' broader narrative aims, they contradict the storytelling convention within network drama of visually depicting storyworlds, not only via a slick style, but also in a generally unambiguous way so as not to confound viewers.

Despite being developed in an advertiser-supported context, narrative designers of basic cable drama series also sometimes take an unorthodox approach to both their plotting and style in relation to commercial break placement. In many cases, narrative designers within the basic cable sphere conform to network convention by positioning act-end scenes immediately prior to commercial breaks and ensuring that these scenes conclude abruptly. This practice is evident in a scene in *The Americans* episode 'Pests' (5:2), which contains a storyline turning point concerning KGB officer Oleg Burov. As part of the Moscow-set scene, Oleg receives covert instructions from the CIA, a consequence of his previous unauthorised interactions with this American intelligence agency, thereby placing Oleg in a precarious position within the Motherland. Conforming to advertiser-supported conventions of storytelling, the scene ceases very shortly after Oleg has read the CIA's instructions; the scene therefore concludes at a point of peak tension. Backed by a stress-inducing soundscape of high-pitched strings and a tuneless, reverberating drone, the scene's final shot frames Oleg as he rubs his temples and forms a distressed expression before the swift cut to the commercial break that follows.

Other narrative design processes in the basic cable sphere, however, suggest a failure to anticipate commercial break insertion as part of the plotting of act structures and the forming of visual styles, indicating an apparent lack of prioritisation for the commercial loads that series carry. *Fargo* showrunner Noah Hawley, for example, acknowledges writing episodes of the series without caring where commercial breaks might be inserted.[176] So too does Matthew Weiner with regards to the plotting of *Mad Men*'s episodes, noting that consideration for commercial interruption occurred during a given episode's post-production phase. Speaking during the series run, he claimed, 'I write the show straight through … And then we find, when we're editing, where the breaks go.'[177] Such lack of regard for storytelling conventions around commercial break placement is evident in the *Mad Men* episode 'The Rejected' (4:4). In said episode, the final seconds of the scene that (in original transmission form) precedes the first commercial break feature office manager Joan Harris switching off lights and drawing the curtains of the advertising agency's empty consultation room. The sequence is clearly not an especially compelling one, and was not conceived to provide suspense and/or to entice viewers to the narrative to come.

Just as it hadn't with *The Sopranos*, this failure to position and present act-break events in a manner traditional to advertiser-supported programming does not, however, equate to an abandonment of conventional act structure within the *Mad Men* narrative design process. 'The Rejected', for example, features key turning-point events that divide the episode into an evenly paced five-act plot structure (in common with some twenty-first century network drama series) within its 46-minute duration. At 9:20, junior partner at the firm Pete Campbell is surprised to learn from his father-in-law that his wife is pregnant. At 19:50, advertising guru Don Draper's secretary Allison, bitter after a one-night stand with her boss, breaks down in tears during a focus group for Ponds cold cream, with Don looking anxiously on. At 28:20, Allison confronts Don and quits before storming out of the agency's doors. At 37:10, a bohemian gathering attended by another of the agency's junior partners, Peggy Olsen, is subject to a police raid. Within the narrative design traditions of network television, many if not all of these turning-point events would be plotted so as to synchronise with the advent of a commercial break. Yet, perversely, *Mad Men* narrative designers opted against arranging even a single one of these story events to pre-empt commercials. Such practice is a clear departure from traditions in advertiser-supported environments; however, by plotting storyworlds in such a way, and so avoiding act-break editing/shooting convention associated with the positioning of act-break scenes prior to commercials, *Mad Men* style thus appears more akin to that utilised within a subscriber service context.

As the above analysis suggests, FX and AMC, with series such as *Fargo*, *Legion*, *Mad Men* and *Better Call Saul*, developed episode plots and visual styles that reflect these channels' HBO-influenced aims to enhance their brands via the creation of narratives that appear highly distinctive within an advertiser-supported context. These efforts have furthermore paid off, with FX and AMC's original series frequently serving their designated purpose by raising their respective institutional profiles through column inches, social media chatter, and numerous Emmy award wins. As Collier observes of AMC, the channel's drama series commissions have garnered 'the brand more of a halo effect than any other acquisition could've given us'.[178]

The question remains regarding how the previously discussed techniques of episode plotting and visual style within FX and AMC series relate to the economic specificities of the basic cable revenue model. Through many of its distinctive original drama series commissions, HBO and Netflix market their services as culturally invaluable to an affluent demographic. But if, how, and when subscribers opt to view such brand-boosting content is of secondary concern to subscriber service institutions. FX and AMC have also targeted upscale audiences with original series commissions such as *Fargo*, *Damages* (2007–2012), *Mad Men* and *Breaking Bad*. However, in contrast to HBO and Netflix, the ad-supported component in FX and AMC's economic models depends, to some degree, upon the commoditisation of these audiences and the subsequent marketing of these lucrative 'eyeballs' to the appropriate advertisers. Commercial breaks typically need to be viewed. Why, then, do FX and AMC countenance narratives that—due to their episode plots and visual styles—do not appear engineered to complement commercial interruption within episodes?

One key reason is that AMC and FX have often relied on a strategy whereby the ad revenues particular to those primetime hours in which its series air are often relatively insignificant to the economic logics that underpin these institutions' commissions. While their air-time can sometimes be of marginal value, FX and AMC's original series can serve these institutions by increasing the worth of FX and AMC's respective overall line-ups (to advertisers) and the FX and AMC brand (to cable operators). There are clear exceptions to this general trend. In 2015, AMC's *The Walking Dead*, for example, was able, due to its remarkably high ratings among desirable demographics, to charge more money ($502,500) per 30-second commercial spot than any other scripted series on US television.[179] This series' extraordinary economic performance should not, however, be considered reflective of the economic underpinnings of all FX and AMC drama series.

Mad Men serves as a counter-example to *The Walking Dead*, demonstrating how high-profile basic cable drama series can struggle to garner large amounts of advertising revenue during the hours in which they air. AMC's efforts to lure, via this series, upscale audiences and the advertisers willing to pay a premium to access them, proved successful only up to a point. For instance, the overall advertiser revenues *Mad Men* generated ($2.25 million approximately for season one airings, $2.8 million approximately for season two, $1.98 million for season three) are low compared to those which high-profile network series typically commanded during that period.[180] For example, while in 2010, ABC was charging advertisers $222,113 per 30-second spot included during *Grey's Anatomy* broadcasts,

AMC was charging around \$20,000–25,000 for an equivalent spot in *Mad Men* transmissions during the same year.[181] *Mad Men*'s ad-earnings, in fact, offered only a minor contribution to the license fees—an estimated \$2–3 million per episode—that AMC paid Lionsgate Entertainment (*Mad Men*'s production company) for the right to transmit the series.[182] As such, the income *Mad Men* recouped per hour did not come close to covering the money that AMC invested in the series. Neither has AMC benefited from Lionsgate's sales of *Mad Men* to international distributors, while the cable institution has received only a share from sales of *Mad Men* DVDs, merchandise and digital downloads.[183] But, crucially, series such as *Mad Men*, along with other AMC and FX series, have enabled these channels to generate greater revenues for these institutions via two other means that together reflect the specificities of basic cable's twin revenue source of advertiser support and carriage fees.

The first of these sources concerns the advertising revenue that FX and AMC's original series bring to each channel's schedule in its entirety, with the brand buzz that FX and AMC series generate, enabling each institution to attract interest in its wider schedules from both viewers and advertisers. As Lotz notes of FX, its distinctive dramas, through garnering awards, acclaim and publicity, and thereby elevating the channel's identity, have likely increased ratings for the channel's entire schedule.[184] By distinguishing the FX brand as a site for risk-taking, convention-breaking narrative, these series help make the FX brand as a whole, and therefore the entire FX schedule, desirable to advertisers, rather than just a given drama series' timeslot. As media analyst Bill Carroll observes concerning the benefits advertisers can gain by connecting their products and services to the FX brand, 'There is a positive rub off of being associated with something of that quality.'[185] An objective to strengthen the value of its entire schedule has similarly driven AMC's commissioning policy. As Collier notes, AMC aims to create 'interplay between a great stable of films and high-end originals', with its series recontextualising for both audiences and advertisers the films with which they share AMC's schedules. As Collier puts it, AMC's aim has been to use the profile boost its original series provide to 'set us up in a way that all boats could rise'.[186]

AMC's scheduling, accordingly, develops associations between its original series and its catalogue of feature films. On the premiere weekend of espionage drama *Rubicon*'s third episode, for example, AMC scheduled four movies similar in theme, namely *JFK* (1991), *Michael Clayton* (2007), *Charlie Wilson's War* (2007) and *Three Days of the Condor* (1975).[187] Such scheduling strategy potentially enhanced AMC's prospects in luring an upscale TV audience towards the feature film transmissions that comprise part of its schedules, thus raising the value of such programming to advertisers. By forming a thematic association between *Rubicon* and awards-nominated, critically acclaimed films such as those listed above, AMC's scheduling furthermore raised the drama series' cultural value.

FX has adopted a similar approach to developing synergies with its drama series and transmissions of feature films. While FX, unlike AMC, did not originate as a dedicated film channel, movies have become a large part of its schedule, accounting for 84 per cent of its primetime line-up in 2013, for example.[188] FX has accordingly looked to develop, via its scheduling practices, connections between its film and drama series episode transmissions, thereby maximising the value of both. In the hours leading up to the premiere of the pilot episode of *Legion*, a series that forms part of 21st Century Fox's film and television X-Men storyworld, two 20th Century Fox movies were scheduled that contribute to this same shared fictional universe: *The Wolverine* (2013) and *X-Men: Days of Future Past* (2014).[189] While the two movies served as a logical lead in for the *Legion* episode, the high anticipation that developed around *Legion* prior to its premiere raised the cultural relevance of these two film transmissions, potentially making them more attractive to viewers.[190]

In the case of AMC, its approach to balancing commercial loads within its schedule is emblematic of this economic strategy of developing distinctive television drama as a means to generate value for the schedule as a whole. For some of its drama series, including *Mad Men*, *Breaking Bad* and *Better Call Saul*, the channel carried a reduced commercial inventory within the hours in which they were transmitted. Consequently, episodes of these series range from around 46–52 minutes, contrasting with the 40–43 minute (approx.) episode durations standard in network and basic cable primetime schedules.[191] The wider institutional intent to emulate aspects of HBO's policies motivated this particular approach. As Collier confirms, AMC has aimed to ensure that the hours in which episodes of original series air remain 'uncluttered' so as to support its efforts to develop 'an environment that's premium television on basic cable'.[192] But, conversely, AMC has, in the case of its feature film transmissions, increased the volume of commercial breaks they carry so as to capitalise on the greater value (to advertisers) that its series potentially lend its entire schedule.[193] This strategy has proved economically fruitful. For example, in 2010, *Mad Men*'s advertising revenue comprised only 1.5 per cent of AMC's ad income, yet the institution's total ad revenues had risen by 23 per cent (to $204.6 million) since the series 2007 debut.[194] AMC's ad earnings for *Mad Men* transmissions are unimpressive when considered in isolation, but the series operated more successfully as a loss-leader product, generating profitability for all timeslots.[195]

The example of *Mad Men* suggests that the boosts that original series bring to ad-sales across basic cable channel schedules have the potential to significantly outweigh the value these series bring to their own respective timeslots. Yet the enhancement in institutional profiles, which original drama series can bring about, additionally enables channels to capitalise on basic cable's alternative means of revenue, providing institutions leverage in their negotiations with cable operators over the carriage fees they charge.[196] For example, in 2006, the revenue amount AMC received from cable providers per subscriber (per month) was 21 cents, a decline on the 22 cents per subscriber (per month) it received in 2005. But, following *Mad Men*'s debut, the amount AMC charged cable providers rose from 22 cents to 24 cents per subscriber (per month) in 2010.[197] According to industry analyst Robert Seidman's estimates, this three cent per subscriber increase earned the institution somewhere within the region of an additional $33 million per annum.[198]

Thus, while the unconventional narratives of FX and AMC original series might sometimes seem poorly configured to deliver 'eyeballs' to commercial breaks, the brand elevation they provide these channels has rendered them more attractive to basic cable providers. By contributing to the institutions' carriage fee rises, by increasing the value of its entire schedule to advertisers, the profitability of FX and AMC's original series often proves both indirect and specific to a basic cable context. These complex economic logics that have enabled FX and AMC to reconcile their series' idiosyncratic episode plots and styles with an advertiser-supported context underline the importance of basic cable's twin revenue streams to these programming strategies. The following section considers the manner in which FX and AMC's strategy of brand-enhancing programming has informed techniques of serial storytelling, and furthermore ascertains to what extent the specificities of the basic cable model facilitate these approaches.

Basic Cable: Serialised Plots

In some cases, basic cable channels mandate that their MSS drama series emulate networks' conventional patterns of serial plotting by balancing episode-length standalone conflicts against serial storylines. For example, as *Battlestar Galactica*'s (Syfy, 2004–2009) showrunner Ronald D. Moore observes, the basic cable channel SyFy pressured its narrative designers to use standalone storylines within episodes as a means to reduce the amount of 'hurdles for new viewers to overcome to watch the show'; this pressure led Moore to pledge to always 'try to provide at least an episodic quality to each show'.[199] As basic cable institutions are, similar to networks, reliant on advertiser support, it makes sound economic sense that channels have used these strategies to maximise the widest possible audience from the intended demographic.

The heavy serialisation within various FX and AMC series that have been transmitted over the last ten years or so, including *Fargo*, *Legion*, *Damages*, *The Killing*, *Breaking Bad* and *Better Call Saul*, indicates that neither institution imposes a mandate similar to that imposed on Moore. Similar to those of HBO and Netflix, these series are dominated by multiple-episode narrative. The storylines that comprise *Breaking Bad*, for example, which typically concern Walter's continued effort to survive and thrive within the methamphetamine trade, as well as the ongoing struggles of those characters within his near orbit, usually thread through one episode to the next. *The Killing* displays a similar commitment to seriality, with each episode of the first season representing a different day of the same single murder investigation.

This general preference for serial storylines within FX and AMC drama series is an integral element of the institution's HBO-inspired attempts to commission content that is recognised as culturally significant. As Newman and Levine observe, HBO's original programming has contributed to a process whereby serial storytelling has become privileged as culturally superior, with much of the critical kudos this programming receives resulting from its celebrated long-form narrative.[200] In this cultural climate, it follows that FX and AMC, as institutions seeking to commission brand-enhancing content, have permitted an overriding dominance of serial storylines within the narratives of their series. Again speaking to the importance of the twin revenue streams of basic cable, however, the chief risk of serialisation—that of alienating casual viewers—is (in contrast with networks) offset for FX and AMC by the supplementary income that carriage fees provide. As Hilmes observes, this additional revenue stream permits basic cable programming to function on the kind of relatively low ratings that would prove untenable within the context of a network business model.[201] So, for example, while in 2017 *Better Call Saul*'s third season averaged 1.6 million viewers, and *Legion*'s first season averaged fewer than a million viewers, AMC nevertheless saw fit to renew the former series, and FX the latter.[202] In a network context, such viewing figures would very probably have resulted in cancellation. The carriage fee income that the basic cable revenue model provides therefore permits FX and AMC to routinely incorporate a high degree of serial storylines within their drama series, bringing their original programming more in line with many series produced within the subscriber-supported space (as opposed to a network context).

The advent and popularisation of streaming platforms within television culture has further increased the viability of intensely serialised narrative at FX and AMC. Similar to networks, channels such as FX and AMC look to gain increased value from the drama series they not only commission, but also produce or co-produce (and therefore own or co-own streaming rights to). Channels have extracted this value not only by selling series streaming rights to popular streaming services, such as Netflix and Amazon, but also—in some cases—via their own streaming platforms. AMC, for example, in addition to having given Netflix licence to stream older seasons of *The Walking Dead* (which AMC Studios produces), also launched the supplementary streaming service AMC Premiere in 2017, enabling AMC viewers to stream the series ad free (for a fee).[203] FX CEO John Landgraf's acknowledgement in 2014 that he was aiming to restructure the FX model 'so that we own the shows, own the back end' reflects the increased significance channels now place on exploiting the streaming potential of series subsequent to their basic cable transmission.[204]

As previously discussed, serial storytelling has proved to be an approach to plotting that strongly complements the modes of viewer self-scheduling that streaming provides. The intense serialisation within series that AMC and FX own or co-own, such as *Legion* and *The Walking Dead*, therefore increases the potential for such series to perform successfully in a digital afterlife. A further factor motivating serial storytelling within FX and AMC series are the particular season schedules that these channels impose, as the following section details.

Basic Cable: Season Plots

As previously noted, while HBO's reliance on the shorter season format in the late 1990s was unique, the strategy came to greatly influence the commissioning policies of its rivals. As Weiner remarks, due to HBO's introduction of the format, 'a genre was born'.[205] As a consequence of this influence, FX and AMC's drama series have maintained seasons typically ranging from ten to thirteen episodes in length. The particularities of the basic cable model have permitted FX and AMC's commissioning of short series. As Collier notes, while advertisers support basic cable institutions, the channels' ad rates are not set via the sweeps process, and so they have no need to schedule long seasons to span these periods.[206] These shorter seasons may represent a missed opportunity for basic cable channels to fully exploit advertising sales for a given series; however, as noted, FX and AMC are generally each more concerned with raising carriage fees and drawing lucrative demographics to the schedule as a whole then they are with maximising the ad income for a given series via lengthier seasons.[207] The shorter season form that HBO popularised has at least the potential to result in the type of coherently and artistically structured season that critics often valorise. By commissioning shorter seasons, FX and AMC therefore encourage approaches to season narrative design that might result in the enhancement of their respective brands, thereby potentially raising each channel's value to advertisers and cable providers.

Due to these channels' adherence to the shorter season template, certain FX and AMC narrative designers have indeed taken advantage of shorter season lengths to utilise systems of season plotting whereby a season's elements form a narrative unity. Walter's storyline in season four of *Breaking Bad* provides a prime example of the kind of unbroken, slowly unravelling season-long arc associated with series originating from the subscriber service space, such as *The Wire* and *Game of Thrones*. As Vince Gilligan observes, the season plays out 'as a major game of chess' between Walter and his employer, the drugs kingpin Gus Fring.[208] The season begins with Walter in a perilous position; having crossed Fring in the concluding episode of season three, Walter knows he is on borrowed time, with only his expert meth-cookery skills keeping his own execution temporarily at bay. Throughout the season, an increasingly desperate Walter consistently schemes to kill Gus, but is thwarted again and again by his cool and cautious employer. Only in the season finale is the conflict resolved, when Walt's crazed ingenuity finally facilitates Fring's assassination.

In the case of the FX series *Fargo* and *American Horror Story*, narrative designers have taken to extremes this objective of organising each season into a coherent narrative module. Each season of each of these two series presents a storyworld that is, in the main, only very loosely connected to other seasons within its respective series, and therefore operates as a quasi mini-series. While, for example, seasons of *Fargo* are ultimately serially connected, as they each appear to share the same Minnesota-set storyworld as the 1996 Coen brothers' film of the same name, they each largely function as independent narrative units. There are, then, some small instances of storyworld continuity between *Fargo*'s seasons, yet a given season's characters, settings, storylines and time period are largely confined to that season. FX's commissioning policy, which reflects the specificities of basic cable economics, formed the narrative design conditions that have given rise to these particular innovative approaches to season structure. By commissioning shorter season orders, the channel enables *Fargo* and *American Horror Story*'s narrative designers to more easily conceive of each season as a coherent whole. Furthermore, by transmitting episodes without interruption to their weekly frequency, the channel enables audiences to more easily perceive each season as a distinct, unified set of episodes.

Conclusion

This study of the relationship between the contrasting categories of economic models within twenty-first century US television and the narratives they commission underlines the importance of economics as a variable sub-dimension of specificity within a medium. It shows how the specificities of economic models influence narrative design conditions and processes. It also demonstrates how the discrepancy between economic models can facilitate clear distinctions between narratives. This is evident in the manner by which HBO, Netflix, FX and AMC have, due to the respective specificities of their economic models, been able to commission series that represent significant departures from network conventions in matters of plot, style and storyworld. It furthermore shows how, within a national context, a medium's narrative design conditions can vary according to specific uses of technology (such as Netflix's practice of making a series' episodes simultaneously available) and audience-targeting objectives (such as the pursuit of 'quality' viewers) that institutions employ.

The study also indicates, however, that processes of media convergence—particularly the forces of technological convergence—have the potential to lessen previously clear distinctions in television's narrative design conditions and processes. For example, the emergence of online streaming services, and the new content syndication opportunities that this development has afforded more traditional television institutions, has proved to be a factor influencing some change to networks' narrative design conditions. As this chapter's section on network drama suggests, this industrial shift potentially makes the abandonment of standalone storylines more permissible in the network context. These altered industrial contexts therefore have the potential to bring network narrative design conditions more in line with those of subscriber service and basic cable narrative design conditions (wherein short seasons and high degrees of serialisation are now conventional). This example indicates how the increased connection of television culture to an internet base can erode differences in narrative design conditions across a given medium's culture. As this chapter shows, the specificities of particular economic models, targeted audiences, uses of technology, as well as national regulatory systems, still influence variability in narrative design conditions in distinct ways; nevertheless, as the chapter also indicates, the ongoing influence of technological convergence should be accounted for in analyses of twenty-first century narrative design processes.

The study furthermore suggests that the presence of variability in economic models does not *always* equate to clearly contrasting narrative design conditions and processes. Despite their institutions operating via revenue models that are markedly different from one another, the original drama series of HBO and Netflix nevertheless share many similar narrative traits to those of FX and AMC. Contrasts in economic models have certainly ensured some differentiation in narrative design conditions and processes between the two sectors. As noted, for example, unlike HBO and Netflix, basic cable channels do not have the economic motivation to countenance extravagant budgets. However, despite the specificities of basic cable economics, narrative designers working on FX and AMC series have been able to utilise approaches to serial storytelling and season structure that strongly resemble practices developed within the subscriber service space.

This narrative resemblance across economic categories is no coincidence of course. FX and AMC aimed to emulate the particular commissioning policy that HBO pioneered, reconciling it with basic cable's distinct revenue model. FX and AMC's successful strategy here holds an important implication for the dimensions of specificity model. It indicates the potential importance to narrative design processes of shared influence across economic categories. FX and AMC certainly operate in an economic sector distinct from that of Netflix and HBO, but these institutions have not operated in isolation from one another. While this chapter, then, underlines the relevance of economic specificity within a single marketplace, it also signals the need to simultaneously account for the influence that variable economic models potentially share within a given national media industry, or even across multiple national media industries, as part of their commissioning of narratives.

Similar exchanges of influence have passed between the two rival US comic-book publishers Marvel and DC over the years. Since the late 1930s, each of the pair has derived new approaches to both business and narrative from the other. These shifts in institutional and storytelling strategy that have taken place through the decades have often occurred due to publishers' pursuit of new audiences within the market. The following chapter closely examines the connections between such shifts in audience specificity in the US comic-book industry and narrative design conditions and processes.

Notes

1. Amanda D. Lotz, 'If It's Not TV, What is It?': The Case of U.S. Subscription Television', in *Cable Visions: Television Beyond Broadcasting*, ed. Sarah Banet-Weiser, Cynthia Chris and Anthony Freitas (New York: New York University Press, 2007), 87.
2. See, for example, ibid.; Mark C. Rogers, Michael Epstein and Jimmie L. Reeves, '*The Sopranos* as HBO Brand Equity: The Art of Commerce in the Age of Digital Reproduction', in *This Thing of Ours: Investigating The Sopranos*, ed. David Lavery (New York: Columbia University Press, 2002), 42–57; Deborah L. Jaramillo, 'The Family Racket: AOL Time Warner, HBO, *The Sopranos*, and the Construction of a Quality Brand', *Journal of Communication Inquiry* 26, No. 1 (2002), 59–75; Avi Santo, 'Para-Television and Discourses of Distinction: The Culture of Production at HBO', in *It's Not TV: Watching HBO in the Post-Television Era*, ed. Marc Leverette, Brian L. Ott and Cara Louise Buckley (New York: Routledge, 2008), 19–45; Casey J. McCormick, '"Forward Is the Battle Cry": Binge-Viewing Netflix's *House of Cards*', in *The Netflix Effect: Technology and Entertainment in the 21st Century*, ed. Kevin McDonald and Daniel Smith-Rowsey (London: Bloomsbury, 2016), 101–116; Chuck Tryon, 'TV Got Better: Netflix's Original Programming Strategies

and Binge Viewing', *Media Industries* 2, No. 2 (2015), http://quod.lib.
umich.edu/m/mij/15031809.0002.206/--tv-got-better-netflixs-origi-
nal-programming-strategies?rgn=main;view=fulltext.

3. See Robert C. Allen, *Speaking of Soap Operas* (Chapel Hill: University of
North Carolina Press, 1985), 70–71.

4. See ibid.

5. Robin Nelson, *TV Drama in Transition: Forms, Values and Cultural
Change* (Basingstoke: Macmillan, 1997), 31–34.

6. See Marc Dolan, 'The Peaks and Valleys of Serial Creativity', in *Full of
Secrets: Critical Approaches to Twin Peaks*, ed. David Lavery (Detroit:
Wayne State University Press, 1995), 34.

7. See Hilmes, *Only Connect*, 186–187, 217–218.

8. See Dunleavy, *Television Drama*, 133–134. The networks' combined
audience share declined from 90 per cent in the late 1970s to 67 per cent
by the end of the 1980s. Robert J. Thompson, *Television's Second Golden
Age: From* Hill Street Blues *to* ER (Syracuse, NY: Syracuse University
Press, 1997), 36.

The adoption of niche-targeting practices emerged in the 1970s on
networks discovering that a demographic group of urban adults aged
18–49 were the primary purchasers of the majority of products featuring
in commercial spots. Feuer, 'MTM: Enterprises: An Overview', 3–4.

9. Douglas Gomery, *A History of Broadcasting in the United States* (Oxford:
Blackwell, 2008), 266.

10. The ongoing primetime drama series format emerged in the late 1950s.
By the 1960s the format had superseded the networks' more costly live-
anthology plays (which had prevailed through the previous decade). See
William Boddy, *Fifties Television: The Industry and Its Critics* (Urbana:
University of Illinois Press, 1993), 187–188.

11. Examples of seriality in primetime drama series during this period include:
The Fugitive (1963–1967), *Run for Your Life* (1965–1966) and *The
Invaders* (1967–1968), which, though ostensibly episodic dramas, were
each built around a single, suspenseful overarching story thread; science
fiction series such as *Lost in Space* (1965–1968) and *Time Tunnel* (1966–
1967), which utilised cliff-hanger endings redolent of the adventure and
science fiction film serials of the 1930s; and the medical drama series *Ben
Casey* (1961–1966) and *Dr Kildare* (1961–1966), which, from their
fourth seasons onward, began serialising distinct storylines regarding
their respective doctors' romantic lives. See Raymond W. Stedman, *The
Serials: Suspense and Drama by Instalment*, second edition (Norman:
University of Oklahoma Press, 1977), 403–406, 417.

12. Hilmes, *Only Connect*, 268–269.

13. In contrast, ABC's *Peyton Place* (1964–1969), network television's most successful primetime soap prior to *Dallas*, had failed to inspire sustainable imitations, with short-lived rival network projects either flailing in the ratings or failing to ever reach the schedules. See Stedman, *The Serials*, 409–412; Michael Z. Newman and Elana Levine, *Legitimating Television: Media Convergence and Cultural Status* (New York: Routledge, 2012), 83–84.

14. NBC's attempt at a *Dallas*-emulative series, *Flamingo Road* (1981–1982), proved short-lived.

15. See Thompson, *Television's Second Golden Age*, 34–35; Newman and Levine, *Legitimating Television*, 85.

16. See Thompson, *Television's Second Golden Age*, 14, 30, 58.

17. For further discussion of *Hill Street*'s unconventional story elements, see ibid., 65–69.

18. See Nelson, *TV Drama in Transition*, 30–32.

19. Thompson notes that the use of 'quality' as a descriptor emerged within journalistic and scholarly discourse in the early 1980s in response to the emergence of this new type of hour-long drama. Thompson, *Television's Second Golden Age*, 12–13.

20. One example would be soap-style drama series targeted towards teen demographics, pioneering early examples being *Beverley Hills 90210* (FOX, 1990–2000) and *Melrose Place* (FOX, 1992–1999).

21. Jane Feuer, 'HBO and the Concept of Quality TV', in *Quality TV: Contemporary American Television and Beyond*, ed. Janet McCabe and Kim Akass (London: I. B. Tauris, 2007), 151.

22. Mittell, *Complex TV*, 32.

23. Lotz, *The Television Will Be Revolutionized*.

24. Nate Anderson, 'Nielsen Tracks DVR Data, But How Should It Be Used?', *Ars Technica*, 13 February 2006, https://arstechnica.com/uncategorized/2006/02/6169-2/; Anon., 'Milestone Marker: SVOD and DVR Penetration Are Now On Par With One Another', Nielsen, http://www.nielsen.com/us/en/insights/news/2016/milestone-marker-svod-and-dvr-penetration-on-par-with-one-another.html; Cynthia Myers, *TV on Strike: Why Hollywood Went to War Over the Internet* (Syracuse, NY: Syracuse University Press, 2013), 9–10.

25. Jennifer Gillan, *Television and New Media: Must Click TV* (New York: Routledge, 2011), 137–138.

26. Jonathan Storm, 'TV Takes Dramatic Turn for Fall Season; Cinematic Style, Technical Advances—Out of 16 New Dramas, Not a Loser in This Dazzling Broadcast Lineup', *The Philadelphia Inquirer*, 17 September 2006, A01.

27. ABC's 1997–1998 line-up also included two short-lived MSS series, *Push* (1998) and *Nothing Sacred* (1997–1998).

28. The 2007–2008 line-up also includes the following MSS series: *ER, Las Vegas* (NBC, 2003–2008), *Lipstick Jungle* (NBC, 2008–2009), *Big Shots* (ABC, 2007–2008), *Ugly Betty* (ABC, 2006–2010), *Pushing Daisies* (ABC, 2007–2009), *Desperate Housewives* (ABC, 2004–2012), *Brothers & Sisters* (ABC, 2006–2011), *Private Practice* (ABC, 2007–2013), *Dirty Sexy Money* (ABC, 2007–2009), *October Road* (ABC, 2007–2008), *Boston Legal* (ABC, 2004–2008), *Men in Trees* (ABC, 2006–2008) and *Cashmere Mafia* (ABC, 2008).

29. The 2016–2017 line-up also includes the following MSS series: *Chicago Med* (NBC, 2015–present), *Chicago Fire* (NBC, 2012–present), *Shades of Blue* (NBC, 2016–present), *Midnight, Texas* (NBC, 2017–present), *Grey's Anatomy, Quantico* (2015–present), *The Catch* (ABC, 2016–2017) *American Crime* (ABC, 2015–2016), *Emerald City* (2017), *Agents of S.H.I.E.L.D., Secrets and Lies* (ABC, 2015–2016), *Designated Survivor* (ABC, 2016–present) and *How to Get Away With Murder* (ABC, 2014–present).

30. Gary R. Edgerton and Jeffrey P. Jones, 'HBO's Ongoing Legacy', in *The Essential HBO Reader*, ed. Gary R. Edgerton and Jeffrey P. Jones (Lexington: University of Kentucky Press, 2008), 319.

31. Jethro Nededog, '5 Reasons Why TV Networks Are Ordering Shorter Seasons', *Business Insider*, 18 June 2015, http://uk.businessinsider.com/why-tv-networks-are-ordering-shorter-seasons-2015-6.

32. Robert C. Allen, 'Making Sense of Soaps', in *The Television Studies Reader*, ed. Robert C. Allen and Annette Hill (New York: Routledge, 2004), 253.

33. The phrase 'least objectionable programming' is attributed to Paul Klein, vice-president for NBC from 1977 to 1979. See Thompson, *Television's Second Golden Age*, 38–39.

34. Matt Zoller Seitz, 'TV's Serial Drama Slump', *Vulture*, August 2016, http://www.vulture.com/2016/08/serial-drama-slump-c-v-r.html.

35. John Horn, 'Jill Soloway on Transparent and How Lena Dunham's Success Convinced Her to Stop Pretending', *Vulture*, 26 September 2014, http://www.vulture.com/2014/09/jill-soloway-interview-transparent-amazon-lena-dunham-girls-louie.html.   Character   behaviour within networks series is further constrained by the requirement of networks to conform to standards of decency imposed by the Federal Communications Commission (FCC). Network protagonists are, for example, therefore not permitted to utter profanity.

36. Denise Martin, 'Shonda Rhimes Talks *Scandal*'s Brutal Season 3 and the Issue of Likeability', *Vulture*, 6 December 2013, http://www.vulture.com/2013/12/shonda-rhimes-talks-season-3-of-scandal.html.
37. Jason Mittell, 'Lengthy Interactions with Hideous Men: Walter White and the Serial Poetics of Television's Anti-Heroes', in *Storytelling in the Media Convergence Age: Exploring Screen Narratives*, ed. Roberta Pearson and Anthony N. Smith (Basingstoke: Palgrave Macmillan, 2014), 74–92.
38. Brian Steinberg, 'Advertisers Embrace Gory Shows Like *Walking Dead*', *Variety*, 3 April 2013, http://variety.com/2013/biz/news/advertisers-embrace-gory-shows-like-walking-dead-1200332162/.
39. Emily Steel and Bill Marsh, 'Millennials and Cutting the Cord', *The New York Times*, 3 October 2015, https://www.nytimes.com/interactive/2015/10/03/business/media/changing-media-consumption-millenials-cord-cutters.html.
40. TV by the Numbers, 'ABC Scores Series Highs Across the Board', *Screener*, 7 December 2012, http://tvbythenumbers.zap2it.com/network-press-releases/abcs-scandal-scores-series-highs-across-the-board/; Michael Schneider, 'Scandal vs. The Blacklist: Here's How the First Night of TV's Thursday Face Off Fared', *TV Insider*, 6 February 2015, https://www.tvinsider.com/1386/scandal-vs-the-blacklist-heres-how-the-first-night-of-tvs-thursday-face-off-fared/.
41. Michael Z. Newman, 'From Beats to Arcs: Toward a Poetics of Television Narrative', *The Velvet Light Trap* 58 (2006), 17.
42. Ibid.
43. Nelson, *TV in Transition*, 33.
44. See Bordwell, *Narration in the Fiction Film*, 50.
45. Jonathan Lupo, 'Just Three Cameras and We Shoot: Mode of Production and Televisual Style in *Friday Night Lights*' (paper given at SCMS Conference, New Orleans, Louisiana, 12 March 2011).
46. Lupo's analysis of four sample episodes of *24* measures a median ASL of 3.5 seconds; Jeremy G. Butler's analysis of nine sample *CSI* episodes records a median ASL of 4.1 seconds. See Lupo, 'Just Three Cameras and We Shoot'; Butler, *Television Style*, 9–10.
47. See Thompson, *Television's Second Golden Age*, 68.
48. See Butler, *Television Style*, 143–144; Barry Salt, 'Practical Film Theory and its Application to TV Series Dramas', *Journal of Media Practice* 2, No. 2 (2001), 108–109.
49. Lesley Goldberg, '*Scandal* Hits 100 Episodes', *The Hollywood Reporter*, 11 April 2017, http://www.hollywoodreporter.com/features/scandal-hits-100-episodes-casting-secrets-trump-a-battle-abortion-revealed-dishy-oral-histo.
50. See Newman, 'From Beats to Arcs', 20–21.

51. Pamela Douglas, *Writing the TV Drama Series: How to Succeed as a Professional Writer in TV*, second edition (Studio City: MWP, 2007), 74.

52. Jane Espenson, 'The Writing Process', *Fireflyfans*, [no date given], http://www.fireflyfans.net/firefly/espenson.htm.

53. Kristin Thompson, *Storytelling in Film and Television*, 54.

54. See Nelson, *TV Drama in Transition*, 34.

55. See Jason Mittell, 'Narrative Complexity in Contemporary American Television', *The Velvet Light Trap* 58 (Fall 2006), 32.

56. Newman and Levine, *Legitimating Television*, 91–92; Mittell, *Complex TV*, 20.

57. Todd Van Der Werff, 'How NBC's This Is Us Became the Breakout Hit of the Fall', *Vox*, 29 November 2016, https://www.vox.com/2016/11/29/13769520/this-is-us-ratings-nbc.

58. Jeffrey Sconce, 'What If?: Charting Television's New Textual Boundaries', in *Television After TV: Essays on a Medium in Transition*, ed. Lynn Spigel and Jan Olsson (Durham, NC: Duke University Press, 2004), 97–98.

59. Simon Brown and Stacey Abbott, 'Serious Spy Stuff: The Cult Pleasures of *Alias*', in *Investigating Alias: Secrets and Spies*, ed. Stacey Abbott and Simon Brown (London: I. B. Tauris, 2007), 2–3.

60. Sean Axmaker, 'Joss Whedon and the Vampire Detectives', *GreenCine*, 29 October 2007, http://www.greencine.com/central/josswhedon.

61. Newman, 'From Beats to Arcs', 24–25.

62. Peter de Jonge, 'Aaron Sorkin Works his Way Through the Crisis', *The New York Times*, 28 October 2001, 42.

63. Newman, 'From Beats to Arcs', 24.

64. Ibid., 24–25.

65. Nededog, 'Five Reasons Why'.

66. Gordon Kho, 'The Changing Landscape of Television', *Star 2*, 10 July 2015, http://www.star2.com/entertainment/tv/2015/07/10/the-changing-landscape-of-television/.

67. Mark Colvin, '*Mad Men* Creator on American TV's Renaissance', *PM*, 17 November 2009, http://www.abc.net.au/pm/content/2009/s2745489.htm.

68. Newman, 'From Beats to Arcs', 25.

69. Rose Maura Lorre, 'Bryan Fuller on *Hannibal*, Fannibals, and Finally Having a Show Last More Than 2 Seasons', *Vulture*, 16 September 2014, http://www.vulture.com/2014/09/hannibal-bryan-fuller-interview-finally-getting-season-3-mannibals.html.

70. Daniel Holloway, 'TV's New Normal: How Shorter Runs, Fewer Episodes are Revitalizing Primetime', *Variety*, 17 May 2016, http://variety.com/2016/tv/features/primetime-shorter-seasons-fewer-episode-nbc-1201776172/.

71. According to Nielsen Media Research, the average number of channels available to a 'typical' US household escalated from 43.0 in 1997 to 96.4 in 2005. Gary R. Edgerton, 'Introduction' to *The Essential HBO Reader*, ed. Edgerton and Jones, 11.

72. Prior to *Oz*, HBO's original fictional content had taken the form of sitcoms, TV movies and mini-series. For a detailed history of HBO programming, see ibid.

73. Quoted in Andy Meisler, 'Not Even Trying to Appeal to the Masses', *New York Times*, 4 October 1998, 45.

74. Quoted in Janet McCabe and Kim Akass, 'It's Not TV, it's HBO's Original Programming: Producing Quality TV', in *It's Not TV*, ed. Leverette et al., 84.

75. Quoted in Meisler, 'Not Even Trying to Appeal to the Masses', 45.

76. See Rogers et al., '*The Sopranos* as HBO Brand Equity', 47–48; Jaramillo, 'The Family Racket', 59–75; Santo, 'Para-Television and Discourses of Distinction', 19–45; Christopher Anderson, 'Producing an Aristocracy of Culture in American Television', in *The Essential HBO Reader*, ed. Edgerton and Jones, 23–41.

77. See Feuer, 'HBO and the Concept of Quality TV', 145; Jason Mittell, 'All in the Game: *The Wire*, Serial Storytelling, and Procedural Logic', in *Third Person: Authoring and Exploring Vast Narratives*, ed. Pat Harrigan and Noah Wardrip-Fruin (Cambridge, MA: MIT Press, 2009), 429–430; Anthony N. Smith, 'TV or Not TV? *The Sopranos* and Contemporary Episode Architecture in US Network and Premium Cable Drama', *Critical Studies in Television* 6, No. 1 (Spring 2011), 38; Newman and Levine, *Legitimating Television*, 4.

78. John Dempsey, 'Netflix, Starz Strike Streaming Deal', *Variety*, 1 October 2008, http://variety.com/2008/digital/news/netflix-starz-strike-streaming-deal-1117993139/.

79. Netflix, 'Netflix, Inc. Q4 2008 Earnings Call Transcript', *Seeking Alpha*, 27 January 2009, https://seekingalpha.com/article/116612-netflix-inc-q4-2008-earnings-call-transcript; Jason O. Gilbert, 'Netflix Account Losses Much Higher Than Expected After Pricing Backlash', *Huffpost*, 24 October 2011, http://www.huffingtonpost.com/2011/10/24/netflix-account-losses-q3-2011_n_1029269.html; Paul Bond, 'What Hollywood Execs Privately Say About Hollywood', *The Hollywood Reporter*, 14 January 2011, http://www.hollywoodreporter.com/news/hollywood-execs-privately-netflix-71957.

80. Gina Keating, *Netflixed: The Epic Battle for America's Eyeballs* (New York: Penguin, 2013), 261; Tryon, 'TV Got Better', 110.

81. See Keating, *Netflixed*, 261.

82. See ibid.

83. Kevin McDonald, 'From Online Video Store to Global Internet TV Network: Netflix and the Future of Home Entertainment', in *The Netflix Effect*, ed. McDonald and Smith-Rowsey, 210–211.
84. Tryon, 'TV Got Better', 100.
85. Ibid., 110.
86. The clear exception to this rule is *Game of Thrones*, HBO's adaptation of George R. R. Martin's literary series of novels. The series scatters its cast over multiple storyworld settings, each separated from the other by great distance; the storyworld thus fails to provide its cast with easy opportunity to interconnect with one another. The ambitious scope of this setting, however, probably reflects less HBO's economic specificity and more the fact that the source material was never conceived as an ongoing TV drama series.
87. Rebecca Hawkes, '*Game of Thrones* Now Costs Over $10 Million Per Episode', *The Telegraph*, 30 March 2016, http://www.telegraph.co.uk/tv/2016/03/30/game-of-thrones-now-costs-over-10-million-an-episode/.
88. Sharon Waxman, 'HBO's Rocky Roman Adventure', *The New York Times*, 21 October 2004, http://www.nytimes.com/2004/10/21/arts/television/21rome.html; Kim Masters, 'HBO's High-Class Problems: $100m *Vinyl* Disappoints Amid *Westworld*, David Fincher Woes', *The Hollywood Reporter*, 24 February 2016, http://www.hollywoodreporter.com/news/hbos-100m-vinyl-disappoints-westworld-868605.
89. Ben Travers, 'How *Marco Polo*, Netflix's Biggest Bet Yet, Could Forever Change Film and TV', *IndieWire*, 10 December 2014, http://www.indiewire.com/2014/12/how-marco-polo-netflixs-biggest-bet-yet-could-forever-change-film-and-tv-67069/.
90. Hannah Hope, '*The Crown*: A Behind the Scenes Look at Netflix Drama That Has an A-List Cast and Cost £100 Million', *The Mirror*, 3 November 2016, http://www.mirror.co.uk/tv/tv-news/crown-behind-scenes-look-netflix-9184237; Hilary Lewis, '*The Crown* Creator Disputes "Most Expensive Show Ever Made" Rumours, Teases Second Season', *The Hollywood Reporter*, 5 November 2016, http://www.hollywoodreporter.com/live-feed/crown-not-expensive-show-ever-made-creator-says-as-peter-morgan-matt-smith-claire-foy-talk.
91. Bill Carter, 'Weighty Dramas Flourish on Cable', *The New York Times*, 4 April 2010, http://www.nytimes.com/2010/04/05/business/media/05cable.html; Andrew Wallenstein, 'Netflix Series Spending Revealed', *Variety*, 8 March 2013, http://variety.com/2013/digital/news/caa-agent-discloses-netflix-series-spending-1200006100/.
92. Toby Miller, foreword in *It's Not TV*, ed. Leverette et al., x.

93. James Hibberd, '*Game of Thrones*: How Producers Pulled off "Blackwater"', *Entertainment Weekly*, 27 May 2012, http://ew.com/article/2012/05/27/game-of-thrones-blackwater-2/; James Hibberd, '*Game of Thrones*: Battle of the Bastards Director Speaks Out', *Entertainment Weekly*, 19 June 2016, http://ew.com/article/2016/06/19/game-thrones-battle-director/.

94. See Marc Leverette on the importance of sex, profanity and violence to HBO's original programming. Marc Leverette, '"Cocksucker, Motherfucker, Tits"', in *It's Not TV*, ed. Leverette et al., 125.

95. Steve Hewlett, *The Media Show*, BBC Radio 4 broadcast, 18 March 2015.

96. This observation is based on use of the Netflix UK platform on 9 July 2017.

97. Leo Barraclough, '*Orange is the New Black*: Picked Up by the Sony Channel in UK', *Variety*, 24 March 2017, http://variety.com/2017/tv/global/orange-is-the-new-black-sony-channel-uk-1202015467/.

98. Jason Mittell, 'The Scenic Rhythms of *Game of Thrones*', *Just TV*, 5 June 2012, http://justtv.wordpress.com/2012/06/05/the-scenic-rhythms-of-game-of-thrones/.

99. Ibid.

100. Peter Biskind, 'The Family that Preys Together', *Vanity Fair*, 13 March 2007, http://www.vanityfair.com/culture/features/2007/03/chase200703.

101. Peter Bogdanovich, 'David Chase interview', bonus feature in *The Sopranos: The Complete First Season* DVD box set, HBO video, 2002.

102. Dana Polan, 'Cable Watching: HBO, *The Sopranos*, and Discourses of Distinction', in *Cable Visions*, ed. Banet-Weiser et al., 278.

103. David Simon, audio commentary for 'The Target', in *The Wire: The Complete First Season* DVD box set, HBO video, 2004.

104. Sarah Le, 'Beautiful Florida Keys is a Major Star in Netflix's New Series *Bloodline*', *Locations Hub*, 10 April 2015, http://www.locationshub.com/blog/2015/4/10/beautiful-florida-keys-is-a-major-star-in-netflixs-bloodline.

105. Lotz, *The Television Will Be Revolutionized*, 89.

106. Ibid., 88–89.

107. An exception to this trend in HBO scene plotting and style is *True Blood*, which typically possesses a frantic pace of editing and performance.

108. Quoted in Steven Hullfish, *The Art of the Cut: Conversations with Film and TV Editors* (New York: Routledge, 2017), 118.

109. Quoted in Neil Landau, *TV Outside the Box: Trailblazing in the Digital Television Revolution* (New York: Focal, 2016), 391.

110. See ibid.

111. Kristin Thompson, *Storytelling in Film and Television*, 54; Smith, 'TV or Not TV?'.

112. James Hibberd, '*Game of Thrones* Showrunners Season 7 Interview: "The War is Here"', *Entertainment Weekly*, 28 June 2017, http://ew.com/tv/2017/06/28/game-of-thrones-showrunners-season-7/.

113. Amy Dawes, '*Orange is the New Black* Creator Jenji Kohan Aims for "a Real Ride"', *Los Angeles Times*, 21 November 2013, http://articles.latimes.com/2013/nov/21/entertainment/la-et-mn-jenji-kohan-orange-new-black-20131121.

114. Jill Golick, '*The Sopranos* Finale', *Running with my Eyes Closed*, 11 June 2007, http://www.jillgolick.com/2007/06/the-sopranos-finale/.

115. The use of standalone storylines within *The Sopranos* is, according to Chase, a consequence of his own storytelling preferences. Bogdanovich, 'David Chase Interview'.

116. Ryan McGee, 'Did *The Sopranos* Do More Harm than Good?: HBO and the Decline of the Episode', *A.V. Club*, 20 February 2012, http://www.avclub.com/articles/did-the-sopranos-do-more-harm-than-good-hbo-and-th,69596/.

117. Chapelle and Pelecanos, audio commentary for 'Middle Ground', in *The Wire: The Complete Third Season* DVD box set. HBO video, 2007.

118. Meghan O'Rourke, 'Interrogation: Behind *The Wire*, David Simon on where the show goes next', *Slate*, 1 December 2006, http://www.slate.com/id/2154694/pagenum/all/.

119. Despite this writing practice, however, individual *Wire* episodes are, nonetheless, not without some consistency, achieving a sense of unity, Mittell argues, through both a persistent 'mood and tone' and the occurrence of 'thematic and character-related parallels across plot-lines'. Mittell, *Complex TV*, 31.

120. Lauren Laverne, *The Culture Show*, BBC 2, 15 July 2008, http://www.bbc.co.uk/cultureshow/videos/2008/07/s5_e7_wire/.

121. Stuart Levine, 'HBO brings in the big guns', *Variety*, 11 July 2008, 3.

122. For example, while HBO's first transmission of the *Game of Thrones* season two premiere attracted 3.9 million viewers, *The Leftovers*' season two premiere attracted a mere 713,000 viewers. James Hibberd, '*Game of Thrones* Returns to Biggest Ratings Yet', *Entertainment Weekly*, 3 April 2012, http://ew.com/article/2012/04/03/game-of-thrones-ratings-season-2/; Lisa de Moraes, '*The Leftovers* Opens Season 2 With Early 713k Tuned Into Premiere in L+SD', *Deadline Hollywood*, 6 October 2015, http://deadline.com/2015/04/game-of-thrones-logs-series-best-opener-despite-leak-of-first-four-episodes-1201408949/.

123. Cynthia Littleton, '*The Leftovers* Renewed for Third and Final Season at HBO', *Variety*, 10 December 2015, http://variety.com/2015/tv/news/hbo-the-leftovers-season-3-end-1201658594/.

124. Rogers et al., '*The Sopranos* as HBO Brand Equity', 54.

125. James Poniewozik, 'TV 101: They're not TV numbers. They're HBO numbers', *Time*, 10 October 2007, http://time-blog.com/tuned_in/2007/10/tv_101_theyre_not_tv_numbers_t_1.html.

126. Josef Adalian, '*Westworld* Is Shaping Up to Be an Early Ratings Success for HBO', *Vulture*, 4 October 2016, http://www.vulture.com/2016/10/westworld-premiere-ratings-early-success-for-hbo.html; Nellie Andreeva, '*Westworld* Sets Ratings Highs in Week 3', *Deadline Hollywood*, 18 October 2017, http://deadline.com/2016/10/westworld-ratings-high-week-3-1201838478/.

127. Jason Lynch, 'Here's the Recipe Netflix Uses to Make Binge-Worthy TV', *Quartz*, 20 March 2015, https://qz.com/367117/heres-the-recipe-netflix-uses-to-make-binge-worthy-tv/.

128. Steve 'Frosty' Weintraub, 'Beau Willimon talks *House of Cards*, the Different Production Schedule of Season 2, "Hyper-Serialized" Storytelling, the Show's Directors, and More', *Collider*, 11 August 2014, http://collider.com/beau-willimon-house-of-cards-interview/.

129. Emily Buder, 'Beau Willimon on *House of Cards*, Bad Television and His "Crazy" Next Project', *IndieWire*, 15 September 2014, http://www.indiewire.com/2014/09/beau-willimon-on-house-of-cards-bad-television-and-his-crazy-next-project-22198/.

130. Daniel Feinberg, 'Interview: *Orange is the New Black* Creator Jenji Kohan Talks Prison, Netflix and Jodie Foster', *Uproxx*, 10 July 2013, http://uproxx.com/hitfix/interview-orange-is-the-new-black-creator-jenji-kohan-talks-prison-netflix-and-jodie-foster/DRVY6vZLH2OQqJxl.99; Jethro Nededog, '*Orange is the New Black* Creator on Getting Renewed Ahead of Debut: "Netflix Has Balls"', *The Wrap*, 3 July 2013, http://www.thewrap.com/orange-new-black-creator-talks-early-season-2-renewal-netflix-has-balls-101166/.

131. Linda K. Hughes and Michael Lund, *The Victorian Serial* (Charlottesville: University Press of Virginia, 1991), 8.

132. An obvious exception to this convention is the Fox drama *24*; a given season's plot concerns a mere day's worth of storyworld time.

133. Buder, 'Beau Willimon on *House of Cards*'.

134. Josef Adalian, '10 Episodes is the New 13 (Was the New 22)', *Vulture*, 12 June 2017, http://www.vulture.com/2015/06/10-episodes-is-the-new-13-was-the-new-22.html.

135. Jaramillo, 'The Family Racket', 63.

136. Dean J. DeFino, *The HBO Effect* (New York: Bloomsbury, 2014), 122.

137. Brian G. Rose, '*The Wire*', in *The Essential HBO Reader*, ed. Edgerton and Jones, 83.

138. David Simon, audio commentary for 'The Target'.

139. Lynch, 'Here's the Recipe Netflix Uses'; Axel Alonso, 'Cup O' Joe Returns!', *Comic Book Resources*, 9 May 2014, http://www.cbr.com/cup-o-joe-returns/; Nathan Mattise, 'House of Cards: The "13-Hour Movie" Defining the Netflix Experience', *Ars Technica*, 1 February 2013, https://arstechnica.com/information-technology/2013/02/house-of-cards-the-13-hour-movie-defining-the-netflix-experience/.

140. In contrast to HBO, many of Netflix's series are produced by external companies; with regard to such series, Netflix is unlikely to be receiving significant DVD revenues.

141. Mittell, *Complex TV*, 39.

142. This is according to the movie business data site the-numbers.com.

143. The success of *The Sopranos*, for example, enabled HBO to expand its subscriber base from 24 million households when the mob saga debuted in 1999 to 28 million in 2005. Michael M. Epstein, Jimmie L. Reeves and Mark C. Rogers, 'Surviving "the Hit": Will *The Sopranos* Still Sing for HBO', in *Reading the Sopranos: Hit TV by HBO*, ed. David Lavery (London: I. B. Tauris, 2006), 16.

144. Rogers et al., '*The Sopranos* as HBO Brand Equity', 47–48.

145. Concepcion Cascajosa Virino, 'The Derivation of a Television Crime Drama', in *Interrogating* The Shield, ed. Nicholas Ray (Syracuse, NY: Syracuse University Press, 2013), 12.

146. Ibid., 13.

147. Alan Sepinwall, *The Revolution was Televised* (New York: Touchstone, 2012), 139–140, 145.

148. Ray Richmond, 'AMC serious about its series', *The Hollywood Reporter*, 18 July 2008.

149. Alex Witchel, '*Mad Men* Has Its Moment', *The New York Times*, 22 June 2008, http://www.nytimes.com/2008/06/22/magazine/22madmen-t.html.

150. McCabe and Akass, 'It's Not TV, it's HBO's Original Programming', 84.

151. Quoted in Gary R. Edgerton, 'The Selling of *Mad Men*: A Production History', in Mad Men: *Dream Come True TV*, ed. Gary R. Edgerton (London: I. B. Tauris, 2011), 8.

152. See Lorna Jowett and Stacy Abbott, *TV Horror: Investigating the Darker Side of the Small Screen* (London: I. B. Tauris, 2012).

153. Each episode of *Mad Men* and *Breaking Bad* cost, on average, $3 million to produce, placing their budgets at the high end of expenditure in basic cable drama. These per episode spends fail, however, to match HBO at its most extravagant. Cynthia Littleton, 'AMC, Sony Make *Bad* Budget Work', *Variety*, 13 June 2010, http://www.variety.com/article/VR1118020572; Brian Steinberg, 'Why *Mad Men* Has so Little to Do With Advertising', *Advertising Age*, 2 August 2010, http://adage.com/mediaworks/article?article_id=145179.

154. See Edgerton, 'The Selling of *Mad Men*', 12.
155. See Lotz, *The Television Will Be Revolutionized*, 247; for more on the provocative storyworlds of FX series and the controversies they have ignited, see Michael Curtin and Jane Shattuc, *The American Television Industry* (London: BFI, 2009), 134–135.
156. Lotz, *The Television Will Be Revolutionized*, 184–185, 228; Tony Kelso, 'And Now No Word from our Sponsor: How HBO puts the Risk Back into Television', in *It's Not TV*, ed. Leverette et al., 56–57.
157. Forty-nine per cent of the first season's audience was earning in excess of $100,000 per annum. Bill Keveney, 'Success suits the *Mad Men* brand; Distinctive drama about the '60s ad game reaches out to today's style', *USA Today*, 14 August 2009, 1D (LIFE Section); BMW has acted as sole sponsors for multiple commercial-interruption-free *Mad Men* episodes.
158. Tom Lowry, 'How *Mad Men* Glammed Up AMC', *Business Week*, 24 July 2008, http://www.businessweek.com/magazine/content/08_31/b4094034647265.htm.
159. Stella Gaynor, 'Made for TV Monsters: Aesthetic Disposition and Socio Political Comment in Contemporary Horror Programming' (paper given at Fear 2000: 21st Century Horror Conference, Sheffield, 1 April 2016).
160. Lotz, *The Television Will Be Revolutionized*, 229.
161. See Mittell, 'The Scenic Rhythms of *Game of Thrones*'.
162. Narrative designers working within the HBO context have occasionally taken a similar approach to plotting. The second half of *The Sopranos* episode 'Whoever Did This' (4:9), for example, is devoted entirely to a sequence in which Tony and Christopher dispose of a corpse, while *The Leftovers* episode 'Guest' focuses throughout on a single intense storyline concerning Nora's attempts to deal with the grief she endures for her lost family.
163. David Carbonara and Tim Hunter, audio commentary for 'Long Weekend', in *Mad Men* Season One DVD box set, Lions Gate Home Entertainment, 2007.
164. Style within these particular scenes is similar to that within corresponding scenes in *Forbrydelsen* (2007–2012), the Danish drama series that *The Killing* adapts.
165. Randee Dawn, '*The Killing*: Quiet, Slow, Methodical and, yet, Popular', *Los Angeles Times*, 16 June 2011, http://articles.latimes.com/2011/jun/16/news/la-en-the-killing-20110616.
166. Alan Sepinwall, 'How Rubicon Became Much More than a Conspiracy Thriller', *Hitfix*, 10 September 2010, http://www.hitfix.com/blogs/whats-alan-watching/posts/how-rubicon-became-much-more-than-a-conspiracy-thriller; Tim Goodman, '*The Killing*: TV Review', *The Hollywood Reporter*, 27 March 2011, http://www.hollywoodreporter.com/review/killing-tv-review-171764.

167. Christine Fell, 'Q&A—Michael Slovis (Director of Photography)', amctv.com, 14 April 2009, http://blogs.amctv.com/breaking-bad/2009/04/michael-slovis-interview.php.

168. Josh Gajewski, '*Breaking Bad*: Michael Slovis, a Visual Storyteller', *Los Angeles Times*, 16 May 2010, http://latimesblogs.latimes.com/showtracker/2010/05/breaking-bad-michael-slovis-a-visual-storyteller.html.

169. Todd Van DerWerff, 'Interview: *Rubicon* Executive Producer Henry Bromell', *A.V. Club*, 15 October 2010, http://www.avclub.com/articles/rubicon-executive-producer-henry-bromell,46389/.

170. The three episode ASLs I measured were: 'The Outsider' (1:4, ASL: 6.0), 'Look to the Ant' (1.6, ASL: 8.2) and 'Caught in the Suck' (1.8, ASL: 4.9). In comparison to *Rubicon*, Butler's analysis of *Mad Men*'s cutting pace reveals a higher editing tempo; but its median ASL of 5.2 seconds (for the first season) is, relative to most contemporary ad-supported drama series, unhurried. Jeremy G. Butler, *'Smoke Gets in Your Eyes': Historicizing Visual Style in* Mad Men', in Mad Men: *Dream Come True TV*, ed. Edgerton, 67–68.

171. Butler, *Television Style*, 144.

172. Graeme Virtue, 'A Trippy, Decadent Fever Dream: Why *Legion* is the Best Superhero Show on TV', *The Guardian*, 27 March 2017, https://www.theguardian.com/tv-and-radio/2017/mar/27/noah-hawley-legion-marvel-x-men-dan-stevens.

173. Hugh Hart, 'Extreme Contrast: DP Shoots FX's *Fargo* and *Legion*', *Where to Watch*, 10 July 2017, https://www.wheretowatch.com/2017/07/extreme-contrast-dp-shoots-fxs-fargo-and-legion.

174. Ibid.

175. Mittell, *Complex TV*.

176. Christina Radish, 'Noah Hawley Talks *Fargo*, Showing the Total Story to the Audience, Input from the Coens, Changes in Storytelling, and Possible Second Season Ideas', *Collider*, 10 June 2014, http://collider.com/noah-hawley-fargo-interview/.

177. Scott Tobias, '*Mad Men* creator Matthew Weiner', *A.V. Club*, 27 July 2008, http://www.avclub.com/content/interview/mad_men_creator_matthew.

178. David B. Wilkerson, 'AMC uses original shows, scheduling to expand audience', *MarketWatch*, 8 April 2009, http://www.marketwatch.com/story/amc-uses-original-shows-scheduling.

179. Madeline Berg, '*The Walking Dead* Returns to Impressive Ratings', *Forbes*, 25 October 2016, https://www.forbes.com/sites/maddieberg/2016/10/25/the-viewers-of-the-walking-dead-are-very-much-alive/#66f79c42516b; Brian Steinberg, 'TV Ad Prices: Football

Hikes, *Walking Dead* Stumbles, *Chicago Fire*, *Goldbergs* on the Rise',
Variety, 17 October 2016, http://variety.com/2016/tv/news/
tv-ad-prices-football-walking-dead-empire-advertising-1201890660/.

180. Steinberg, 'Why *Mad Men* Has so Little to Do With Advertising'.

181. Brian Steinberg, 'Simon Who? *Idol* Spots Still Priciest in Prime Time',
Advertising Age, 18 October 2010, http://adage.com/article/ad-
age-graphics/american-idol-spots-priciest-prime-time/146495/; John
Lafayette, 'The *Mad Men* Lesson: Buzz Lights Up a Network', *Broadcasting
& Cable*, 19 July 2010, http://www.broadcastingcable.com/news/pro-
gramming/mad-men-lesson-buzz-lights-network/36595.

182. Steinberg, 'Why *Mad Men* Has so Little to Do With Advertising'.

183. Ibid.

184. Lotz, *The Television Will Be Revolutionized*, 248.

185. Marc Berman, 'Why Advertisers Still Love *Fargo* After Fans Have
Changed the Channel', *Campaign*, 21 June 2017, http://www.cam-
paignlive.com/article/why-advertisers-love-fargo-fans-changed-
channel/1437111.

186. Wilkerson, 'AMC uses original shows'.

187. The unorthodox narrative style of AMC's series sometimes strengthens
these associations. In the case of *Rubicon*, as Bromell acknowledged, DP
Gordon Willis' meditative shooting style on the 1970s Hollywood conspiracy thrillers *The Parallax View* (1974) and *All the President's Men*
(1976) proved an important influence on the series' visual aesthetic.
David Zurawik, '*Homicide* Producer Takes on a Political Thriller', *The
Baltimore Sun*, 30 July 2010, http://articles.baltimoresun.com/2010-
07-30/entertainment/bs-ae-zontv-rubicon-20100730_1_political-
thriller-henry-bromell-cia-officer/2.

188. Robert Marich, 'FX at 20: Cabler's Revenue Soars on Movies, Original
Series', *Variety*, 15 May 2014, http://variety.com/2014/tv/features/
fx-revenue-soars-on-movies-original-series-1201182522/.

189. On *Legion*'s connection to the X-Men cinematic universe, see Josh
Wigler, '*Legion* Premiere Previewed at NYCC: A Look Inside FX's
Upcoming X-Men Series', *The Hollywood Reporter*, 9 October 2016,
http://www.hollywoodreporter.com/live-feed/legion-premiere-
previewed-at-nycc-936647.

190. On the anticipation for *Legion* that developed prior to its series premiere,
see Alex Welch, 'Legion Does Not Take Place in X-Men Movies
Continuity', *ScreenRant*, 17 January 2017, http://screenrant.com/
legion-tv-show-x-men-movies-no-connections/.

191. The extended episode running times could be a further factor enabling the decelerated storytelling to be found within many *Mad Men, Breaking Bad* and *Better Call Saul* scenes.

192. Lafayette, 'The *Mad Men* Lesson'.

193. Steinberg, 'Why *Mad Men* Has so Little to Do With Advertising'.

194. Lafayette, 'The *Mad Men* Lesson'.

195. The extent to which AMC marginalises the commercial value of its air-time during the hours in which original series air has limits, as the case of *Rubicon* suggests. According to Bromell, the difficulty AMC endured trying to sell advertising time during *Rubicon*'s slot factored into the series' cancellation following the airing of its first season. Jon Weisman, 'Holes in Basic Cable's Safety Net', *Variety*, 14 December 2010, http://www.variety.com/article/VR1118028452.

196. Adam Davidson, 'The *Mad Men* Economic Miracle', *The New York Times*, 4 December 2012, http://www.nytimes.com/2012/12/09/magazine/the-mad-men-economic-miracle.html.

197. Lafayette, 'The *Mad Men* Lesson'.

198. Robert Seidman, 'Is *Mad Men* Worth it for AMC?', *TV by the Numbers*, 1 September 2009, http://tvbythenumbers.com/2009/09/01/is-mad-men-worth-it-for-amc/26024.

199. Adam B. Vary, 'Four-Ward, Cylons', *EW.com*, 27 March 2007, http://www.ew.com/ew/article/0,,20015932,00.html.

200. Newman and Levine, *Legitimating Television*, 80–81.

201. Hilmes, *Only Connect*, 253.

202. Anon., '*Better Call Saul*: Season Three Ratings', *TV Series Finale*, 27 June 2017, http://tvseriesfinale.com/tv-show/better-call-saul-season-three-ratings/; Anon., '*Legion*: Season One Ratings', *TV Series Finale*, 30 March 2017, http://tvseriesfinale.com/tv-show/legion-tv-show-fx-season-one-ratings/.

203. George Szalai, '*The Walking Dead* Coming Exclusively to Netflix Under Multi-Year Streaming Deal', *The Hollywood Reporter*, 10 July 2011, http://www.hollywoodreporter.com/news/walking-dead-coming-exclusively-netflix-245539; Mallory Locklear, 'AMC Premiere Will Let You Stream *The Walking Dead* Ad-Free', *Engadget*, 29 June 2017, https://www.engadget.com/2017/06/29/amc-premiere-stream-walking-dead-ad-free/.

204. Anthony Crupi, 'FX is the Edgiest and Most Prolific Drama Producer on Ad-Supported TV', *Adweek*, 2 March 2014, http://www.adweek.com/tv-video/fx-edgiest-and-most-prolific-drama-producer-ad-supported-tv-156028/.

205. Colvin, '*Mad Men* Creator'.

206. Adalian, '10 Episodes is the New 13 (Was the New 22)'.

207. AMC's approach to *The Walking Dead* is an exception here. The channel's commissioning of sixteen episode seasons of the series is no doubt the channel's attempt to fully capitalise on the series' extraordinarily high desirability to advertisers.
208. Todd Van Der Werff, 'Vince Gilligan Walks Us Through Season Four of *Breaking Bad* (Part 1 of 4)', *A.V. Club*, 10 October 2011, http://www.avclub.com/articles/vince-gilligan-walks-us-through-season-four-of-bre,63013/.

CHAPTER 4

Audience Specificity in Narrative Design: Comic-Book Storytelling in the Inclusivity Era

INTRODUCTION

The comic-book industry's trajectory in the 1980s and 1990s echoes trends within US television within the same period. Just as television networks and advertisers increasingly came to prefer niche audience-targeting strategies during this era, comic-book publishers similarly veered away from a mass-market approach. Prior to this time, following its emergence in the 1930s as a distinct entertainment business centred on the distribution and consumption of periodically produced pamphlets, the comic-book industry marketed its product widely via newsstand outlets.[1] But, as Bradford W. Wright and Matthew J. Pustz each note, publishers came to prize and prioritise a small but heavily dedicated (and thus lucrative) consumer base following a major shift in distributional mode from newsstands to speciality comic shops during the late 1970s and early 1980s.[2] Due to major failings within the comic-shop distribution model, however, publishers were, by the dawn of the twenty-first century, committed to reversing this trajectory and the narrowing of its audience. Publishers have since pursued a far broader mix of readers, chiefly through the increased distribution of *collected editions* (graphic novel formats containing compiled periodical comic-book material) via both comic shops and mass-market bookstores (both online and off).[3] More recently, publishers have also looked to address a wider audience through the distribution of comic-book material in digital form via online e-reading platforms that can be accessed via tablets and smartphones. Newly targeted consumers have

© The Author(s) 2018
A. N. Smith, *Storytelling Industries,*
https://doi.org/10.1007/978-3-319-70597-2_4

included particular demographic segments previously neglected (such as teens, females and people of colour), as well as, more generally, casual, less committed readers.

This chapter focuses on this recent period within the US comic-book industry, which is labelled here the *inclusivity era* (and which commences from approximately 2000 onwards). It fully explores the ways in which publishers' pursuit of new types of readers has influenced comic-book writing and illustrating practices, thus comprehensively testing the relevance of the sub-dimension of audience specificity to narrative design conditions and processes. As Wright and Pustz each observe, prior to the inclusivity era, the specificities of the industry's intended consumer base held major importance for storytelling in the period. Just as television networks' niche-targeting tactics influenced the proliferation of primetime serial narratives within the 1980s and 1990s, comic-book publishers during the same period maximised the expenditure of deeply loyal comic-shop consumers via the increased utilisation of the serial mode within comic-book narratives. But how has the subsequent shift in audience specificity, whereby publishers have not only continued to serve an exclusive core of deeply invested readers, but also simultaneously addressed new reader types via alternative means of format and distribution, influenced these narrative design conditions and processes? By engaging with this question, the chapter not only serves this book's wider aim to ascertain the connections between a medium's industrial dimensions of specificity and its narratives, it also updates the existing small field of scholarship regarding the interrelation between the comic-book industry and its storytelling.

Prior to examining the relationship between audience and narrative in the inclusivity era, the following section provides a necessary foundation via its overview of the US comic-book industry's practices past and present. It surveys the specificities of publishers' intended audiences and narrative design conditions and processes within the respective eras of newsstand and comic-shop distribution; it furthermore outlines the development of the collected edition and digital comics formats in the industry, detailing how these formats have come to offer publishers a key means of address to consumers beyond comic-shop points of sale. The chapter goes on to consider how the perceived requirements of intended audiences in the inclusivity era have informed comic-book narrative components of plot, style and storyworld. The chapter as a whole concentrates on the practices and narratives of DC and Marvel Comics, in particular. This is an appropriate choice as the two publishers have dominated the commercial comic-book sector's market share since the 1970s,[4] together shaping the direction of the industry.

CHANGE AND CONTINUITY: AN HISTORICAL OVERVIEW OF THE US COMIC-BOOK INDUSTRY AND ITS NARRATIVES

Iteration to Continuity: The Newsstand Era

While the superhero genre has remained the dominant storyworld archetype within the comic-book industry since the 1960s, the late 1940s and 1950s saw a far greater balance of genres within the industry.[5] Marvel (then Timely) and DC (then National Allied), for example, diversified during this period with a variety of themes traditional to American pulp, such as crime, horror, war, sci-fi, western and 'true-romance' tales.[6] But a particular commonality linked narrative production conditions and processes regardless of storyworld types; that is, narrative designers were required to eschew the serial form.[7] As Umberto Eco suggested of the *Superman* series (in 1962), each of its issue's storylines, though focused on recurrent characters, retain an *iterative* quality; each issue represents 'a virtual beginning, ignoring where the preceding event left off', he observed.[8] As is typical of the narratives of primetime network drama series episodes in the 1960s and 1970s, each single-issue storyline is thus, via this iterative mode, a self-contained tale that fails to imply a progression of events beyond a given single issue. 'The very structure of time falls apart [as a consequence of this narrative mode] ... that is, the notion of time that ties one episode to another', Eco observed.[9]

There are two key explanations for the institutional enforcement of this iterative mode during this period. Firstly, as former Marvel and DC writer/editor Dennis O'Neil suggests, the unreliability of newsstand distribution rendered continuing, multiple-issue storylines untenable. 'Single-issue stories were not only common, they were all but required', says O'Neil; 'publishers believed that readers couldn't be sure of getting two consecutive issues—newsstand distribution was erratic at best—and so they wanted everything complete in one issue'.[10] Due to the specificities of the newsstand audience, there was also zero imperative for narrative designers to repair the 'broken time' of the iterative mode by suggesting within narratives (either explicitly or implicitly) that an accumulation of single-issue storylines contributed to a coherent chronology. As children/adolescents represented the primary target audience in this period, the market experienced a general customer turnover every three years.[11] The perception of comic books as disposable entertainment additionally led to an absence of back issues within reading cultures; thus there was little available prior narrative to which consumers might refer.[12] Superman was given no recourse to recall events that had (at least in terms of publication) occurred years earlier for the simple reason that his readers typically had no recall of such events either.

In the 1960s, however, an important transition in audience specificity relating to consumer practice induced publishers' strategic turn towards seriality, and thus underpinned a major shift in narrative design conditions. Whereas periodical comic books had previously been regarded as ephemeral artefacts to be discarded, traded, or just handed around from friend to friend, the decade saw the origins of a dedicated niche seeking to collect and preserve back issues.[13] This trend was due in part to the emergence of an audience of older comic-book consumers looking to source and celebrate their favourite books from earlier decades.[14] Comic-book narratives slyly acknowledged this change in reader practice. Marvel's *The Avengers* #28 (1966), for example, introduced The Collector, an alien intent on hoarding a collection of superheroes. But the plotting of comic-book narratives further reflected this shift in audience habits. While single-issue conflicts remained the industry norm during the 1960s, narrative designers at DC, and even more so at Marvel, began experimenting with the serial form. The techniques developed in this period were not only well suited to the beginnings of an intensification in reader dedication, they would also greatly inform comic-book narratives in subsequent decades.

Narrative designers' installation of an explicit memory within publishers' fictional universes during this period, via the plotting of overarching storyworlds, represents the most pervasive implementation of the serial mode of production during the 1960s, with characters beginning to make reference to events in other series and from earlier storylines. For example, when Marvel resurrected Captain America in *Avengers* #3 (1964), writer (and editor-in-chief) Stan Lee established Cap's earliest manifestation (from Timely's *Captain America* run [1941–1950]) as part of the character's chronology.[15] In a subsequent storyline, in *Tales of Suspense* #75 (1966), Captain America recalls his war-days' derring-do, lamenting the loss of his former sidekick Bucky Barnes (a partnership that featured in the original Timely series). Such storytelling, by implying that depicted conflicts and relationships contribute to a single unified history, represents the origins of what is popularly known as comic-book *continuity*, that is, the generally consistent storyworld frameworks that the DC and Marvel comic-book narratives each form.[16]

The implementation of continuity complemented this period in which a segment of comic-book readership began to accumulate and revisit its own collection of comic-book experiences. The burgeoning dedicated readership was, in fact, in part directly responsible for instigating this trend towards continuity, with readers in the 1960s lobbying editors with demands for narrative consistency within a given series and between separate series.[17] The continued growth of the practice of comic-book collecting, combined with a simultaneous decline in newsstand sales, precipitated a major industrial transition that began in the late 1970s when publishers moved towards a *direct market* method of distribution. Via this system, speciality comic shops, opened so as to meet the growing demand for back issues, replaced traditional retail outlets as the primary conduit for comic books. This change led to publishers relying increasingly on serial narrative design processes that serviced a growing audience of dedicated consumers.

Complex Continuities: The Rise and Fall of Direct Market Dominance

The direct market manifested in the 1970s due to failings in the newsstand distribution system and the simultaneous emergence of a committed consumer subculture focused primarily on Marvel and DC's superhero narratives. Via the newsstand distribution system, publishers had flooded the market with more issues of a given periodical than they could ever realistically hope to sell, offering distributors credit on unsold issues (which were subsequently destroyed).[18] While in the 1940s and 1950s publishers had frequently sold more than 70 per cent of a given series, publishers in the 1970s often failed to sell even 40 per cent of a given title's print run, which led to publishers struggling to break even.[19] Yet the growth of speciality comic shops in the 1970s, which occurred in response to the collecting practices of consumers, came to offer publishers an alternative distribution model by which to operate. Rather than seek reimbursement for unsold product from publishers, these businesses sold back issues alongside recently published material. For the publishers, the opportunity to sell without any obligation to credit returns was highly preferable to the increasingly problematic newsstand model; thus they shifted focus to the direct market in the late 1970s and early 1980s.[20]

The direct market model, notes Wright, corrected the haphazard nature of newsstand distribution as it ensured that a highly concentrated consumer base was consistently addressed with the wide range of a publisher's output.[21] Publishers, provided with this means of address, utilised the serial mode of production as a means to maximise the expenditure of this target audience.[22] By the late 1980s and early 1990s, single-issue storylines were only sporadically punctuating the narratives of many ongoing series. Instead, serialised storylines, journeying through multiple issues and/or between multiple different series, dominated comic-book publishing. The 14-part Spider-Man conflict, 'Maximum Carnage' (1993), for example, which alternates through issues of five separate Spider-Man series, required, via its periodical publication, a high degree of reader dedication.[23]

Complementing such efforts to exploit a dedicated consumer base, narrative designers in this period also increasingly emphasised continuity within long-running series and between different series (outside of the auspices of serialised storylines). The single-issue storyline 'Transition', from *New Titans* #55 (1989), for example, functions as an amplification to *Batman* #428 (1988), in which DC's second Robin, Jason Todd, is killed. As part of the *New Titans* storyline, Dick Grayson, the first Robin, learns of Jason's death. The angst-ridden Dick visits Bruce Wayne (Batman), and the pair row, each betraying the guilt they feel regarding Jason's death, while making myriad explicit references, via dialogue, to their years of shared history.[24] The specificities of publishers' target audience continued to drive this service to continuity, as such narratives had become central to the experience of the industry's deeply committed consumers. As Pustz observes, 'Information based on continuity becomes the source of discussion, jokes and arguments, making it the raw material for the interactive glue that holds comic-book culture together.'[25]

These narrative production strategies within the era of direct market dominance helped publishers establish a dedicated audience of twenty-something males, with such consumers habitually purchasing multiple periodical comic books on a weekly basis.[26] But, as Pustz suggests, publishers' 'increasing reliance on this kind of [narrative] complexity … has limited the comics audience'.[27] While the direct market system enabled year-on-year increases in sales through the 1980s and early 1990s, this consumer base, observes Wright, nevertheless 'remained precariously narrow'.[28] The danger of an overriding dependence on this isolated consumer niche was exposed in the mid-1990s; industry sales reached $1 billion in 1993, but, due to the collapse of an artificially inflated collector/

speculator market, revenues had declined to $450 million by 1996.[29] Faced with a contracted market, publishers placed priority on reaching out to a wider readership. Yet the direct market system and the editorial strategies publishers had developed to complement this economic model proved counterproductive to this aim of audience broadening. As former Marvel publisher Bill Jemas recalls, the complicated, continuity-heavy narratives of mainstream comics in the 1990s were 'almost unintelligible' to anyone other than dedicated consumers.[30]

But the direct market's retail and consumption cultures have proved equally as prohibitive to new and/or casual readers as the publishers' convoluted narratives. As Pustz observes, the retail switch from newsstand to specialist comic shop 'helped to remove [comics] from the daily lives of most Americans' thereby making comics less physically accessible to new and/or casual consumers.[31] In addition to the geographical ghettoisation of comic books' points of sale, the perceived nature of comic shops and their customer base has also restricted publishers from engaging a wider audience. As Pustz notes, comic shops have traditionally performed the function of 'a clubhouse for regular readers', generating an environment that is potentially 'intimidating' for consumers outside of these committed reading communities.[32] As former DC president and publisher Paul Levitz's comments suggest, the direct market culture had, during the 1990s, ultimately erected a series of obstacles preventing publishers from appealing to a wider audience:

> The store was too far away, the stuff might get sold out before people came in, the product itself wasn't editorially satisfying unless you really immersed yourself in it and made sure you read every issue; a whole host of things kind of came together to create that 'You're in the pool or you're not in the pool'. It's been my view that no matter how much we could grow that segment of the population, there was still going to be a limit to how many people could commit that heavily to comics.[33]

The impenetrability of periodical comic-book narratives and the culture within which they were predominantly consumed proved at odds with the imperative that publishers developed at the beginning of the twenty-first century to incorporate new and/or casual readers into the fold. In response to this industrial climate, publishers in this period have continued to service dedicated readers with periodical comic books via the direct market, but they have simultaneously moved to target new audiences via the development of large 'backlists' (or in-print back catalogues) of collected editions. The distribution of this format through not only comic shops but also mass-market channels has widened publishers' address, while the backlist model has, as I will show, permitted more casual modes of consumer purchasing. The industry's more recent development of a market for digital comics has further broadened publisher reach, enabling the sale of digitised comic books via online platforms. As with the collected edition, digital comics also encourage casual modes of consumption; readers are able to gain access to such content on their screen-based digital devices at their convenience. The following section charts the development of the collected edition and digital comics formats within the industry.

Building the Backlist: The Emergence of the Collected Edition and Digital Comics Markets

The reprinting of comics narratives in the graphic novel format dates back to the beginning of the twentieth century when news syndicates distributed hardcover compilations of reprinted strips to bookstores.[34] But, for comic-book companies, the practice of publishing periodical material as part of collected editions only began gaining traction in the 1980s as the term 'graphic novel' came to develop a cultural cachet among a maturing comic-shop clientele.[35] As Charles Hatfield observes, the term appealed to a direct market audience, which 'was increasingly self-conscious, relatively affluent and eager for belated recognition of the comic book as "art"'. The label, with its connotation of prestigious fiction, suggests Hatfield, became a 'wish-fulfilling totem' for the industry.[36] Marvel, tapping into this sensibility, appropriated the term in 1982 with the launch of its 'Marvel Graphic Novel' line. The imprint utilised a slim, glossy, oversized magazine-style format, and published standalone narratives (ranging from 48 to 64 pages in length) that had not previously been serialised in periodical form. (Such non-serialised narratives have since come to be known within the industry as 'original graphic novels' or 'OGNs'.) The books were distinguishable from periodical comic-book narratives of the time via their utilisation of 'adult' themes (*The Death of Captain Marvel* [1982] concerns a superhero's battle with cancer, for example) and sophisticated artwork enabled by new print technologies (such as Bill Sienkiewicz's use of paint for *Daredevil: Love and War* [1986]). The line sold well within the direct market, but made little impact outside of comic shops.[37]

The collected edition of the DC mini-series *Batman: The Dark Knight Returns* (1986), however, achieved unprecedented success within the sphere of mass-market bookstores. Each of the four instalments of *The Dark Knight Returns* serial narrative had been marketed towards the comic-shop consumer base as a pseudo graphic novel; with each possessing a card cover, square spine and unique moniker.[38] The narrative, which subverts generic convention by depicting the Caped Crusader, not as a virtuous crime fighter but as a crazed vigilante, was appropriate to the late-teen/adult audience for which it was intended. The artwork, in addition, was suitably refined, courtesy of its unusually slick paper, which permitted a high degree of colour subtlety uncommon for the period.[39] But, reissued by DC as a single collected edition (after having speedily sold out in periodical form), the series proved appropriate not only to the segment of the direct market audience that craved sophistication but also to an adult audience beyond the direct market.

For adult consumers outside the increasingly marginalised comic-shop scene, superhero comics and the periodical format were typically regarded as being of poor cultural value.[40] But in its collected edition format *The Dark Knight Returns* was the first superhero comic to be considered seriously within 'mainstream' media, thus encouraging audiences outside a direct market context to perceive the narrative as culturally prominent.[41] The *New York Times* review headline, 'The Funnies Grow Up', is indicative of this altered perception.[42] The narrative's unorthodox themes and general moral ambiguity contributed to this process of legitimisation. But the collected edition format was also instrumental to the work's celebration within a wider culture. Paratextual trappings such as the format's 'graphic novel' descriptor, card cover and high quality paper grade, an absence of advertisements punctuating its narrative, and the product's presence within Barnes & Noble bookstores all dispelled associations between *The Dark Knight Returns* and the derided periodical comic book.

The cultural reverence of certain serial comics narratives published in graphic novel form adheres to what Mittell regards as the 'pattern of validation through bound publication' that is also present within literature and television.[43] Within twenty-first century television culture, the DVD box set format, observes Mittell, raises the cultural value of a given serialised narrative by 'detaching it from the industrial-controlled, commercially-saturated flow of broadcasting', inviting audiences to regard it as a 'bound collectable object' analogous to a lauded novel or classic film.[44] In a similar vein, the graphic novel became, for those outside the direct market niche, a legitimate format with which to consume otherwise culturally marginalised narrative content.

The Dark Knight Returns was not the only graphic novel to achieve mainstream media 'buzz' and establish a mass-market bookstore presence during this period. Others include the first *Maus* volume (1986), a surreal biography of holocaust experience in which its characters are portrayed as rodents, and DC's collected edition of its twelve-part limited series *Watchmen* (1987), which, similar to *The Dark Knight Returns*, provides a grimly pessimistic deconstruction of superhero archetypes. These three products, notes Hatfield, 'established a beachhead for "graphic novels" in the booktrade'.[45] But all three in addition demonstrated a simple and specific lesson: the reformatting of a given periodical narrative into the graphic novel format offered the potential to wring further revenues from said narrative—not only within the direct market, but via mass-market bookstores as well. Yet, despite DC's realisation of the potential of the collected edition, the publisher exploited the format in the late 1980s and early 1990s only selectively, reserving it for high-profile storylines. Marvel, meanwhile, save exceptions such as the 'Marvel Masterworks' line (which collected material from the 1960s and 1970s into a graphic novel format), largely neglected the collected edition altogether during this period. These publishers' economic policies at the time were reflective of the tremendously healthy state of direct market periodical sales, which remained DC and Marvel's core concern.

DC's Vertigo imprint, launched in 1993, however, represented an alternative approach, with the division establishing the collected edition format and the backlist system as an integral component to its economic model. The imprint, which has always been intended 'for mature readers' (as its publications' advisory label states), has traditionally specialised in dark, strange and sometimes violent narratives, often with a fantasy-horror bent, such as *Hellblazer* (1988–present) and *Preacher* (1995–2000), which, observes Will Brooker, 'can be traced back to *Dark Knight*'s adult-oriented revisionism'.[46] Vertigo, regarding the graphic novel format as particularly appropriate for its mature target audience, compiled the majority of its ongoing series into collected editions, while also maintaining an in-print backlist. As former Vertigo executive editor (and founder) Karen Berger acknowledges, the sales of collected editions represented (and continue to represent) a highly significant revenue stream for the imprint; while Vertigo's periodical sales have consistently ranked below superhero titles, 50 per cent of its consumer base has traditionally comprised those who purchase the imprint's narratives exclusively in trade paperback format.[47] As the 1990s wore on, DC's wider culture, inspired by Vertigo's precedent, began utilising the collected edition more consistently.[48] Smaller publishers, such as Dark Horse, also started to rely more upon the collected edition, with the company regularly putting out its *Hellboy* and *Sin City* mini-series in trade paperback, for example.

This increased prominence of the collected edition through the 1980s and 1990s contributed to the emergence of a sustainable US graphic novel market. However, in 2001, this market's revenues ($43 million via comic shops, $32 million via mass-market bookstores)[49] were still dwarfed by direct market periodical sales.[50] Yet, at this juncture, perceiving the graphic novel market as the key means with which to lure new consumers and thus widen contracted consumer bases, publishers looked to maximise their production and distribution of collected editions. Marvel's backlist of in-print titles grew, for example, from approximately 250 in 2001 to upwards of 1100 in 2011.[51] As publishers have expanded their backlists, sales of graphic novels have not only grown substantially but also eclipsed those of periodical comic books. For example, in 2016, North American sales of graphic novels reached $590 million, easily exceeding those of print periodical comic books ($405 million).[52]

Speaking to the technological specificity of the early twenty-first century, Alisa Perren observes that the emergence of online's 'long tail' economics has facilitated this expansion of the collected edition market. The internet-based retail system of distribution (by which Amazon operates), whereby vast ranges of unique products are sold, each in small quantities, has rendered Marvel and DC's flooding of the market with hardcovers and trade paperbacks viable.[53] Yet the endeavour to develop new audiences has driven this increased emphasis on the backlist model. At DC, for example, Levitz (in 2001) specifically regarded the collected edition as a format with which to nurture a new breed of 'casual or mild purchasers of comics'.[54] At Marvel, the opinion was shared. As former editor-in-chief Joe Quesada recalls, he envisioned at the start of the 2000s that collected editions 'would attract a different kind of consumer to the [comic books]', permitting the publisher to 'reach out to a whole new clientele that was unavailable to us in the past. I like to refer to them as the casual comic book reader.'[55] While Marvel intended to continue serving what Quesada refers to as the 'habitual' consumer via periodicals sold through comic shops, the collected edition format was intended for the 'casual' reader.[56]

For publishers, the collected edition format and its distribution through mass-market channels have removed three major obstacles to entry for those consumers lacking investment in comic-book culture. Firstly, the cultural capital the graphic novel format accrued over the 1980s and 1990s has imbued collected editions with the legitimacy that periodicals lack outside of the direct market. Secondly, due to the availability of a comprehensive backlist of collected editions in print, consumers are not obliged to keep pace with the rate of periodical production and distribution. Instead, the easy availability of a great deal of comic-book narratives in collected edition form, years after their periodical publication, permits casual modes of consumption. As Levitz notes, it's easier to attract new readers 'when they don't have to commit to the blood oath of coming in every week'.[57] Thirdly, by marketing collected editions through mass-market channels, publishers have provided those consumers who perceive comic shops as inconvenient and/or forbidding with a more accessible point of sale.

Concern for the bottom line, then, led to publishers putting weight behind the backlists and their targeting of new and/or casual consumers. But a predilection among narrative designers for the collected edition format has complemented this process. The writer Warren Ellis, for example, has privileged the graphic novel format over the periodical monthlies, regarding the former as the 'optimized form of comics'.[58] Comments by the writer Jeph Loeb, with regards to DC's attempts to halt delays in periodical publication, demonstrates a bias, not only towards the graphic novel format, but its mode of consumption also. Loeb became frustrated by DC's decision to recruit a replacement ('fill-in') penciller so as to help complete an issue of Loeb and illustrator Carlos Pacheco's *Superman/Batman* run (2003–2005). DC editorial had hired the fill-in to avoid disrupting the frequency of the periodical's publication, but Loeb's concern was that the fill-in work would lead to inconsistency to his run, marring the narrative experience of reading the collected edition as a discrete text.[59] For Loeb, serving the requirements of the periodical market became secondary to enhancing graphic novel consumption.

But narrative designers' taste culture has not only favoured the graphic novel but also the wider audience that the collected edition format offers a means to address. The writer Devin Grayson suggests that narrative designers have shared publishers' desire to increase focus on collected editions, as the format 'changes the entire audience that their stories can reach'.[60] Grant Morrison, on a similar note, revealed, in his proposal to Marvel regarding his *New X-Men* run (2001–2004), an antipathy towards the industry's dedicated readership while demonstrating his preference for a wider potential audience. 'The only people reading [X-Men comics] are fanboys who don't count', he wrote. 'We have to stop talking to the shrinking fan audience and reengage the attention of the mainstream.'[61]

As we have seen, at the beginning of the twenty-first century publishers were motivated to attract a broader consumer mix, and were relying on the collected edition format, and the mode of retail consumption it facilitates, as a means to do so. But, having developed one market sector better suited to a wider audience of new and/or casual consumers, publishers have more recently moved to rapidly grow another—the digital comics market. The 1990s saw the emergence of the digital comics form as independent comics creators, influenced by the popularisation of the internet, began to develop and circulate digital comics content as a means to reach wide audiences without incurring the production and distribution costs that print comics entail.[62] Mainstream publishers, too, dipped their toes into digital comics during this period. For example, Marvel Comics launched its 'Cybercomics' service in 1996, which included content custom-built for online viewing.[63]

In the twenty-first century, however, publishers have developed a burgeoning market for digital versions of monthly comic-book issues. These digital remediations of printed periodicals are sold to readers via such online platforms as Amazon and Comixology or alternatively made available via online subscription services, such as Marvel Unlimited. The format and its distribution mode has enabled a new and/or casual readership to conveniently consume such content via computers and, more recently, tablets and smartphones, and so avoid the more intensive consumption practices of direct market culture. Publishers have focused resources on digitally reproducing back issues, releasing digital versions of their collected editions and ensuring that the digital version of any new issue is published simultaneously with its print incarnation. The digital market has grown rapidly from the late 2000s onwards, with North American revenues escalating from a mere estimated $1 million in 2009 to $90 million in 2016.[64] As the publishers intended, the format has proved especially attractive to new and casual readers. For example, DC Comics' 2012 data concerning consumption of its titles indicated that casual readers are more attracted to issues in digital form, as opposed to in print.[65]

Reflecting the importance of technological specificity to narrative design conditions within a given medium, the development of digital comics has afforded narrative designers the opportunity to develop new narrative design processes that are not available to those constructing narratives for the printed page. Accordingly, notes Daniel M. Goodbrey, pioneering independent creators have, particularly since the early 2000s, made efforts to 'push at the boundaries of the fledgling form and … explore the potential of the digital medium'.[66] Mainstream publishers, too, have made some effort to commission content that experiments with the specific narrative affordances of the digital context. In 2012, for example, Marvel Comics launched its 'Infinite Comics' imprint, which publishes narratives created exclusively for digital screen-based devices.[67] According to the rhetoric of the Marvel.com website, the imprint takes 'full advantage of the latest technology … Showcasing new storytelling possibilities and techniques'.[68] One way in which Infinite Comics narrative designers have fulfilled this rhetoric is by developing approaches to page layout composition that are impossible in the printed form. Goodbrey's analysis of *Guardians of the Galaxy: Infinite Comic* #1 (2013) provides an example of such approaches: as part of a particular sequence in this digital comic's narrative, each click of the mouse or tap of the screen overlays a further small panel onto a previously revealed full-'page' establishing shot.[69] This is, of course, a technique that printed comics cannot permit due to the 'fixed' nature of the printed page.

Despite such innovations, however, while almost all new comics narratives that DC and Marvel Comics now produce are made available for digital consumption, they are, due to the relative economic insignificance of the digital comics market compared to the total market for printed comics, typically intended for print retail also. In most cases therefore, the content that narrative designers create must be suitable for print in comic book and/or graphic novel form. As Goodbrey acknowledges, in the comics medium, the 'computer screen serves primarily as a new means of accessing a pre-existing format'.[70] For publishers, then, the digital comics market is of most immediate value as a conduit to reach new and/or casual readers via product conceived to also serve the more sizeable print sectors. While the contexts of technological convergence have therefore laid conditions for narrative design innovation in the twenty-first century, the particularities of economic contexts of the mainstream comic-book industry in this period have so far restricted the widespread adoption of such new storytelling techniques. Applying the dimensions of specificity model to DC and Marvel's digital comics production, it appears that the sub-dimension of economic specificity has taken precedence over the sub-dimension of technological specificity in the formation of narrative design conditions.

With the development of the collected edition and the digital comics markets, publishers have established the industrial means to reach new and/or casual consumers. But what narrative design processes have been developed to make comic-book narratives more accessible to those consumers that publishers aim to address via these distributional avenues? The following section, which updates prior understandings concerning the connections between comic-book continuity and industrial conditions, begins to address this question by surveying, at a macro level, publisher-wide branded initiatives carried out in the 2010s so as to appeal to targeted audiences.

All-New, All-Different: Configuring Continuities in the Inclusivity Era

Marvel and DC have each carried out multiple publisher-wide narrative reboots or revamps in the 2010s designed to increase the accessibility of their comic-book titles. Supported by extensive branding and marketing pushes, and frequently reported on by mainstream media news sources, these initiatives have, in most cases, been clearly conceived and configured as outreaches to new and/or casual readers. Altered editorial approaches to continuity management, which have been designed to meet the needs of targeted audiences, have been central to these initiatives.

The first of these publisher-wide initiatives occurred in 2011 when DC rebooted its entire line of comic books, resetting the issue numbering of long-enduring superhero titles and streamlining the narrative continuity that its characters had accumulated and shared over decades.[71] In the case of Superman, for example, the only significant backstory material that remained following this streamlining was a version of his standard origin story. Dubbed 'The New 52'—the new comic-book line's simplified continuity was intended in part to attract new readers to the DC universe.[72] As the company's co-publisher Jim Lee explained, the line's prior high issue numbers (*Detective Comics*, for example, had reached #881 prior to the reset) and complicated character biographies had 'made the world of comic books a little more daunting to jump into'. The changes, the company hoped, would enable 'new readers' to 'jump in and understand what's going on from the very first issue'.[73] DC Comics executed a further branded initiative—'DC You'—in 2015, which according to co-publisher Dan DiDio, was designed to 'broaden the appeal' of its narratives to new readers. Central to this DC You strategy was the publication of 24 standalone mini-series that, while furthering New 52 storyworld continuity, were conceived as 'small, accessible arcs'.[74]

Marvel Comics has so far neglected to hollow out its storyworld continuity as DC did as part of its New 52 launch. It has, however, via its 'Marvel NOW!' initiative (which launched in 2012), and its 'All-New, All-Different' initiative (which began in 2015), made significant efforts to make its continuity more accessible. With Marvel NOW!, for example, issue numbering for ongoing series was reset, while—across the company—narratives of #1 issues were configured so as to be easy for readers unversed in continuity to comprehend, as was the case with the initiative's *Daredevil* #1 (2014), for instance. Prior to the Marvel NOW! revamp, Mark Waid had written a 37-issue run on *Daredevil* (2011–2014) that serialises Matt Murdock's New York-based adventures. However, to commence his subsequent Marvel NOW! *Daredevil* run (2014–2015), Waid relocated Murdock to San Francisco, starting a new chapter in The Man Without Fear's crime-fighting career. In so doing, Waid structured for *Daredevil* #1 a useful 'jumping-on point' for those readers not up to speed with the character's continuity.

As former Marvel Comics editor-in-chief Axel Alonso noted during the Marvel Now! launch, an appeal to new and/or casual readers was central to this initiative. 'We want lapsed readers—the guy who likes, say, Captain America, but doesn't know where to start—to know this is a great place to jump on', he said. 'And, of course, we want the stories to be accessible to anyone who saw a Marvel movie or heard the buzz about Marvel NOW!'[75] Alonso orchestrated a similar approach to storyworld continuity as part of the All-New, All-Different initiative, which again reset the publisher's issue numbering. While 'we are not erasing Marvel's history', Alonso stressed prior to the initiative's launch, each new #1 launched under the initiative would nevertheless 'be structured so it's completely accessible to new readers. We don't want to make you feel like you're coming into the middle of the story, and that you need to have read a comic before.'[76]

As these publisher-wide initiatives demonstrate, the inclusivity era aims of broadening publisher readerships, by influencing changes to storyworlds (with The New 52) and plot structures (with Marvel NOW! and All-New, All-Different), significantly determined narrative design conditions and processes. We must keep in mind, however, that publishers in this period have not only looked to attract new readers, but also to keep loyal, dedicated readers satisfied by their product. This concurrent aim also informs narrative design conditions and processes within the inclusivity era. For example, as Alonso's comments during the build-up to 'Marvel NOW!' imply, consideration for the reading pleasures of dedicated Marvel fans influenced the initiative's retention of existing storyworld continuity: 'Our bread and butter are the people who go to comic stores every Wednesday', he acknowledged, 'and Marvel NOW! respects them and the investment they've made—emotionally and financially—in the Marvel Universe.'[77] A more recent example of a publisher-wide initiative—'DC Rebirth'—further demonstrates the influence that the objective to appease dedicated readers exerts. Launched in 2016, DC Rebirth has reinstalled to DC Comics' continuity the great wealth of storyworld material that The New 52 had previously jettisoned, a move conceived to appeal to long-time direct market readers, rather than new and/or casual readers. Pledging the company's commitment to the 'core comics fan', DiDio claimed that 'Rebirth was designed to bring back the best of DC's past'.[78] As DC Chief Creative Officer Geoff Johns further explained, certain DC Rebirth titles, such as *The Flash: Rebirth* and *Green Lantern: Rebirth*, are, due to their referencing of reinstated continuity, 'targeted towards fans who have read a lot of comics'.[79] As Alonso acknowledges, and as the accumulation of the above examples suggests, comic-book publishers in the inclusivity era are each 'walking a tightrope between serving longtime comics devotees and offering access points to new readers'.[80]

While this section has provided a brief overview of some of the broad editorial changes that have occurred so as to meet inclusivity era audience-targeting aims, the remainder of this chapter examines more closely the narrative design processes that have developed in this period. As part of this detailed study, the chapter observes the degrees to which publishers have been able to successfully 'walk the tightrope' and achieve the balance of audience-targeting aims that Alonso identifies. The following section considers in particular how publishers and narrative designers have contrived storyworld elements so as to be appropriate for audiences outside the dedicated niche. As the section demonstrates, key to this practice have been: (1) efforts to increase the gender, racial, ethnic and generational diversity of comic-book storyworlds, which have formed part of some of the aforementioned publisher-wide initiatives; and (2) narrative designers' frequent sourcing of storyworld components from elsewhere within the comics medium (Japanese manga narratives, in particular) and also other media (notably film).

MANGA, MOVIES AND DEMOGRAPHIC DIVERSITY: STORYWORLD TRANSFORMATIONS IN THE INCLUSIVITY ERA

As the previous chapter's discussion of contemporary US television drama series indicates, storyworlds are geared to the perceived requirements of audiences. Flawed, morally ambiguous anti-hero characters such as Walter White, Tony Soprano and *Damages'* Patty Hewes, for example, were, due to their complex and unconventional natures, intended to appeal to an educated, upscale audience. But, if storyworlds are crafted to suit the preferences of particular audiences, what are the perceived requirements of the potential readers that comic-book publishers mean to attract in the inclusivity era, and in what ways have storyworlds been configured so as to meet these requirements? One important audience group outside of the industry's dedicated core of adult males that publishers have looked to reach in the inclusivity era is the teenage demographic, a market they increasingly neglected throughout the 1990s. Editorially enforced storyworlds have come to reflect the pursuit of this audience, as is evident with the narratives of Marvel's Ultimate line, for example, which was launched in 2000. Comprising titles featuring Marvel's most popular properties, such as *Ultimate X-Men*, *Ultimate Iron Man* and *Ultimate Spider-Man*, the Ultimate storyworld complemented Marvel's teen-targeting strategy in two major ways. Firstly, the storyworld exists outside the 'regular' (and very complicated) Marvel Universe (MU) continuity, its lighter continuity thus providing ease of comprehension for younger readers who might be familiar with the characters but who will likely be ignorant of decades' worth of backstory.[81] Secondly, the Ultimate narratives provide versions of these characters with ages younger than those of their MU equivalents, thus potentially rendering the characters appropriate for the intended audience. While, for example, Reed Richards of the Fantastic Four has, in the MU, long been (not always happily) married with children, Ultimate Reed was introduced as a school-age teen with a dictatorial father to overcome.

Following the closure of the Ultimate line in 2015, Marvel's teen-targeting aims have more recently influenced narrative designers to place a greater emphasis on young heroes within the MU. For example, while the MU primary Avengers team has, in recent decades, most typically comprised experienced heroes, three out of the seven Avengers that Marvel Comics assembled in 2015 for the launch of its All-New, All-Different line were teenage characters (Kamala Kahn, Miles Morales and Sam Alexander).[82]

In the twenty-first century, Marvel and DC have also each consistently targeted teenage females specifically, a strategy first influenced by patterns of manga consumption in the US. Reflecting the insular philosophies of the era of direct market dominance, both Marvel and DC had, by the end of the 1990s, little in the way of comic-book content directed towards a female demographic of any age.[83] But the emergence in the early 2000s of a strong US teen-female audience for manga led to publishers striving to capitalise on this new market of comics readers, which was being accessed through mass-market channels. Translated manga had originally been distributed in the US in periodical form through the direct market by the likes of First Comics and Epic (a former Marvel imprint) in the 1980s and 1990s.[84] However, publishers such as Tokyopop built an alternative model in the late 1990s distributing manga collected editions (known as 'tankoubons') through mass-market bookstores.[85] These publishers enjoyed particular success marketing 'shojo' manga towards a female demographic. The term shojo, used within the manga industry to denote serial comics that are targeted towards female teens, covers a broad range of generic storyworld themes—such as comedy, romance and fantasy; but a strong focus on female teen protagonists and their friendships and romances often defines and unites these disparate narratives.

Marvel's efforts to produce narratives for manga's US teen-female audience led, on the one hand, to the publisher emulating its 'Ultimisation' method by extracting pre-existing characters from MU storyworld continuity and reshaping them for the US shojo audience. While the 'regular' Mary Jane Watson, for example, was (in the issues of the early 2000s) married to Peter Parker (aka Spider-Man), the storyworld of *Spider-Man Loves Mary Jane* series (2005–2007) emulates shojo themes by incorporating the social/romantic experiences of a teenage Mary Jane. The *Emma Frost* series (2003–2004) was a similar project, the storyworld containing the titular X-lady's turbulent teen years at home and school, while also including the process of her coming to terms with her mutant powers.[86] But, on the other hand, Marvel, in its endeavours to court the shojo readership, also created new characters to insert *into* MU continuity via such series as *Spellbinders* (2005) and *Runaways* (2003–2009).[87] The latter, with a storyworld comprising a group of teens (each of whom has fled from super-villain parents), has proved a particularly popular and enduring example of such narratives.

Ostensibly the super-powered teen-team at the heart of the series (created by writer Brian K. Vaughan) is part of a lineage of young-hero groups within comic-book history.[88] But the *Runaways* demonstrates ways in which narrative designers, in line with institutional aims, tweaked their own generic formulas so as to present a storyworld more in tune with shojo traditions. For example, core character elements distinguish *Runaways* from its forebears. Firstly, the gender balance of Vaughan's gang is, unusually for superhero teams, weighted towards females, with the original line-up comprising three girls and two boys. This emphasis placed on young female protagonists is thus in keeping with shojo. Secondly, Vaughan's characters are bereft of the bold, functional, modernist costumes representative of contemporary superheroes. Instead the group's leader, Nico Minoru, a Japanese-American sorceress, sports a variety of baroque outfits comprising combinations of laced boots, striped tights, neck chokers, large collars, lacy dresses and buck-led jackets. Nico's sartorial preferences echo not the functional, clean-lined leotards and bodysuits traditional to the superhero fraternity, but rather the ornate and elaborate chic typical of manga heroines.

The *Runaways* provides a clear example of the way in which Marvel in the 2000s modified its traditional superhero storyworld so as to better suit a shojo audience. Complementing these institutionally enforced efforts in storyworld design, the publisher also ensured that the collected edition's physical form was suitable for the intended audience. Whereas collected editions generally adhere to the page dimensions of the periodical comic books, the *Runaways* collected editions (along with those of *Emma Frost*, *Spellbinders* and *Spider-Man Loves Mary Jane*) were published in a smaller 'digest' size similar to that of the tankoubon format. As former Marvel publisher Dan Buckley acknowledged, 'We are doing digest-formatted books because that's where we think the manga reader is.'[89] Sharing Marvel's perception that US shojo consumers are best reached via graphic novel formats, DC bypassed periodical issues altogether in its attempts to appeal to the shojo readership. Instead it published, under its Minx imprint (launched in 2007), a range of OGNs intended for this audience.[90] The storyworlds of Minx titles, such as *Kimmie66* (2007), *The New York Four* (2008) and *The P.L.A.I.N. Janes* (2007), eschew super-heroics, and instead largely concern teen-female relationships.

As part of its further efforts to appeal to female consumers, Marvel Comics has, in the 2010s, increased female representation at the core of the MU continuity. For example, in 2013, the publisher put together an all-female X-Men team for the Marvel NOW! relaunch of its *X-Men* title, while in 2014, Jane Foster became the MU's Thor. According to Marvel's press release, the new female Thunder God would 'speak directly to an audience that long was not the target for superhero comic books in America: women and girls'.[91] In 2015, furthermore, Marvel Comics' *A-Force* title, which was launched in conjunction with that year's 'Secret Wars' event, assembled an all-woman version of the Avengers. As Carolyn Cocca usefully indicates via her analysis of the 2015 All-New, All-Different title line-up, Marvel Comics significantly (if not sufficiently) increased the prominence of female characters within its storyworld during the 2010s: 'Of the seventy titles launched or relaunched in the ... initiative', she observes, 'fifteen have female leads, up from zero only four years previous.'[92] As Anne F. Peppard notes, this increase in female representation within the MU has not always resulted in especially positive or progressive representations of women during this period.[93] Nevertheless, this outreach to female consumers appears to have achieved at least some success in terms of meeting audience-targeting objectives; for example, according to Alonso, the female-led *Mighty Thor* title has attracted 'new readers—most of whom are female'.[94]

In the 2010s, both DC and Marvel have additionally increased diversity within their storyworlds in terms of race and ethnicity as a means to broaden the demographic make-up of its audience base. In terms of the achievement of racial diversity, for example, DC Comics introduced, in 2013, Duke Thomas, Batman's first-ever black protégé; the publisher subsequently launched, in 2017, a title—*Batman & The Signal*—focusing on the sidekick's exploits. In 2014, DC introduced Val-Zod, a black Kryptonian who would adopt the Superman moniker, while, in conjunction with the 2015 DC You initiative, the publisher launched the first solo title concerning Justice League's sole black member, Cyborg.

As part of Marvel Comics' efforts to render its own storyworld more racially diverse, the publisher, in 2011, replaced Peter Parker in Ultimate continuity with the black/Latino character Miles Morales. Miles has, since 2015, become a central figure within MU continuity. As previously noted, he has featured in an Avengers line-up, and is also the subject of Marvel's ongoing *Spider-Man* title (2016–present). The publisher also introduced, in 2015, the Korean-American teen-genius Amadeus Cho as a new incarnation of the Hulk, whose adventures are conveyed in the pages of *The Totally Awesome Hulk* (2015–present). In 2016, the publisher introduced a further highly intelligent hero, the black teen Riri Williams, to take the Iron Man mantle—under the alias of Ironheart. In addition to reconfiguring its storyworld so as to include more people of colour, Marvel has increased the ethnic diversity of the MU. This has chiefly occurred via the publisher's introduction, in 2014, of Kamala Khan as the storyworld's new Ms. Marvel in 2014. A Pakistani-American Muslim teenager, Khan's faith and heritage partly motivate her, such as when her recollection of a passage from the Qur'an provides her with courage to perform heroics.[95] Critics have routinely celebrated the Kahn-led ongoing *Ms. Marvel* (2014–present) series for its positive and respectful portrayal of American Muslims.[96]

Marvel Comics' fairly significant moves to increase the gender, racial, ethnic and generational diversity within its titles have not always been met with enthusiasm by dedicated direct market readers, some of whom have been unimpressed by the resulting marginalisation of long-time characters within the MU. Marvel Vice President of Sales David Gabriel indeed identified reader antipathy towards those titles designed to increase storyworld diversity as a cause of Marvel's 2017 decline in direct market sales.[97] It appears, then, that the publisher's sustained strategy of attracting new readers beyond the direct market via increased storyworld diversity has taken precedence over the goal of appeasing dedicated readers. The strong digital and trade paperback sales performance of some of the titles that have resulted from this editorial strategy, as in the case of *Ms. Marvel*, furthermore indicates that the strategy to reach a wider audience has found some success.[98]

Alongside moves to develop a more diverse range of cultural identities within their storyworlds, publishers have, in the inclusivity era, also attempted to broaden their audience base by adapting the storyworlds of narrative properties from other media. There are precedents for such industrial practice in the era of direct market dominance. As Wright observes, Dark Horse's extensive use of IP licensed from films, such as *Aliens* (1986) and *Star Wars* (1977), distinguished the publisher through the late 1980s and 1990s.[99] But such strategy has since become more uniformly adopted within the industry.

Publishers in the inclusivity era target consumers of popular genres in literature, for example, with IDW publishing adaptations of Richard Stark's series of 'Parker' crime books and Marvel angling for consumers of horror and sci-fi literature with its many adaptations of Stephen King and Orson Scott Card novels. As a means to widen their audience appeal, publishers have also turned en masse to storyworld material originating in videogames. Marvel, for example, has augmented the space-operatic storyworld of Microsoft's *Halo* series; Dark Horse has adapted the sci-fi universe of *Mass Effect*; DC has expanded the storyworld of the time-hopping *Assassin's Creed* adventures and also those of the rugged futuristic shooter *Gears of*

War, while IDW has extended the epic fantasy realm of the *Dragon Age* series and the macabre horror storyworld of the *Silent Hill* games. Publishers promote these comics to consumers invested within these game franchises by promising vital transmedia storyworld crossover between the comics and games texts. IDW, for example, for *Silent Hill: Past Life* (2011), advertised its inclusion of an 'in game' character from a forthcoming *Silent Hill* game, while Dark Horse suggested that its *Mass Effect: Evolution* (2011) was, 'for existing *Mass Effect* fans ... an important piece of the story they are already following'.[100] DC Comics has also produced comic-book series that expand the titles of DC superhero storyworlds native to video-games, including the distinct fictional worlds of the *Injustice* fighting games (2013–present) and the *Batman: Arkham* action-adventure games (2009–present).[101] These transmedia extension comic-book titles include *Injustice: Gods Among Us* (2013–2016) and *Batman: Arkham Knight* (2015–2016). As Warner Bros. Interactive Entertainment publishes both the *Injustice* and *Batman: Arkham* videogame series, these comic-book titles serve not only DC Comics' objective of appealing to videogame enthusiasts but also its parent company Warner Bros.' goal of generating synergies between the content that its various divisions produce.

Publishers not only tie into storyworld material from videogames, they rely on the storytellers of these narratives also. DC, for example, hired Joshua Ortega, a writer from the *Gears of War 2* game (2008), to script its comic-book addition to the *GoW* narrative, while Dark Horse employed Mac Walters, lead writer on the second and third *Mass Effect* games, to map out its contribution to *Mass Effect* storyworld continuity. Recruiting these narrative designers, and promoting their recruitment (via press releases and other means), potentially legitimises these comics in the eyes of the targeted gamer audience. The use of narrative designers from outside of comics as a means to reach new audiences is not restricted to the adaptation of game series; rather it is part of a broader industrial pattern that feeds into publishers' core superhero series also. For example, DC signed up cult filmmaker Kevin Smith and bestselling thriller author June Brad Meltzer to write *Green Arrow* runs, while Marvel, in contrast, has employed high-profile television showrunners such as Joss Whedon (*Buffy*) and Damon Lindelof (*Lost*), the former as writer on *Astonishing X-Men* (Vol. 3, 2004–2008), the latter on *Ultimate Wolverine vs. Hulk* (2005–2009).[102] As Quesada and DiDio each acknowledges, the policy of hiring such personnel, similar to the approach of co-opting narratives from other media, is intended to draw newcomers to its publications.[103] By frequently electing to import storyworlds and narrative designers associated with genres such as horror, crime, sci-fi and fantasy, publishers not only reach out to potential new audiences; they also, via their invocation of generic themes ingrained within the comic-book industry's DNA, simultaneously address those consumers steeped in comic-book culture's traditions.

While publishers have developed associations with a diversity of media in their efforts to reach new audiences, film has most consistently exerted a transmedia influence upon storyworld within the inclusivity era. Yet the direction of influence has not been one way between the two; rather, the relationship between film studios and comic-book publishers has remained largely dialogical. A 'feedback loop' exists between comics and film, as Martin Flanagan et al. observe.[104] The comic-book industry has influenced film, providing studios (with which DC and Marvel are now each horizontally integrated) with storyworld material for a slew of superhero blockbusters in the 2000s and 2010s. These include such adaptations as *X-Men* (2000), *Spider-Man* (2002), *Daredevil* (2003), *The Punisher* (2004), *Catwoman* (2004), *Fantastic Four* (2005), *Batman Begins* (2005), *Superman Returns* (2006), *Ghost Rider* (2007), *Iron Man* (2008), *The Incredible Hulk* (2008), *Thor* (2011), *Green Lantern* (2011), *Captain America* (2011), *The Avengers* (2012), *Guardians of the Galaxy* (2014), *Ant-Man* (2015), *Doctor Strange* (2016) and *Wonder Woman* (2017), along with various associated sequels and reboots. But, as I will demonstrate, these films have informed storyworld detail within superhero comic-books as a consequence of publishers' efforts to engage mainstream cinema-going audiences.

While movie adaptations of comic-book superheroes generally have minimal impact on periodical sales, the interest they generate usually spikes revenues for collected editions.[105] Levitz, for example, attributes the 20 per cent increase in revenues (on the previous year) that DC's backlist enjoyed in 2005 to the release of the *Batman Begins* movie.[106] Publishers systematically exploit these consumption patterns by ensuring that a range of graphic novels featuring an adapted hero is available in the mass market in the year of a film's release. DC, for example, published, along with various Batman collected editions, two Joker-themed OGNs (*Joker¹* and the 'Deluxe Edition' of 1988s *Batman: The Killing Joke*) in 2008, the year of *The Dark Knight* film (within which the Caped Crusader faces off against the Clown Prince of Crime). The two publications went on to become the second and third bestselling graphic novels of that year.[107] Marvel, in contrast, commenced five different Thor-starring mini-series in 2010, alongside its ongoing *Thor* series, so as to ensure a variety of relevant new material was available for publication in collected edition format on the eve of the Thunder God's screen debut.[108] The publisher, signalling its adherence to the philosophy of 'long tail' economics, had, in total, 61 different Thor-featured collected editions in print in the year of the film's release.[109]

The storyworlds of superhero comics have often come to reflect these attempts by publishers to cater for the new and/or casual consumers who arrive at a comic-book narrative via their interest in superhero film adaptations. Sometimes, for example, comic-book storyworlds serve as transmedia storytelling extensions for film. For instance, as noted in Chap. 2, Marvel publishes comic books that expand the Marvel Cinematic Universe storyworld.[110] More commonly, however, narrative designers (sometimes in line with editorial mandates) adjust storyworld components within existing comic-book storyworld continuities so as to ensure that comic-book narratives achieve degrees of similitude with movie adaptations. In so doing, therefore, narrative designers create, not transmedia storytelling connections between the storyworlds of comic books and those of film, but rather intertextual resonances between distinct storyworlds. By creating a closer affinity between comic-book storyworlds and those of superhero films, publishers hope to drive up sales by reaching a wider audience. DC's DiDio bluntly asserts this line of reasoning: 'The closer the source material is to whatever the adaptation is, the better the source material sells.'[111]

Instances of comic-book storyworlds being altered so as to achieve intertextual resonances between comic books and superhero films include narrative designers reconfiguring characters' sartorial preferences. Writer Grant Morrison's response to the release of 20th Century Fox's first X-Men movie serves as an example of this type of approach to narrative design. The choice of the film's producers to replace the X-Men's garish-coloured spandex costumes with black leather apparel had been met with consternation by many dedicated readers.[112] Yet the movie subsequently inspired Morrison, embarking on his *New X-Men* run, to jettison the mutants' primary-coloured garb and to instead have their attire mimic that of the film.[113] As Derek Johnson shows, Marvel Comics' efforts to ensure similarity between its comic-book storyworld and that of the X-movies also led to Marvel editorial mandating for a 'less short and ugly' Wolverine (who is performed by the handsome Hugh Jackman in the movie franchise). In this case, perceived audience requirements influenced physiological change within the storyworld.[114]

Movies have also influenced the identities of the villains that heroes face. For example, on learning that 'Iron Monger' Obadiah Stane was to serve as Tony Stark's foe in Marvel Studio's *Iron Man* film, writer Matt Fraction decided he 'should bring a Stane back' for Iron Man to battle.[115] While Obadiah was unavailable (having committed suicide in *Iron Man* #200, 1985), Fraction opted to introduce to the storyworld the bitter and vengeful son Ezekiel Stane so as to set up a confrontation that resonates with the film's narrative.[116] Marvel's objective to have comic-book storyworlds align more closely with those of film has also led to shifts in superhero settings, as evidenced by the pages of *Peter Parker: The Spectacular Spider-Man*. Despite Peter having developed (in MU continuity) into a globe-trotting business man, this title—which launched a month prior to the release of the *Spider-Man: Homecoming* film—returned the hero to his traditional New York City milieu, thereby matching *Homecoming*'s strong focus on New York environments. As Alonso acknowledges, the *Peter Parker* title results from the publisher's efforts to ensure that it has books available that are thematically similar to films featuring Marvel heroes.[117]

Marvel editorial has even gone as far as altering the identity of one of its superheroes—Ghost Rider—so as to ensure congruity with a movie adaptation. In MU continuity, original Ghost Rider alias Johnny Blaze ceased his role in *Ghost Rider* #81 (1983), and was succeeded by Danny Ketch. Marvel, however, opted to restore Blaze as Ghost Rider for its 2006 relaunch of the series (which was motivated by the scheduled release of Columbia's *Ghost Rider* movie the following year). As Quesada admitted, the decision to restore Blaze to the storyworld was influenced by the filmmakers' use of the character as Ghost Rider's alias in the movie.[118] Marvel wanted neither to confuse nor deter those consumers, ignorant of Ghost Rider continuity, whose interest had been piqued by the film.

Publishers' aims to develop an affinity with superhero movies have furthermore determined the compositions of superhero teams, as in the case of the Guardians of the Galaxy comic-book storyworld. In the second volume of the *Guardians of the Galaxy* comic-book series (2008–2010), the galactic team comprises a deep roster of members; however, since launching a third *Guardians* volume in 2013 in preparation for the release of the first *Guardians of the Galaxy* film (in 2014), Marvel Comics has ensured that the comic-book Guardians mirror those of the film. In this period, therefore, the quintet of Star-Lord, Gamora, Drax, Groot and Rocket-Racoon has remained the core Guardians team, as it does in the Guardians movie adaptations.[119] For its launch of a new volume of the

Suicide Squad series in 2016, DC Comics similarly configured the titular team's roster to resemble the character line-up included in the *Suicide Squad* film released in the same year.

Comic-book publishers have also more generally ensured that a range of accessible, continuity-free and or continuity-light storyworlds are available to new and/or casual consumers who arrive at comic books or collected editions via the films. For example, publishers have frequently commissioned limited and ongoing series centred on the origins of characters in the process of being adapted for the screen, such as *Wolverine: Origin* (2001–2003), *Daredevil: Yellow* (2001), *The Punisher: Born* (2003), *Superman: Birthright* (2003–2004), *All-Star Batman and Robin: The Boy Wonder* (2005–2008), *Ghost Rider: Road to Damnation* (2006), *Thor: First Thunder* (2010–2011), *Superman: American Alien* (2016) and *Wonder Woman: Earth One* (2016–present). Due to their absence of accumulated continuity, these storylines, which mostly represent adaptations and/or elaborations on previously published tales regarding how heroes came to be, offer an easy entry point for new and/or casual consumers.

Due to the smart ways by which narrative designers sometimes augment and adjust a given character's beginnings, however, retold origins are of potential interest to dedicated readers also. *Punisher: Born*, for example, posits that (the Punisher) Frank Castle's zero-tolerance vigilantism is not, as had been put forward in previous interpretations of the character, a product of his family having been murdered via a mob war's crossfire; rather, the *Born* storyworld, written by Garth Ennis, suggests that Frank's dark, murderous instincts were unleashed years earlier during the Vietnam conflict. For readers unfamiliar or only casually acquainted with Punisher narratives, the origin tale operates as a discrete storyline detailing Castle's final tour of duty. But Ennis' deconstruction of the standard Punisher myth potentially functions as a significant paradigm shift for those dedicated consumers with years of investment in the character. By undermining the easy justification for hoodlum-murder that the slaughter of Frank's family previously provided, Ennis renders a more complex and inscrutable protagonist. Thus publishers, via such origin tales, are potentially able to engage both dedicated and casual readers simultaneously.

The presentation of heroes' origins as a means to address newcomers is not a recent phenomenon. As veteran Marvel writer Peter David notes, editors during the newsstand era would, in anticipation of the high turnover of its child audience, have narrative designers re-convey a superhero's origins every few years so as to bring new consumers up to speed.[120] But, as DC's marketing of a Green Lantern origin story demonstrates, publishers in the inclusivity era rely on origin tales as a means to target those new and/or casual consumers whose interest stems from a given superhero movie. The cover for a collected edition of the 'Secret Origin' arc (taken from the ongoing *Green Lantern* series, Vol. 4 #29–35, 2008), which was published in 2011 so as to coincide with the Warner Bros. *Green Lantern* film release, incorporates a portrait of the film's star, Ryan Reynolds. It also advertises its inclusion of a Reynolds-penned introduction.

While it is clear from the above that DC and Marvel Comics' aim to appeal to new and/or casual consumers has frequently configured storyworlds to complement the release of movie adaptations of superhero narratives, wider industrial pressures have led Marvel Comics to sometimes take an alternative approach. As the above examples of changes made to X-Men and Ghost Rider characters suggest, Marvel Comics storyworlds in the 2000s were, notes Johnson, 'subordinated' to licensed Marvel superhero movies (distributed by Columbia and 20th Century Fox).[121] Since the launch of the Marvel Cinematic Universe in 2008 (with the first *Iron Man* film), and Disney's subsequent acquisition of Marvel Entertainment in 2009, Marvel Comics has made some clear efforts to avoid synergies between its storyworlds and those of licensed film adaptations of Marvel characters. For example, rather than align its Fantastic Four storyworld with that of Fox's 2015 *Fantastic Four* film, Marvel Comics opted instead to end its venerable *Fantastic Four* comic-book series during the build-up to the film's release. According to former *Fantastic Four* comic-book writer Jonathan Hickman, a dispute between Marvel Entertainment and 20th Century Fox concerning Fantastic Four film rights motivated Marvel Comics' decision to cancel its *Fantastic Four* title and to marginalise the Fantastic Four characters within MU continuity.[122]

Much of the discussion here concerning the interactions between film and comic-book storyworlds raises questions about the significance of the specificities of a medium's culture in the formation of narrative design conditions. The instances of comic-book storyworlds aligning with those of film adaptations might suggest these storyworlds' complete subservience to media conglomerate structures, cross-media licensing agreements and the strategies driving transmedia entertainment franchises. The above case of Marvel Comics side-lining the Fantastic Four furthermore indicates that media conglomerates' cross-media interests can, in certain circumstances, take precedence over (medium-specific) priorities within the comic-book industry.[123] The above summary of narrative design processes might therefore be interpreted as indicative of the ways in which processes of media convergence erode the differences between the narratives formed across media. One might conclude, on that basis, that a cultural approach to medium specificity is redundant when considering the relationship of comic-book storyworlds to the comics medium within the broader context of transmedia entertainment franchises.

However, as Chap. 2 indicates, while it is important to account for how media convergence influences twenty-first century narrative design processes, it is equally necessary to acknowledge and separate the industrial/cultural pressures upon narrative design conditions, such as audience-targeting aims that can be internal and specific to a medium. Comic-book publishers have, within the cases discussed above, produced storyworlds that complement conglomerates' cross-media objectives through their achievement of narrative synergies. Yet these narrative design processes are largely driven by the publishers' industry-specific audience-targeting priorities at the beginning of the twenty-first century as much as they are by wider conglomerate interests. This is an important distinction to make because, while publishers' internal audience-targeting pressures have, as we have seen, sometimes resulted in clear similarities between superhero storyworlds across media, they have equally resulted in comic-book storyworlds' inclusion of elements that are clearly distinct from those of film and other media.

For example, Marvel Comics' aforementioned introduction of a range of new characters, including Miles Morales, Kamala Kahn, Riri Williams, Amadeus Cho and a female Thor, has, as previously noted, helped to increase the gender, racial, ethnic and generational diversity of the MU. But the installation of these characters to this storyworld, which medium-specific audience-targeting aims motivated, has contributed to a line-up of heroes that is clearly distinguishable from that of the Marvel movies, which largely comprises (white, male) characters that Marvel Comics created in the twentieth century. A further example: the DC Rebirth initiative's reinstatement of storyworld continuity, which was inspired by the audience-targeting aim of appeasing long-time dedicated readers, clearly distinguishes the DC Comics storyworld from that of the DC Extended Universe (which DC Entertainment's superhero films contribute to). Unlike the former, the latter is not built on, and does not draw from, decades' worth of character chronology.

Speaking with regards to Marvel Comics' editorial approach, Alonso claims that, while the institution looks to 'take advantage' of a Marvel superhero movie's release by 'having something available for readers that approximates the flavour [of that movie]', the institution does not 'march in lockstep with the studios'.[124] Geoff Johns stresses that DC Comics adopts a similar position: DC Comics may 'want to nod to or bring over' elements from film adaptations 'but comics are their own thing'.[125] Such discourses, which are conveyed via comic-book specialist press, should be treated with caution, of course, as they are partly designed to reassure dedicated readers that their beloved storyworlds are not to be homogenised as part of broader transmedia entertainment franchises. These comments nevertheless reflect a clear truth that, in part due to audience-targeting aims specific to the US comic-book industry, the storyworlds of DC and Marvel Comics are far from facsimiles of, respectively, the Marvel Cinematic Universe and the DC Extended Universe. Yet, conversely, this truth does not alter the fact that both Marvel and DC Comics have, in the twenty-first century, each repeatedly looked to build resonances between comic-book narratives and the universally popular medium of film so as to appeal to a wider group of potential consumers. Furthermore, publishers' aims here to court a mainstream cinema-going audience not only echo within the storyworlds that narrative designers convey, but also in *how* they are conveyed, as the next section demonstrates.

Privileging the 'Cinematic': Filmmaking Style in the Inclusivity Era

Publishers in the inclusivity era have often permitted narrative designers to draw extensively upon techniques of visual style more redolent of filmmaking practices than of those traditional to the comic-book industry. By utilising such techniques, narrative designers support publishers' audience-broadening imperatives in two key ways. Firstly the style complements publishers' efforts to develop a greater resonance between comic-book narrative and on-screen presentations of superheroes; secondly, the style's association with filmmaking, more generally, culturally legitimises comic-book narrative within 'mainstream' entertainment culture, wherein film (and also television drama) is generally held in higher regard than comics.

In order to outline the 'cinematic' style ubiquitous within the inclusivity era, and the ways in which this storytelling marks a transition, I will first outline earlier traditions of style within the comic-book industry. As Charles Hatfield observes, the fundamental role of the narrative designer in comics 'is to evoke an imagined [temporal] sequence by creating a visual series'.[126] The particular manner by which a narrative designer utilises the semiotic phenomena of image and language in the process of fulfilling this role constitutes the narrative's style. In turn, a reader's role is to infer the relationship between images and 'translate the given series [of images] into a narrative sequence'.[127] Robert C. Harvey terms this presentation of a temporal sequence via a series of panels (each containing images), as a *breakdown*,[128] a process that, notes Hatfield, 'necessarily entails omitting [the visual presentation of storyworld action] as well as including'.[129] According to Scott McCloud, writers and/or pencillers within the comic-book industry have traditionally relied upon a relatively high omission rate; that is, narrative designers have usually ensured that each successive panel within a given series of panels depicts an action related to but distinct from a previous panel.[130] Consequently, each panel from a breakdown represents a unique action within the evoked temporal sequence, with each panel transition within such a breakdown representing what McCloud refers to as an *action-to-action* progression.[131]

A series of three panels in *Amazing Spider-Man* #313 (written by David Michelinie, pencilled by Todd McFarlane, 1989) provides an example of this process. In said issue, Spider-Man battles a giant inflatable version of himself. Subsequent to a skirmish in which the hero fails to vanquish this foe, Spider-Man, in the first of the three panels, reasons that 'a very big pin' would be the best means by which to defeat this menacing balloon. The second panel depicts Spider-Man atop the Chrysler Building, holding aloft the structure's snapped-off spire (with the action of Spidey snapping off the spire only implied). In the third panel, Spider-Man is depicted hanging in mid-air, poised to bring down the 'very big pin' upon the inflatable enemy that he descends towards.

A key condition of comic-book production—comic-book page length—has historically motivated this traditional mode of visual style. Whether working on the 13-page (approx.) lead stories of the newsstand era or the 22-page (approx.) narratives of the era of direct market dominance, comic-book narrative designers have been obliged to ensure that each periodical delivers a briskly paced, *compressed* package of storyworld action and drama. As the pace of storytelling within comics is dictated by the amount of page space consumed, highly economical action-to-action progressions have enabled narrative designers to compress a high rate of events within the restricted space of a single comic book.[132]

But many narrative designers in the inclusivity era have eschewed these logics of compression, utilising instead a narrative style that remediates cinematographic and editing practice. Two key features define this 'cinematic' style. Firstly, such storytelling is characterised by breakdowns that forgo action-to-action progressions. Instead a distinct storyworld action is broken down into incremental stages via a series of multiple panels, with each panel providing a different perspective on the depicted action. Such breakdown technique echoes the philosophies of contemporary Hollywood cutting and shooting. As David Bordwell explains, a key facet of visual style in modern American film is its high rate of editing between the myriad perspectives of different set-ups that typify big-budget Hollywood productions.[133] But, secondly, comic-book narrative designers' page-layout methods complement their adaptation of film cinematographic and editing practice. Writers and pencillers, in their invocation of action, rely consistently on large page-wide panels that are often akin to film ratio. This combination of breakdown and page layout practice results in pages that appear to comprise selected stills from a particular movie sequence.

A particular breakdown from *Nightwing* #150 (2009), in which writer Peter Tomasi and penciller Don Kramer depict the action of (former Robin) Dick Grayson swinging through a windowpane so as to thwart Harvey 'Two-Face' Dent, serves as an example of 'cinematic' storytelling within the inclusivity era. So as to demonstrate this breakdown's departure from industry convention, the following analysis of a breakdown from *Detective Comics* #571 (1987) shows how an analogous storyworld action has been presented by more traditional means in the era of direct market dominance. In said issue, Jason Todd, as (the second) Robin, similarly swings through a window, in this case so as to confront the Scarecrow. The breakdown begins as Robin is shown waiting atop a hospital roof for the arrival of the Scarecrow at a patient's room. In subsequent panels the Scarecrow is shown to visit the room and explain his intent to harm the patient. Scarecrow's scheming is subsequently interrupted by The Boy Wonder's entrance. The entire action of Jason Todd's swinging outside the window, to crashing through the windowpane, to entering the space of the room, is depicted via a single action-to-action progression, with motion lines economically implying Robin's trajectory. The issue's writer, Mike Barr, and illustrator, Alan Davis, thus compress the action of the Robin swing into a single panel comprising a sixth of a page.

In their (later) depiction of the analogous event in *Nightwing*, Tomasi and Kramer decompress the action of Dick, as he swings on a blimp mooring rope so as to smash through the windowpane of the vehicle's cockpit (occupied by Harvey), via their utilisation of five wide panels. The plot duration of the depicted event encompasses approximately one and a half pages. Tomasi and Kramer fragment their depiction of the swing into successive increments, with each panel offering a new perspective on the action; the breakdown is suggestive of the multiple edits between different camera set-ups.[134] Tomasi and Kramer present the first two increments of the swing via the filmmaking shot/reverse-shot convention. The perspective of the first of these two panels is located behind Harvey as he watches Dick swing towards him. This panel is then succeeded by a reverse-shot panel—in this case, a reaction shot—that reveals Harvey's incredulity towards Dick's trademark bravura. The subsequent two panels provide further different perspectives on Dick as he swings closer to his target, before the fifth panel depicts his moment of impact with the window.

As part of their visual style, however, narrative designers in the inclusivity era not only frequently fragment their presentation of storyworld action via Hollywood's cutting and shooting logics; they also implement styles that adapt the filmmaking convention of camera movement. Warren Ellis and penciller Stuart Immonen's evocation of the Fantastic Four's 'Fantasticar' launch in *Ultimate Fantastic Four* #10 (2004) provides an example of the integration of pseudo camera movement within their work. Again, a separate example of a more conventional breakdown from the era of direct market dominance—in this case, from *Fantastic Four* #343 (1990)—provides a useful point of comparison. Said issue depicts an event similar to that of the Fantasticar launch; that is, the take-off of the Four's Pogo Plane from within the Baxter Building (the Fantastic Four's base of operations), which writer/penciller Walter Simonson conveys via an action-to-action progression, not over two panels, but within a *single* panel. Having used one panel to depict the Four readying for take-off, Simonson compresses the evocation of both the aircraft's launch ignition (via dialogue: '3-2-1-launch') and the subsequent launch itself (via an image of thruster flames emerging from beneath the aircraft and a linguistic sound effect: 'FWHROOSH'), into a large single panel comprising two-thirds of the page.

In contrast, Ellis and Immonen, in *Ultimate Fantastic Four* #10, convey the Fantasticar launch across three pages, and provide the suggestion of camera motion in the process. The depiction of the launch begins with a four-panel breakdown. Each panel shows the roof of the Baxter Building from distinct perspectives, with the fourth panel evoking the opening of the roof (which enables the Fantasticar launch from within). But, in contrast with the multiple perspectives of the above *Nightwing* breakdown, each panel is not suggestive of the vantage point of a separate camera set-up; rather, the four panels comprise the illusion of a single helicopter shot, with each image akin to a distinct frame from the same shot. The subsequent three panels in the evoked temporal sequence provide perspectives situated within the building, with each panel depicting three incremental stages of the vehicle's lift-off, each from a different perspective. Again, each new panel is analogous with a single frame from the same moving camera. In this instance, the series of panels generates the illusion of a vertically tilting shot, with each successive panel providing a higher-angled perspective on the Fantisticar launch from the same vantage point. Concluding the evocation of the launch on a third page, Ellis and Immonen switch perspective again to an extreme wide shot of the Fantasticar ascending above the Baxter Building. Ellis and Immonen finally augment their highly nuanced evocation of take-off via a three-panel series depicting Reed's altering of the craft's trajectory via the igniting of the Fantisticar's main engine.

The influence of manga has proved a determining factor in the utilisation of this 'cinematic' style in the US. Similar approaches to storytelling have maintained a consistent presence within Japanese comics since Osamu Tezuka modelled breakdown techniques on the storytelling practices of Disney animations and Charlie Chaplin movies in the late 1940s.[135] In an example of transnational cultural feedback, this influence has since directed westwards via manga's increased exposure within comic-book production culture in recent decades. Frank Miller, an early adopter of 'cinematic' style in the US with his DC mini-series *Ronin* (1983), took inspiration for his work from the expansive storytelling of the Japanese *Lone Wolf & Cub* series (1970–1976).[136] But comic-book narrative designers' discursive framing of their techniques often elides this influence, emphasising instead the associations between their storytelling and conventions of visual style in contemporary American filmmaking. Thus they contribute to a potential process of cultural legitimisation within a wider consumer culture. Ellis, for example, coined 'widescreen comics' as a term to define his techniques,[137] while Peter David labels comic-book narrative production in the 2000s as 'cinematic storytelling';[138] writer Mark Millar refers to his own 'cinematic style',[139] while writer Brian Michael Bendis acknowledges the strong influence cinematographic methods bear on his practices.[140] By couching their narratives in such terms, these writers echo television narrative designers' positioning of their drama series as emulative of other media more valorised than television (see Chap. 3). As with discourses surrounding television drama, 'cinematic' becomes not only a definitional term, but also a positively evaluative one. This combination of visual style and paratextual framing potentially lends comic books a greater cultural worth beyond their consumer base, thus serving publishers' imperatives within the inclusivity era.

Yet this 'cinematic' style has, due to the uneconomical plot durations that its combination of large panel sizes and multiple-perspective break-downs necessitate, left many dedicated comic-book periodical readers dis-contented due to the resultant deliberate narrative pacing. Many readers regard the decompressed 'cinematic' style, and the resultant extended plot durations, to be ill suited to their consumption of narrative via monthly issues. This dissatisfaction is evident in, for example, consumers' online comments regarding Warren Ellis and penciller Chris Sprouse's six-part mini-series *Ocean* (2004–2005, DC/Wildstorm), which relies on 'cine-matic' storytelling techniques similar to those Ellis deployed as part of his *Ultimate Fantastic Four* run. One blogger acknowledged that the slow-paced sci-fi narrative might read well in graphic novel form 'because you know you can read the whole story in one sitting', but concluded that 'reading it in 6 issue chunks [via monthly comic-book consumption] is unbelievably frustrating'.[141]

Due to the deliberate pacing that the storytelling necessitates, such negative receptions among dedicated consumers to 'cinematic' narrative styles have been common in the twenty-first century, with readers fre-quently venting ire in blog posts and on message boards.[142] Nevertheless, by permitting the immoderate implementation of 'cinematic' techniques, publishers strengthen the association between the culturally marginalised comic-book industry and the more popular medium of film. Narrative designers, through this style, support their aims, and those of their pub-lishers, to lend relevance to comic-book narratives within the larger public sphere. But, while the 'cinematic' style specifically serves the perceived requirements of the wider audiences that publishers seek, so too does the accompanying slow-paced plots that have so irked many periodical read-ers. As the above reader feedback regarding *Ocean* suggests, unhurried pacing has the capacity to suit the collected edition in particular (due to the format's far greater page length). That narrative designers have been permitted to plot serial storylines in ways that can be perceived as more appropriate for consumption via collected editions reflects the precedence publishers have given to nurturing the collected edition market and its potential for widening audiences. The following section explores further the processes of plotting within the inclusivity era, ascertaining the degree to which the perceived requirements of the collected edition format and a potential casual readership have influenced approaches to serial storytelling.

MARSHALLING CONFLICT: SERIAL PLOTS IN THE INCLUSIVITY ERA

The growth in relevance of the collected edition market in the twenty-first century has strongly influenced narrative designers' plotting of distinct serial storylines, or 'arcs' as they are referred to within the industry. A key resulting narrative production practice is that arcs of ongoing series are now often conceived and plotted not only to provide dedicated readers with serial narratives but also to support their future publication in collected editions. To help demonstrate this significant shift in storytelling technique, this section first provides a point of comparison via its analysis of plotting methods within the era of direct market dominance. As noted previously, serial narrative pervaded this era, but it will be useful for this section's purposes to distinguish between the distinct serial plot types of the period. To this end, the below taxonomy of serial plotting methods in the 1980s and 1990s observes this range of techniques and also notes how it complemented the perceived requirements of a dedicated audience.

- *Single-issue storyline.* A 'one-and-done' conflict contained within the boundary of an individual issue. Example: *Batman* #487 (1992), in which the Dark Knight thwarts an assassination attempt on Commissioner Gordon. Reflecting publishers' focus on serving a dedicated readership, single-issue storylines had become, by the 1990s, the exception to the rule of multiple-issue storylines.
- *Same-series arcs.* A distinct storyline told over multiple consecutive issues of the *same* series. Example: *Incredible Hulk* #421–423 (1994), in which the Hulk is transported to Asgard to fight various Nordic mythological adversaries (in an arc entitled, 'Myth of Conceptions'). Lengths of same-series arcs in this period are highly variable. In

1994, for example, the *Incredible Hulk* series comprised a two-parter, a three-parter and a four-parter (and three single-issue storylines also).

- *Crossover arc.* A distinct storyline plotted over multiple consecutive issues of multiple separate series. Example: DC's four-part 'Gorilla Warfare' arc (1992), wherein The Flash and Green Lantern team up to do battle with Gorilla Grodd. First and third instalments appear in the pages of *Green Lantern* (#30–31, Vol. 3), while second and fourth instalments of the storyline were published in *Flash* (#69–70, Vol. 2).

- *Crossover event.* An epic, often non-linear and multiple-stranded conflict plotted across an array of titles. By the 1990s, crossover events represented highly complex narrative networks, containing multiple interlocking storylines under the banner of a single designation. Example: Marvel's 'Onslaught' event (1996). One of this event's storylines, concerning Mister Sinister's opaque attempts to shield X-Man from Onslaught (the villain of the piece) appears in the pages of *X-Man* and *X-Force*. But, published within a similar time frame, a parallel storyline concerning Onslaught's abduction of Franklin Richards threads through issues of *Cable*, *Fantastic Four*, *X-Men* and *Uncanny X-Men*, with both storylines subsequently merging within the pages of *X-Men* #56.[143] Such complicated plots oblige readers to buy multiple issues from a range of different series within the space of a few months so as to discern narrative coherence.

- *Subsidiary storyline.* A distinct storyline operating parallel to single/multiple-issue conflicts. These storylines occupy less page space per issue than a primary conflict but they often endure for far longer. Example: a mystery surrounding the reappearance of Peter Parker's parents is drip-fed through a 22-issue *Amazing Spider-Man* run of single-issue storylines, same-series arcs and crossover arcs in the early 1990s.[144] Such storylines provide readers an extra incentive to continue purchasing from one arc to the next.

In the inclusivity era, narrative designers still rely on these methods of plotting to greater or lesser degrees, but the ways in which they are utilised are often shaped by consideration for the collected edition format. Narrative designers usually regiment a given series in such a way as to ensure that each collected edition volume incorporates at least one complete arc (and no incomplete arcs). At Marvel, at least, this has been editorially enforced. 'The real goal starting from day one of my term as [editor-in-chief, in 2000]', Quesada recalls, 'was to make sure that every book is ... written with [collected editions] in mind.'[145] As part of this obligation to keep the collected edition format 'in mind', writers, according to Quesada, would be expected to ensure that each collected edition volume contains a 'complete story', or, more specifically, a distinct arc.[146]

The technique of ensuring that arcs are contained within the boundaries of a collected edition (and not segmented over multiple collected-edition volumes) is appropriate for the graphic novel format (and thus also potential new readers) in two distinct regards. Firstly, the practice complements the frequency by which publishers put out the collected edition volumes of an ongoing series (usually every five or six months). Just as television drama series producers plot sub-conflicts so as to begin and end in between hiatuses in season transmission (see Chap. 3), comic-book writers ensure that those reading a series via collected editions are not obliged to wait half a year for the continuation of a distinct dramatic conflict. Secondly, this plotting ensures that, while the narrative of a given periodical issue is still appropriate for the dedicated consumer, the narrative of the collected edition is suited to the requirements of the casual consumer. The given periodical issue of an ongoing series still, then, (usually) represents a serial instalment of an arc and encourages continued investment. In contrast, a given collected edition, absent of incomplete dramatic conflicts, offers a high degree of narrative coherence and is appropriate for sought-after casual consumers.

The methods by which editors paratextually parcel these narratives as collected editions indicate the imperative publishers place on conveying each collected edition as a coherent narrative experience. *Action Comics* #866–870 (2008), for example, represents a sequence of issues in which, among other events (concerning, for example, Supergirl and Pa Kent), the intergalactic hoarder Brainiac attempts to acquire Superman. For the marketing of the collected edition of this arc, DC focussed solely on this conflict, distilling it to its elemental core; the collection is branded as *Superman: Brainiac,* with the title complemented by Gary Frank's cover art, which depicts the long-time foes squaring off.

Many writers in the inclusivity era have complemented the publishers' tactic of marketing collected editions as discrete storylines by favouring five- and six-issue arcs (which are regular lengths for the collected edition format). As writer J. Michael Straczynski acknowledged (in 2004), 'I'm writing most of my stories these days in six-issue arcs … because they work well that way for the trades.'[147] This preference for five/six-issue arcs results in many collected editions in the inclusivity era each containing a single coherent storyline, and is in sync with publishers' aims. Such plotting practices contrast with those of the late twentieth century, when a given ongoing series would likely have comprised a combination of single-issue storylines, fragments of crossover arcs and same-series arcs varying in length. In the inclusivity era ongoing series are often instead dominated by successions of five/six-issue same-series arcs. A comparison between Marvel's *The Punisher* in the late 1980s/early 1990s (see Fig. 4.1) with that of the 2000s (see Fig. 4.2) emphasises such discrepancies in plotting during the two eras. But it also speaks to the way in which the collected edition format has shaped the plotting of ongoing series in the inclusivity era. While the earlier *Punisher* run is primarily broken down into one and two same-series conflicts, with five- and six-issue same-series arcs being the exception, the first 42 issues of the latter *Punisher* run is configured neatly into seven six-issue same-series arcs.

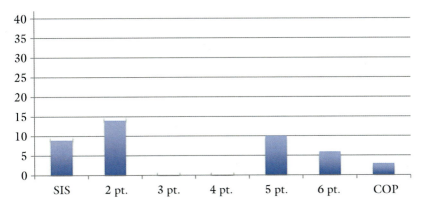

Fig. 4.1 *The Punisher*, Vol. 2 #1–42 (1987–1990). Horizontal axis determines to which category of storyline a sample issue belongs; that is, whether a sample issue represents a single-issue storyline (SIS), part of a multi-part same-series arc (2 pt., 3 pt., etc.) or a part of a crossover arc (COP). Vertical axis measures the amount of sample issues within each category

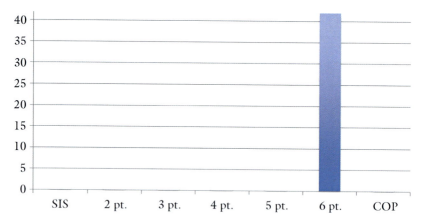

Fig. 4.2 *The Punisher*, Vol. 6 #1–42 (2004–2007)

Statistical analysis of early issues from Marvel's reprise of the *X-Men* series in the early 1990s, and those of two X-Men related series launched in the 2000s, reveals a similar contrast between the respective plot lengths of the two eras. The first 25 issues of *X-Men* (1991–1993) are composed of same-series arcs, two four-issues in length, and various instalments of crossover arcs (Fig. 4.3). In contrast, the first 25 issues of both *Ultimate X-Men* and *Astonishing X-Men* (2001–2003 and 2004–2008, respectively) reveal a clear bias towards five/six-issue arcs (Figs. 4.4 and 4.5). These latter two series plots thus complement the collected edition formatting process.

While many narrative designers in the inclusivity era utilise the five/six-issue arc as a default unit of plotting, it is important to acknowledge that others operate via different methods. Ellis, for example, opted (against type) to arrange his quirky satire of superhero teams, *Nextwave: Agents of H.A.T.E.* (Marvel, 2006–2007), into successive two-issue same-series arcs. The plotting of the series into punchy, two-part blasts is well suited to the frenetic saga; as Ellis proclaims, 'NEXTWAVE is not about Character Arcs and Learning and Morals and Hugs … It is most especially about THINGS BLOWING UP and PEOPLE GETTING KICKED.'[148] But, as the writer's 'pitch' document for the series reveals, consideration for the compatibility of *Nextwave*'s plot with the requirements of the collected edition still permeated the project's conception process. As part of the pitch, Ellis proposed the standard structure of two-issue arcs and suggested to Marvel

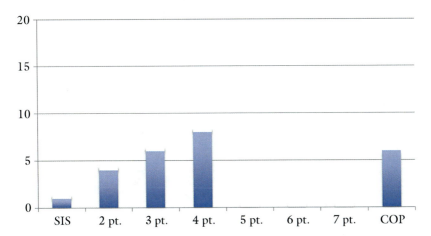

Fig. 4.3   *X-Men*, Vol. 2 #1–25 (1991–1993)

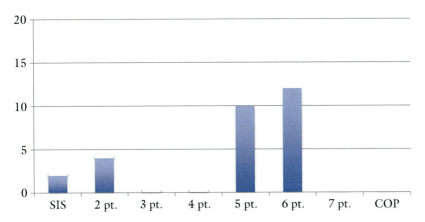

Fig. 4.4   *Ultimate X-Men* #1–25 (2001–2003)

editors that each consecutive trio of arcs be repackaged as collected editions (a suggestion that Marvel subsequently acted upon).[149] While, then, variability in arc-lengths can be discerned, the obligation to provide narratives appropriate to the collected edition format nevertheless holds strong influence over series plotting in the inclusivity era.

The ways in which company-wide crossover events are plotted also strongly reflect the requirements of the collected edition market. These

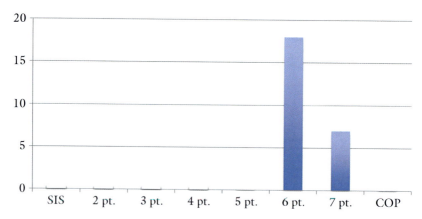

Fig. 4.5 *Astonishing X-Men,* Vol. 2 #1–24 (2004–2008), plus *Giant-Size Astonishing X-Men* #1 (2008)

immense storylines continue to be a vital element of direct market sales, with issues from crossover event mini-series usually ranking among a given year's bestselling items.[150] But, in contrast with the era of direct market dominance, narrative designers in the inclusivity era, in their plotting of these colossal events, often make efforts to cater simultaneously for both dedicated and casual modes of consumption. Marvel's 'Secret Invasion' event (2008) provides an example of such an approach. Over 100 periodical issues, taken from dozens of different series, incorporate the 'Secret Invasion' banner on their covers, with each contributing to this behemoth narrative in which the alien Skrull-race attacks Earth. Yet much of the overall event is organised into self-contained narrative units that complement the central storyline but that readers are able to comprehend in isolation also.

For example, Marvel published myriad mini-series, such as *Secret Invasion: Inhumans* and *Secret Invasion: X-Men* (both 2008), each featuring characters facing their own distinct Skrull-related threat. So whereas *Secret Invasion: Thor* (2008), for example, concerns the Norse deity's defence of small-town Missouri, *Secret Invasion: Frontline* (2008) focuses on a New York cab-driver's fight for survival as a Skrull fleet descends upon Manhattan. While these linear arcs each reflect and acknowledge the meta-arc of the Skrull attack taking place simultaneously across Earth and beyond, they each operate within the boundaries of their respective limited series and do not require readers of one series to invest in another.

Due to this method of plotting, Marvel has subsequently been able to publish collected editions of each of these limited series, with each possessive of a coherent arc. The combination of the distinct storylines that comprise 'Secret Invasion' offers the dedicated reader a remarkable panorama of perspectives upon a single focused period of a storyworld's story time, thus conveying the tremendous scale of the Skrull attack. But the plotting of this prismatic narrative is such that many of its individual components can be extracted and marketed to casual consumers as discrete storylines via collected editions.

The obligation to cater to both dedicated and casual modes of consumption, and more specifically, to ensure that distinct dramatic conflicts are contained within the parameters of single collected editions has therefore influenced the plot structure of ongoing series and crossover events. But the requirement to provide for both new and/or casual consumers also influences the way by which writers engineer and acknowledge the continuity that binds arcs together. Narrative designers in the twenty-first century have, as the next section demonstrates, developed deftly subtle techniques so as to connect a given arc to a greater continuity. By applying such delicate approaches, narrative designers in the inclusivity era provide for the requirements of not only dedicated readers but also new and/or casual consumers.

DELICATE CONNECTIVE TISSUE: IMPLIED CONTINUITY IN THE INCLUSIVITY ERA

In his analysis of the regenerated BBC Television series *Doctor Who* (1963–1989, 2005–present), Matt Hills identifies the subtle way by which the programme's narrative simultaneously meets the requirements of both casual and dedicated viewers.[151] Hills observes that, during Russell T. Davies' tenure as showrunner, individual *Who* episodes, which usually each comprise a standalone conflict, are linked to one another by 'implied story arcs'.[152] These implied arcs do not take the form of linear storylines, but rather they represent the repeated manifestation of a 'specific signifier', planted 'relatively unobtrusively into background details or the dialogue of characters'.[153] Hills suggests that 'this type of narrative does not alienate mainstream audiences who might otherwise feel they are lacking in story knowledge, as it is sufficiently peripheral and marginal ... to potentially not even register for casual viewers'.[154] This approach to storytelling is similar in goal but clearly distinct from the common television-drama plotting technique whereby single episodes comprise both single- and multiple-episode storylines (see Chap. 3).

This notion of *implied* seriality is useful to understanding the methods on which contemporary comic-book narrative designers have relied so as to provide for both new and/or casual consumers. But in contrast with the implied *Who* arcs to which Hills refers, a given comic-book arc (which will likely be put out as—or as part of—a single collected edition subsequent to publication in instalments) is explicitly present rather than implied, taking the form of a clear, linear sequence of depicted events. Any subsidiary storylines that thread through successive arcs of a given series might also be similarly overt. For example, an ongoing subsidiary storyline concerning Spider-Man's relationships with Gwen Stacy and Mary Jane Watson endures through many arcs of *Ultimate Spider-Man* in the 2000s.[155] But narrative designers in the inclusivity era have simultaneously taken a delicate approach in their establishing of a series' storylines within the grander structure of an overarching storyworld. Via this system of *implied continuity*, which utilises the narrative elements of plot and storyworld, narrative designers frequently forgo the copious explicit references to prior events that typify narratives in the era of direct market dominance; instead they subtly allude to continuity. This technique neither threatens the apparent narrative independence of each serialised arc nor alerts new and/or casual consumers to their own ignorance of aspects of continuity, yet it still rewards dedicated readers for their investment of time and money.

One of the means by which implied continuity manifests is through the subtle ways in which some narrative designers reintroduce pre-existent characters to an ongoing narrative. In the era of direct market dominance narrative designers would, as noted earlier, usually reference continuity overtly. Reflecting this practice, writers would, when reintroducing characters, explicitly flag these characters' backstories via expository dialogue and captions, thus calling attention to prior events. *Uncanny X-Men* #294 (1992), which reintroduces Caliban, a former X-Men ally turned enemy, provides such an example. In said issue the troubled mutant makes a dramatic entrance, descending upon X-Men Jean Grey and Scott Summers. As Caliban brawls with Jean and Scott in the subsequent panels, a dialogue exchange references Caliban's backstory. Scott refers to the period in which he, Jean and Caliban stood side by side in the pages of *X-Factor* (#17–24, 1987–1988); 'Caliban, we were friends', he whimpers, his head jammed underneath Caliban's knee. Scott also tells his former ally that

Apocalypse, the villain who had previously tempted Caliban away from the X-Factor team (#24), is no more; 'Apocalypse is *dead*, Caliban—I killed him *myself*.' An editorial note within the same panel reminds readers that said incident occurred in *X-Factor* #68 (1991). During the exchange, Caliban also speaks to his history, bitterly recalling his X-Factor tenure.

That continuity should have been foregrounded in such a way was appropriate for the narrative design conditions of the period in which the issue was written. But, as writer Matt Fraction suggests, 'There are ways to bring [characters] in without the burden of all the decades of continuity.'[156] Fraction demonstrates this as part of his own *Uncanny* run via his retrieval of Simon Trask, the character whose endeavours prove the catalyst for a future conflict between the X-Men and the Dark Avengers (as part of Marvel's 'Utopia' crossover event, published in 2009). In *Uncanny X-Men* #505 (2009), Fraction introduces Trask, an anti-mutant lobbyist, via the depiction of a television campaign-ad for Trask's Humanity Now Coalition. Neither Trask nor the seasoned X-Men viewing the ad acknowledge Trask's prior anti-mutant movement (Humanity's Last Stand), which he led in *The Uncanny X-Men Annual* #19 (1995).[157] Neither is Simon's sibling, Bolivar, who holds a prominent position within X-lore, referred to. Rather, Trask subtly alludes to his brother's legacy as part of his ad rhetoric. 'For years my family name has been synonymous with putting human safety first', he suggests; this claim being an oblique inference to Bolivar's inventing of the Sentinels—the towering robots designed to slaughter mutants only (and leave humans unharmed), and which maintain a consistent presence within X-continuity.[158] Trask's presence within the issue's storyworld, then, along with his non-expository dialogue, merely implies continuity.

By implementing his mode of subtle seriality, Fraction simultaneously serves the contrasting requirements of the different segments of his readership. New and/or casual readers are able to enjoy a storyline seemingly unencumbered with references to backstory, while dedicated readers are provided with the pleasures of not only continuity but also of being 'in the know'. As Fraction, regarding his incorporation of Trask, suggests:

> [These] are rewards for the people who enjoy the heavy continuity. Most readers may not know who [Trask] is—but the long time readers can remember that he's been in the background before ... Only three people might get the joke, so to speak, but it's those three folks who are going to high-five us at conventions for using a rare character that only they remember.[159]

Fraction's reintroduction of this pre-existent character as part of his *Uncanny* run represents one method by which narrative designers can delicately trace connections through the fictional history of a venerable ongoing series. But the writer Brian Michael Bendis, through simultaneous runs on Marvel's *New Avengers* and *Mighty Avengers* series, demonstrates how narrative designers are able to plot continuity between the arcs of distinct ongoing series—but to do so in ways that do not undermine the narrative coherence of each series' storylines. As Bendis observes:

> I thought I could do something subtly unique, and have almost the same story told in *New Avengers* and *Mighty Avengers*, but the points of view were so different that you couldn't even tell it was the same story unless you read both books.[160]

An example of Bendis' technique is apparent in the way that events in the pages of *Mighty Avengers* influence further events in *New Avengers* #32 (2007). In said *New Avengers* issue, the New Avengers super-team, incorporating, among others, Doctor Strange, Spider-Man, and its leader Luke Cage, are flown back from Japan courtesy of Iron Fist Danny Rand's corporate jet. The issue's establishing shot depicts the plane cutting through billowing grey cloud, lit up by strands of lightning; lexica punctuating the issue's pages ('RRRUUMMMMMMMBBBLLLEEEE') invoke the presence of thunder. These stormy conditions function as an apt metaphor for the disharmony within the group dynamic, as the heroes, after having discovered evidence of Skrull infiltration on Earth, accuse one another of being Skrull agents in disguise. Subsequent to these exchanges, the jet engines fail and the piloting Rand crash-lands his aircraft on a Chicago golf course. The cause of engine failure is never made explicit within the series, and the absence of a concrete explanation plays into the characters' ongoing paranoia with regard to a Skrull conspiracy. In the following issue (#33, 2007), for example, Luke suspects that the jet crash was the result of Skrull sabotage.

The *Mighty Avengers'* first arc (#1–6, 2007–2008), the publication of which (in periodical form) was coincident with that of *New Avengers* #32, appears largely unrelated to the events of the *New Avengers* issue. Set in New York City, the arc's conflict depicts the Mighty Avengers, an Iron Man-led superhero team distinct from—and rival to—the New Avengers, attempting to subdue the threat of the villainous robot Ultron. But readers of both the *Mighty* and *New Avengers* are able to infer the ways in which Bendis has events in *Mighty Avengers* determine those of *New Avengers* #32. For example, within *Mighty Avengers* #1–4, Ultron wreaks havoc with global weather patterns via her hijacking of experimental satellite technology, thus creating the hazardous conditions that provide a dramatic backdrop to *New Avengers* #32. Then in *Mighty Avengers* #4, Ultron's switch in tactics provides the explanation for the engine failure on Rand's jet. In said issue, published fourteen days subsequent to the publication of *New Avengers* #32, Ultron unleashes an electromagnetic pulse that disables electronic devices across the US, resulting in the Mighty Avengers racing to catch various aircraft as they drop from the sky. For readers consuming both series, the cause-and-effect between Ultron's action in *Mighty* and the jet engine failure in *New* is easily deduced. While, then, a casual reader is able to consume either one of the same-series arcs in isolation from the other, the dedicated reader is able to discern how each arc interrelates within the wider storyworld.

While Bendis establishes continuity between the two parallel *Avengers* arcs via a deftly plotted causal chain of events, the writer Grant Morrison and illustrator Frank Quitely subtly establish the *Batman & Robin* series as part of DC's greater serial structure via the use of the storyworld's setting. As Karen Lury observes of soap opera, recurrent storyworld locations 'can, for the long-term viewer, become imbued with a series of visually inspired memories of different characters and plot lines', emphasising the continuity that these storyworld components share.[161] Morrison and Quitely, in their retrieval of a particular environment from Batman mythology, rely on the resonating power of storyworld settings as a means to faintly contextualise *Batman & Robin*'s maiden arc, 'Batman Reborn' (#1–3, 2009), within Bat-related history.[162]

In said arc, Batman battles Professor Pyg, a deranged, snout-faced adversary holed up at a dilapidated amusement park. This same-series arc represents Pyg's first appearance in DC narrative and also Dick Grayson's first outing under the Bat cowl (after having replaced a deceased Bruce Wayne). But, contrasting with the newness of both this Batman and his opponent, the amusement park setting is resurrected from the 1988 OGN *Batman: The Killing Joke*. In this earlier narrative, by Alan Moore (writer) and Brian Bolland (penciller), the Caped Crusader's enduring nemesis, the Joker, acquires an amusement park, subsequently utilising its ghost train as part of his elaborate torture of Commissioner Gordon. The storyworld events of 'Batman Reborn' bear little relation to those of *The Killing Joke* but Morrison and Quitely's choice of setting emphasises the vast sequence of events that connect the two storylines. Quitely's depictions of the amusement park environment are sometimes acutely similar to those of *The Killing Joke*; for example, his ghost train façade, which features the word 'GHOST TRAIN' spelled out in blood red letters and imposed upon a dingy white/yellow background, is near identical to Bolland's. Such recreations of Bolland's original depictions of the same setting signal to dedicated readers this particular link between the two narratives.

This implied connection between *The Killing Joke* and the 'Batman Reborn' arc is further invoked by the latter's final issue (#3). Subsequent to Batman and Robin defeating Pyg and his menacing circus troupe, Commissioner Gordon oversees the police round-up of Pyg's henchmen at the amusement park. In a dialogue exchange with Batman, Gordon mutters in an aside, 'I hate this place'. For the reader unfamiliar with Gordon's biography, the commissioner's unremarked upon comment might be slightly baffling, but would do little to derail the new and/or casual readers' comprehension of the arc's sequence of events. But, for the dedicated consumer, Gordon's comment accentuates the continuity shared between the arc and *The Killing Joke*. *Batman & Robin*'s subtle allusion to *The Killing Joke* reflects Morrison's philosophies regarding continuity, which he suggests should merely operate as 'background window dressing' within a given narrative so as not to turn off newcomers.[163]

Within these examples, narrative designers—through the particular ways they present events, characters and setting—subtly imply links within the vast chronological event sequences that populate superhero storyworlds. Such connections operate on what Allen refers to as a *syntagmatic* axis of the narrative, that is, connections form via chains of events.[164] Simon Trask's most recent bout of anti-mutant campaigning within the pages of *Uncanny*, for example, represents a continuation of his earlier efforts; Ultron's EPM detonation in *Mighty Avengers* is shown not only to precede but also to cause the jet crash in *New Avengers*; Commissioner Gordon's display of antipathy towards Gotham's condemned fairground is subsequent to and a consequence of his earlier ordeal. But contemporary narrative designers also imply layers of seriality across what Allen refers to as the *paradigmatic* narrative axis, wherein association between distinct storylines are not tied to a chronology of depicted events, but are instead dependent on an inferred thematic parallelism.[165]

Such paradigmatic seriality is in evidence, for example, in the implied continuity between the *Batman & Robin* series and DC's 'Blackest Night' crossover event (2009–2010). In the latter narrative, Green

Lantern and his allies defend the universe from a possessed legion of heroes and villains resurrected from their graves. In the sixth issue of the eight-part *Blackest Night* mini-series, published February 2010, Bruce Wayne rises to join the undead's fold in Coast City, California. The first issue of Morrison's slyly titled 'Blackest Knight' arc in *Batman & Robin* (#7–9) landed in stores the following month. Within said issue, Batman (Dick Grayson) attempts to bring a deceased Bruce Wayne clone back to life courtesy of a 'Lazarus pit' located in a Northumbrian mine. In the subsequent issue, the reanimated Wayne-clone proves to be a demented zombie, resulting in Batman having to quell the threat. According to Morrison, his arc was designed to complement 'Blackest Night'. But, 'rather than tie directly into the main event', he recalls, 'we chose to reflect it in a more thematic way with this story of a walking dead man'.[166]

While the events of the 'Blackest Knight' arc fail to directly link to those of the 'Blackest Night' plot via the syntagmatic axis, their shared similarities in storyworld theme encourage dedicated DC readers to invoke a paradigmatic association between the two different storylines. The coincidence in publication times of the respective periodicals further encouraged this paradigmatic link. So too did Frank Quitely's cover art for the first issue of said *Batman and Robin* arc, which features a portrait of the eerie, undead Batman. But, crucially, due to the subtlety of Morrison's acknowledgement of continuity, the casual *Batman & Robin* reader can enjoy the 'Blackest Knight' storyline as a self-contained dramatic conflict without even having to be made aware of the Green Lantern's battles with raised corpses in *Blackest Night*.

A more recent Batman storyline, 'The Court of Owls', provides a further example of this practice of implied continuity via paradigmatic association. The run of *Batman* issues that includes the arc (#1–12, 2011–2012) formed part of DC Comics' New 52. While most DC characters, as part of this initiative, had their histories streamlined, the Batman backstory was exempted from this continuity-simplification process. As Batman writer Scott Snyder stressed shortly after the comic-book line reboot, in contrast to the likes of Superman, many of the significant events that the Caped Crusader had experienced within the prior universe would remain part of DC's newly-created continuity.[167] But Snyder, who took charge of the *Batman* title as part of the New 52 launch, nevertheless ensured that his storytelling approach complemented DC's aim of appealing to new audiences. With the relaunched title, he elected to avoid obvious references to recent and significant storyworld incidents—such as Bruce Wayne's death, along with his subsequent resurrection and reclamation of the Batman identity (in *Batman: The Return of Bruce Wayne*, 2010)—so that 'new fans' would not 'trip over' such potentially confusing material.[168]

Yet, despite his decision not to place any emphasis on continuity in 'The Court of Owls', Snyder did aim to more subtly engage dedicated readers through the establishing of thematic connections with antecedent Batman narratives. The arc concerns Batman's battle with the Court of Owls, a secret criminal society that includes a cadre of deadly assassins—dubbed 'Talons'—within its membership. While the Court—a Snyder creation—is revealed to have manipulated Gotham for centuries, this story arc marks its debut within DC fiction. But 'The Court of Owls' was nonetheless strongly inspired by previous storylines concerning owl-themed characterisations scattered throughout Batman's prior history. 'Everything is a re-imagining of the elements that went into Owl villains [and other characters] in Batman', notes Snyder; 'the whole story, honestly, came flowing out of that'.[169]

Early in 'The Court of Owls', for example, Batman discovers (misleading) evidence suggesting that Dick Grayson (since returned to his Nightwing role) was a former Talon. This plot point evokes the theme of a *Batman* issue storyline published decades previous (#107, 1957) in which a young Dick temporarily adopts the persona of 'Owlman'. As Snyder acknowledges, this type of paradigmatic association is deliberately intended to engage and reward the dedicated reader: 'Within the story itself, the history of Gotham is brought against the heroes of the present ... And then for readers of Batman and lovers of Batman and the Bat-mythology, there are story elements that feel that way on a meta-level, you know? It's like, "Hey, I remember that issue where Robin was Owlman. Look at this, now Dick was supposed to have been a Talon".' But by relying on subtle evocations of thematic continuity—which are unlikely to even register with a new/casual readership—as a means to address loyal and knowledgeable consumers, Snyder is still able to meet his objective of crafting coherent, self-contained story arcs. He ensures therefore that his narratives are also appropriate for those readers less committed to Batman's rich and highly complex storyworld.

CONCLUSION

By demonstrating how comic-book narrative designers have adjusted techniques in accordance with publishers' audience-targeting methods this century, this chapter underlines the relevance of audience specificity to narrative design conditions and processes. The gearing of narrative production to address the perceived requirements of audiences previously neglected, in addition to maintaining an address to dedicated consumers, has influenced many aspects of narrative. Changes in narrative design conditions and processes have informed, for example, increases in serial plot durations, the widespread use of a remediated 'cinematic' style, and significant storyworld changes, such as the MU's clear increase in gender, racial, ethnic and generational diversity. The chapter confirms that the variability of target audiences within a medium can hold important implications for storyworlds and their presentations. It therefore indicates that consideration of the relationship between a narrative and its medium's specificity should take into account both the variability of audiences within that medium, and its range of institutionally configured audience-targeting strategies.

As this chapter also demonstrates, the collected edition has so far this century proved a central part of comic-book publishers' efforts to reach consumers beyond the direct market, going on to become the biggest-selling format for the industry. Related to the format's industrial significance, many approaches to narrative production discussed above—such as the designing of storyworlds so as to appeal to (mass-market bookstore-dwelling) manga readers and the plotting of ongoing series so as to complement their publication in collected edition form—are closely tied to the collected edition's emergence in the 2000s. As the US comic-book industry continues to evolve, it will be useful to further trace connections between publishers' priorities in the marketplace and the narratives these companies disseminate. As publishers look to increasingly expand the digital comics sector, it will be crucial for scholarship to examine, in particular, how publishers' continued development of digital formats and platforms influences future narrative design conditions and processes. The following chapter carries over this concern for the manner by which industries exploit digital technologies; shifting attention to the console videogame marketplace, it explores how publishers' dependence on the perpetual upgrading of digital tech informs videogame narrative.

NOTES

1. This distribution method reflects the comic-book industry's cultural links with the newspaper trade. The industrialised production of comics narrative in the US dates back to the 1890s with the newspaper publication of syndicated humour strips, while the first periodical comic books were reprint compilations of such 'funnies'. Bradford W. Wright, *Comic Book Nation* (Baltimore: Johns Hopkins University Press, 2001), 2, 4.

2. Matthew J. Pustz, *Comic Book Culture: Fanboys and True Believers* (Jackson: University Press of Mississippi, 1999), 131–132; Wright, *Comic Book Nation*, 278.

3. The term 'graphic novel' is popularly used to denote a publication within the medium of comics that is distinguished from standard periodical comic books by its greater bulk and its card or hardback cover. See Charles Hatfield, *Alternative Comics: An Emerging Literature* (Jackson: University Press of Mississippi, 2005), 29; Robert C. Harvey, *The Art of the Funnies: An Aesthetic History* (Jackson: University Press of Mississippi, 1994), 116.

4. In the 2000s, for example, the two publishers' combined comic-book store market share ranged between 60 and 80 per cent (approx.). John Jackson Miller, 'December 2009 Top Sellers: *Blackest Night* Finishes Year on Top', *The Comichron*, 27 January 2010, http://blog.comichron.com/2010/01/december-2009-top-sellers-blackest.html.

5. Wright suggests that the dominance of the superhero genre since the 1960s is attributable to the rise of television as a mass medium. 'In an era of extremely limited special-effects technology (in TV), comic books could present fantastic visual imagery more imaginatively than could a live-action medium.' Wright, *Comic Book Nation*, 183–184. An exception to this rule of superhero ubiquity would be the storyworlds of the alternative/independent comics movement that grew out of the 1970s. For narrative analyses and a cultural history of this distinct scene, see Hatfield, *Alternative Comics*.

6. The origins of pulp's influence on comic books can be traced to *Detective Comics* #1 (1937). The series (which would go on introduce Batman) was, as Wright observes, distinguished from its funnies-dominated rival publications due to its emphasis on mystery and adventure tales derivative of American pulp fiction magazines. Wright, *Comic Book Nation*, 5.

7. US newspaper comic-strips had, in contrast, featured serial storylines since the early 1900s. See Jared Gardner, *Projections: Comics and the History of Twenty-First Century Storytelling* (Stanford, CA: Stanford University Press, 2012), 40–67.

8. Umberto Eco, *The Role of the Reader: Explorations in the Semiotic in Texts* (London: Hutchinson & Co., 1981), 117.

9. Ibid., 113–114.

10. Dennis O'Neil, *The DC Comics Guide to Writing Comics* (New York: Watson-Guptill, 2001), 95–96. See also Henry Jenkins, 'Best Contemporary Mainstream Superhero Comics Writer: Brian Michael Bendis', in *Beautiful Things in Popular Culture*, ed. Alan McKee (Malden, MA: Blackwell, 2007), 23; Henry Jenkins, '"Just Men in Tights": Rewriting Silver Age Comics in an Era of Multiplicity', in *The*

Contemporary Comic Book Superhero, ed. Angela Ndalianis (New York: Routledge, 2009), 20.

11. Roberta E. Pearson and William Uricchio, 'Notes from the Batcave: An Interview with Dennis O'Neil', in *The Many Lives of the Batman: Critical Approaches to a Superhero and His Media*, ed. Roberta E. Pearson and William Uricchio (New York: Routledge, 1991), 24.

12. See Pustz on the transitory status of comic books pre-1960. Pustz, *Comic Book Culture*, 15.

13. By the mid-1960s some bookstores began to sate this demand by specialising in the sale of back issues. Ibid.

14. See Paul Lopes, *Demanding Respect: The Evolution of the American Comic Book* (Philadelphia: Temple University Press, 2009), 93.

15. The *Avengers* narrative suggests that, following the Second World War, Cap had been preserved in ice.

16. See O'Neil on continuity practices. O'Neil, *The DC Comics Guide to Writing Comics*, 113.

17. Catherine Saunders, Heather Scott, Julia March and Alistair Dougall, *Marvel Chronicle: A Year by Year History* (London: DK, 2008), 108. For Marvel, such demands reflected the company's strategy of encouraging reader feedback as a means to increase consumer engagement. See Gardner, *Projections*, 112–113.

18. As the cost of printing was outweighed by the investment into editorial production (writing, pencils, colours, etc.) it made sense that publishers used large print runs to ensure a strong newsstand presence. Chuck Rozanski, 'Evolution of the Direct Market: Part One', *Mile High Comics*, November 2003, http://www.milehighcomics.com/tales/cbg95.html.

19. See Wright, *Comic Book Nation*, 261.

20. See Pustz, *Comic-Book Culture*, 15.

21. Wright, *Comic Book Nation*, 262.

22. See ibid., 278; Pustz, *Comic Book Culture*, 131–132.

23. The five series through which 'Maximum Carnage' plays out are *Spider-Man*, *Web of Spider-Man*, *Spectacular Spider-Man*, *Spider-Man Unlimited* and *The Amazing Spider-Man*.

24. The pair cite prior events within continuity, including instances of Dick's impetuousness and ill-discipline (Bruce: 'When *you* didn't listen to me, *your* injuries weren't fatal'), Bruce's removal of Dick from the Robin role (Bruce: 'I would have had to *fire him* [Jason] as I did you') and Dick's chagrin at Bruce having adopted Jason (Bruce: '*You* told me you resented it that I had adopted *him* and not you').

25. Pustz, *Comic Book Culture*, 134.

26. See Wright, *Comic Book Nation*, 280.

27. Pustz, *Comic Book Culture*, 134.

28. Wright, *Comic Book Nation*, 280.

29. Ibid., 283.

30. Sean T. Collins, 'The Amazing! Incredible! Uncanny Oral History of Marvel Comics', *Maxim*, 12 August 2009, http://www.maxim.com/amg/humor/stupid-fun/83588/amazing-incredible-uncanny-oral-history-marvel-comics.html.

31. Pustz, *Comic Book Culture*, 209.

32. Ibid., 23.

33. Milton Griepp, '20 Questions: Paul Levitz, Part II: DC's Executive VP Talks About the Comic Business', *ICv2*, 10 March 2001, http://www.icv2.com/articles/indepth/759.html.

34. See Wright, *Comic Book Nation*, 3.

35. Veteran writer/illustrator Will Eisner popularised the label in the late 1970s, using it to market his anthology project, *A Contract with God* (1978).

36. Hatfield, *Alternative Comics*, 29.

37. Nat Gerter and Steve Lieber, *The Complete Idiot's Guide to Creating a Graphic Novel* (New York: Alpha Books, 2004), 9–11.

38. This physical format became known as the 'prestige format'. The unique titles for each instalment are (in order), 'The Dark Knight Returns', 'Dark Knight Triumphant', 'Hunt the Dark Knight' and 'The Dark Knight Falls'.

39. Robert Greenburger (ed.), *Batman in the Eighties* (New York: DC, 2004), 185.

40. A 1988 *Time* magazine article illustrates the low status of comic-book culture in this period; it claims 'comic-book' has, as a definitional label, 'suggestions of arrested adolescent development'. Jay Cocks and John E. Gallagher, 'The Passing of Pow! And Blam!', *Time*, 25 January 1988, http://www.time.com/time/magazine/article/0,9171,966542-1,00.html.

41. See Wright, *Comic Book Nation*, 267; Will Brooker, 'The Best Batman Story: *The Dark Knight Returns*', in *Beautiful Things*, ed. McKee, 41.

42. Mordecai Richler, 'Batman at Midlife: Or the Funnies Grow Up', *The New York Times*, 3 May 1987, 35 (section 7).

43. Mittell, *Complex TV*, 37.

44. Ibid.

45. Hatfield, *Alternative Comics*, 30.

46. Brooker, 'The Best Batman Story', 43.

47. Tom Spurgeon, 'CR Holiday Interview #12: Karen Berger', *The Comics Reporter*, 6 January 2008, http://www.comicsreporter.com/index.php/cr_holiday_interview_13/.

48. For example, the publisher ensured that each issue of *JLA* (a late 1990s rebranded Justice League of America series) was reformatted into collected editions.

49. Anon., 'Graphic Novels by the Numbers', *Publishers Weekly*, 3 May 2007, http://www.publishersweekly.com/pw/print/20070305/4192-graphic-novels-by-the-numbers-.html.

50. In comparison, the dollar sales for the top 300 comic books from each month distributed to speciality stores in 2001 totalled $186.98 million. John Jackson Miller, 'Comic Book Sales by Year', *Chomichron*, n.d., http://www.comichron.com/yearlycomicssales.html.

51. Anon., 'Marvel Ratchets Up Book Production', *ICv2*, 12 March 2001, http://www.icv2.com/articles/news/220.html; John Rhett Thomas, *Marvel Backlist Chronology* (New York: Marvel, 2011).

52. John Jackson Miller, 'Comics and Graphic Novels Up 5% in 2016', *Comichron*, n.d., http://www.comichron.com/yearlycomicssales/industrywide/2016-industrywide.html.

53. Alisa Perren, 'Up, Up, and Away? Separating Fact from Fiction in the Comic Book Business', *FlowTV*, 21 August 2008, http://flowtv.org/?p=1635.

54. Griepp, '20 Questions: Paul Levitz'.

55. Owen Vaughan, 'An Interview with Spider-Man's Boss, Marvel Chief Joe Quesada', *The Times*, 21 March 2009, http://www.thetimes.co.uk/tto/arts/books/article2454472.ece.

56. Ibid.

57. Anon., 'Interview with DC's Paul Levitz, Part II: On Comics, Movies and Possibly Manga', *ICv2*, 24 September 2003, http://www.icv2.com/articles/news/3552.html.

58. Warren Ellis, 'Come in Alone: Issue 18', *Comic Book Resources*, 31 March 2000, http://www.comicbookresources.com/?page=article&id=13272.

59. Robert Taylor, 'Reflections: Talking with Jeph Loeb', *Comic Book Resources*, 25 October 2006, http://www.comicbookresources.com/?page=article&id=8426.

60. Douglas Wolk and Calvin Reid, 'Graphic Novels, Tie-Ins Highlight Comic-Con', *Publishers Weekly*, 30 July 2001, 16.

61. Grant Morrison, 'Morrison Manifesto', in *New X-Men* Ultimate Collection Vol. 3, by Grant Morrison (New York: Marvel, 2008).

62. See Daniel M. Goodbrey, 'Distortions in Spacetime: Emergent Narrative Practices in Comics' Transition from Print to Screen', in *Storytelling in the Media Convergence Age: Exploring Screen Narratives*, ed. Roberta Pearson and Anthony N. Smith (Basingstoke: Palgrave Macmillan, 2015), 57.

63. Darren Wershler and Kalervo A. Sinervo, 'Marvel and the Form of Motion Comics', in *Make Ours Marvel: Media Convergence and a Comics Universe*, ed. Matt Yockey (Austin: University of Texas Press, 2017), 193.

64. Seth Rosenblatt, 'Digital comics successful sidekick to print, say publishers', *CNET*, 20 July 2013, http://www.cnet.com/uk/news/digital-comics-successful-sidekick-to-print-say-publishers/; Miller, 'Comics and graphic novel market'; Miller, 'Comics and Graphic Novels Up 5% in 2016'.

65. Heidi McDonald, 'DC's Rood Breaks Down Reader Survey', *Publishers Weekly*, 14 February 2012, http://www.publishersweekly.com/pw/by-topic/booknews/comics/article/50633-dc-s-rood-breaks-down-reader-survey.html.

66. Goodbrey, 'Distortions in Spacetime', 57; see also, T. Campbell, *The History of Webcomics* (San Antonio: Antarctic Press, 2006), 15.

67. See Goodbrey, 'Distortions in Spacetime', 60; Wershler and Sinervo, 'Marvel and the Form of Motion Comics', 198–199.

68. 'Infinite Comics', Marvel.com, http://marvel.com/comics/discover/451/infinite-comics.

69. Goodbrey, 'Distortions in Spacetime', 62.

70. Ibid., 58.

71. The company had carried out a less comprehensive simplification of continuity in 1986.

72. The New 52 moniker reflects the number of #1 books DC simultaneously launched as part of the initiative.

73. Melissa Block, 'Several DC Comics Go Back To Issue No. 1', *NPR*, 31 August 2011, http://www.npr.org/2011/08/31/140093549/several-dc-comics-go-back-to-issue-no-1.

74. Aja Romano, 'DC Comics Steps Up Its Diversity Efforts With "DC You: Lineup"', *The Daily Dot*, 9 July 2015, https://www.dailydot.com/parsec/dan-didio-emphasizes-diversity-in-dc-you-lineup-sdcc/.

75. Albert Ching, 'Alonso on Why the Time is Right for the Marvel NOW! Revamp', *Newsarama*, 5 July 2012, https://www.newsarama.com/9763-alonso-on-why-the-time-is-right-for-the-marvel-now-revamp.html.

76. Noelene Clark, 'Marvel Comics Shaking Up its Superhero Roster to Attract New Readers', *Los Angeles Times*, 4 June 2015, http://www.latimes.com/entertainment/herocomplex/la-et-hc-marvel-comics-axel-alonso-all-new-all-different-lineup-20150603-story.html.

77. Ching, 'Alonso on Why the Time is Right'.

78. Official Press Release, 'DC Entertainment Reveals First Details of "Rebirth" to Retailers at Comics Pro 2016', DC Comics, 18 February 2016, http://www.dccomics.com/blog/2016/02/18/dc-entertainment-reveals-first-details-of-"rebirth"-to-retailers-at-comics-pro-2016.

79. Albert Ching, 'Exclusive: Geoff Johns Details "Rebirth" Plan, Seeks to Restore Legacy to DC Universe', *Comic Book Resources*, 18 February 2016, http://www.cbr.com/exclusive-geoff-johns-details-rebirth-plan-seeks-to-restore-legacy-to-dc-universe/.

80. Clark, 'Marvel Comics Shaking Up its Superhero Roster'.

81. Jenkins discusses further this trend within the industry for multiple parallel superhero universes. Jenkins, '"Just Men in Tights"', 16–42. Sam Ford and Henry Jenkins, 'Managing Multiplicity in Superhero Comics: An Interview with Henry Jenkins', in *Third Person: Authoring and Exploring Vast Narratives*, ed. Pat Harrigan and Noah Wardrip-Fruin (Cambridge, MA: MIT Press, 2009), 303–311.

82. Via his account of Marvel Comics' 'Share Your Universe' promotional campaign, Derek Johnson provides a further example of the way in which the publisher has aimed to strengthen its cross-generational appeal. Derek Johnson, '"Share Your Universe": Generation, Gender, and the Future of Marvel Publishing', in *Make Ours Marvel*, ed. Yockey, 138–163.

83. The exception would be Vertigo's *The Books of Magic* (Vol. 2, 1994–2000). The series is in a similar gothic vein as *Sandman* (both having been created by Neil Gaiman). The *Sandman* audience was, unusually for the industry, well represented by a female demographic (which made up approximately 50 per cent of the readership). Anon., 'DC SVP Karen Berger on Minx', *ICv2*, 30 November 2006, http://www.icv2.com/articles/news/9697.html.

84. First Comics published *Lone Wolf and Cub* from 1987, for example, while Epic published *Akira* from 1989.

85. For a detailed history of the growth of the Japanese manga market in the US, see Casey Brienza, *Manga in America: Transnational Book Publishing and the Domestication of Japanese Comics* (London: Bloomsbury, 2016), 50–67.

86. Marvel provided a more general (and ironic) address to the manga market with its 'Marvel Mangaverse' line, which, notes Jenkins, 'reimagined and resituated [Marvel's] stable of superheroes within Japanese genre traditions'. The line reinterpreted, for example, Spider-Man as a Ninja and expanded the Hulk to Godzilla proportions. Henry Jenkins, *Convergence Culture* (New York: New York University Press, 2006), 112.

87. Anon., 'Interview with Marvel Publisher Dan Buckley 2005, Part 4: Reaching Girls; A Comic Movie Bubble?', *ICv2*, 22 August 2005, http://www.icv2.com/articles/news/7397.html.

88. This lineage includes such teams as Marvel's New Warriors and DC's Teen Titans.

89. Anon., 'Interview with Marvel Publisher Dan Buckley 2005, Part 1: On the Comics and Graphic Novel Market', *ICv2*, 22 August 2005, http://www.icv2.com/articles/news/7394.html.

90. George Gene Gustines, 'For Graphic Novels, a New Frontier: Teenage Girls', *The New York Times*, 25 November 2006, B7.
91. Anon., 'Marvel Proudly Presents Thor', Marvel.com, 15 July, 2014, https://news.marvel.com/comics/22875/marvel_proudly_presents_thor/.
92. Carolyn Cocca, *Superwomen: Gender, Power, and Representation* (New York: Bloomsbury, 2016), 213.
93. Anne F. Peppard, '"This Female Fights Back!" A Feminist History of Marvel Comics', in *Make Ours Marvel*, ed. Yockey, 138–130.
94. Clark, 'Marvel Heroes Shaking Up Its Superhero Roster'.
95. Noah Berlatsky, 'What Makes the Muslim Ms. Marvel Awesome: She's Just Like Everyone', *The Atlantic*, 20 March 2014, https://www.the-atlantic.com/entertainment/archive/2014/03/what-makes-the-muslim-em-ms-marvel-em-awesome-shes-just-like-everyone/284517/.
96. See, for example, Katie M. Logan, 'America Needs Marvel Superhero Kamala Kahn Now More Than Ever, And Here's Why', *Newsweek*, 20 February 2017, http://www.newsweek.com/marvel-kamala-khan-muslim-american-superhero-america-needs-right-now-558943.
97. Sian Cain, 'Marvel Executive Says Emphasis on Diversity May Have Alienated Readers', *The Guardian*, 3 April 2017, https://www.the-guardian.com/books/2017/apr/03/marvel-executive-says-emphasis-on-diversity-may-have-alienated-readers.
98. Stephen Gerding, 'Ms. Marvel Rockets to the #1 Slot on Marvel's Digital Sales Chart', *Comic Book Resources*, 10 February 2014, http://www.cbr.com/ms-marvel-rockets-to-the-1-slot-on-marvels-digital-sales-chart/; Chase Magnett, '*Ms. Marvel* Tops the October Sales Charts (Because Ms. Marvel is Amazing)', *Comicbook*, 7 November 2014, http://comicbook.com/2014/11/07/ms-marvel-tops-the-october-sales-charts-because-ms-marvel-is-ama/.
99. Wright, *Comic Book Nation*, 291.
100. Anon., 'IDW Announces Silent Hill: Past Life', IDW Publishing, 12 August 2010, http://www.idwpublishing.com/news/article/1338/; Anon., 'Video Game Comics Don't Have to Suck', *Dark Horse*, 1 November 2010, http://www.darkhorse.com/Horsepower/1873/Video-Game-Comics-Dont-Have-to-Suck-11-1-10.
101. The *Injustice* videogame series sees a wide range of DC Comics characters pitted against one another in combat.
102. For further details on, and analysis of, Marvel Comics' recruitment of writers from outside of comics, see Deron Overpeck, 'Breaking Brand: From NuMarvel to Marvel NOW! Marvel Comics in the Age of Media Convergence', in *Make Ours Marvel*, ed. Yockey, 173–175.

103. George Gene Gustines, 'Mild-Mannered Literary Guys Transform Into Comics Writers', *The New York Times*, 17 March 2004, E4; Michael Sangiacomo, 'Top Authors Teaming Up With Marvel', *Plain Dealer* (Cleveland), 5 November 2005, E9.
104. Flanagan et al., *The Marvel Studios Phenomenon*, 36.
105. Anon., 'Interview with Dan Buckley, Part Two: Marvel's Digital Initiatives, Tuesday Delivery', *ICv2*, 11 July 2008, http://www.icv2.com/articles/news/13680.html.
106. Anon., 'Interview with DC President Paul Levitz 2005, Part 1', *ICv2*, 1 August 2005, http://www.icv2.com/articles/news/7298.html.
107. CBR News Team, 'Top Comics & Graphic Novels for 2008', *Comic Book Resources*, 12 January 2009, http://www.comicbookresources.com/?page=article&id=19505.
108. The five mini-series are *Thor: First Thunder, Thor: The Mighty Avenger, Iron Man/Thor, Thor: For Asgard* and *Ultimate Comics: Thor* (all 2010–2011).
109. Thomas, *Marvel Backlist Chronology*.
110. For analysis of the MCU transmedia narrative comic-book extensions, see Flanagan et al., *The Marvel Studios Phenomenon*, 191–192.
111. Rich Johnston, 'Axel Alonso Cites Bad Publicity for Marvel Comics as Evidence That Comics are Reaching Out', *Bleeding Cool*, 19 July 2017, https://www.bleedingcool.com/2017/07/19/axel-alonso-bad-publicity-marvel-comics/.
112. Scott Chitwood, 'DeSanto Talks about X-Men Costumes', *IGN*, 10 February 2000, http://uk.movies.ign.com/articles/034/034827p1.html.
113. Morrison, 'Morrison Manifesto'.
114. Johnson, 'Will the Real Wolverine Please Stand Up?', in *Film and Comic Books*, ed. Ian Gordon et al., 80.
115. Alex Zalben, 'Exclusive Interview: Matt Fraction Reflects on His Career, From Fear Itself to Mantooth', *MTV Geek!*, 31 March 2011, http://geek-news.mtv.com/2011/03/31/exclusive-interview-matt-fraction-reflects-on-his-career-from-fear-itself-to-mantooth/.
116. Fraction introduced Ezekiel Stane in *The Order* #8 (2008). The writer subsequently utilised the character as the villain in his first arc on *The Invincible Iron Man*, 'The Five Nightmares' (#1–6, 2008).
117. Johnston, 'Axel Alonso Cites Bad Publicity'.
118. Jerome Maida, 'Make Va-Room for More *GR* Books', (Philadelphia) *Daily News*, 16 February 2007, 46.
119. Jesse Schedeen, 'Between the Panels: The Guardians of the Galaxy Need to Get Bigger', *IGN*, 12 May 2017, http://uk.ign.com/articles/2017/05/12/between-the-panels-the-guardians-of-the-galaxy-need-to-get-bigger.

120. Peter David, *Writing for Comics with Peter David* (Cincinnati: Impact, 2006), 115.
121. Johnson, *Media Franchises*, 98.
122. Hoai-Tran Bui, 'Fantastic Four Comics Were Really Cancelled Over the Film Rights', */Film*, 7 August 2017, http://www.slashfilm.com/marvel-canceled-fantastic-four-comics-jonathan-hickman/.
123. This is not the only example of Marvel Entertainment exerting such pressure. Sean Howe suggests that, in the early 2000s, the parent company influenced Marvel Comics to drop titles so as to protect the broader company's movie-licensing aims. Sean Howe, *Marvel Comics: The Untold Story* (New York: Harper, 2012), 421.
124. Johnston, 'Axel Alonso Cites Bad Publicity'.
125. Ching, 'Exclusive: Geoff Johns Details "Rebirth" Plan'.
126. Hatfield, *Alternative Comics*, 41.
127. Ibid. For further discussion of the reader's role in interpreting the connections between panels, see Scott McCloud, *Understanding Comics: The Invisible Art* (New York: HarperPerennial, 1993), 60–69.
128. Harvey, *The Art of the Funnies*, 14–15.
129. Hatfield, *Alternative Comics*, 41.
130. McCloud, *Understanding Comics*, 74–75. The responsibility for breakdowns as part of the narrative design processes is variable. Sometimes the writer takes responsibility, sometimes the penciller, while other times it is shared.
131. Ibid., 70.
132. Re. the relationship between pace and page space in comics storytelling, see Harvey, *The Art of the Funnies*, 176.
133. David Bordwell, 'Intensified Continuity: Visual Style in Contemporary American Film', *Film Quarterly* 55, No. 3 (2002), 16–17.
134. A thematically analogous scene from the movie *Die Hard* (1988), in which the character John McClane swings on a fire hose through a skyscraper window, provides a good example of this combination of multi-cam set-up and cutting pattern within film.
135. See Paul Gravett, *Manga: Sixty Years of Japanese Comics* (London: Lawrence King, 2004), 24–27.
136. See Gary Marshall, *Studio Space: The World's Greatest Comic Illustrators at Work* (Berkeley: Image, 2008), 189.
137. David Harper, 'The Decade According to Multiversity: Best Artist', *Multiversity Comics*, 9 December 2009, http://www.multiversitycomics.com/2009/12/decade-according-to-multiversity-best_09.html.
138. David, *Writing for Comics*, 115.
139. Samuel Roberts, 'Interview: Mark Millar', *SciFiNow*, 15 November 2010, http://www.scifinow.co.uk/interviews/interview-mark-millar/.

140. Keith Phipps, 'Interview: Brian Michael Bendis', *A.V. Club*, 9 August 2007, http://www.avclub.com/articles/brian-michael-bendis,14138/.

141. Greg Burgas, 'Compressed Storytelling Versus Decompressed Storytelling', Comics Should Be Good, 1 August 2005, http://good-comics.blogspot.com/2005/08/compressed-storytelling-versus.html.

142. Examples of blog posts critical of the 'cinematic' style in comics include Frederik Hautain, 'The Decompression Oppression', *Broken Frontier*, 14 March 2004, http://www.brokenfrontier.com/lowdown/p/detail/the-decompression-oppression; Scipio, 'The War Against the True Enemy of Comic Books', *The Absorbascon*, 15 May 2007, http://absorbascon.blogspot.com/2007/05/war-against-true-enemy-of-comic-books.html.

143. The relevant issues are *Cable* #35, *X-Men* #55, *X-Man* #18–19, *X-Force* #57, *Uncanny X-Men* #336 and *Fantastic Four* #415–416 (all 1996).

144. This subsidiary storyline begins in *Amazing Spider-Man* #365 (1992).

145. Jonathan Ellis, 'Interview: Joe Quesada', *Pop Image*, August 2001, http://www.popimage.com/industrial/080101quesada1.html.

146. Vaughan, 'An Interview with Spider-Man's Boss'.

147. Jonah Welland, 'J. Michael Straczynski to Write Fantastic Four Starting in June', *Comic Book Resources*, 22 December 2004, http://www.comicbookresources.com/?page=article&id=4390.

148. Warren Ellis, 'The *Nextwave* Original Pitch', in *Nextwave: Agents of H.A.T.E.* Ultimate Collection, by Warren Ellis and Stuart Immonen (New York: Marvel, 2010).

149. Ibid.

150. All eight parts of Marvel's *Secret Invasion* mini-series, for example, made the top-ten list of the bestselling comics of 2008, while the first five issues from DC's *Blackest Night* mini-series made the top-ten list of the bestselling comics of 2009. David Colton, 'Comic books sold well in 2008; graphic novels did, too', *USA Today*, 11 January 2009, http://www.usatoday.com/life/books/news/2009-01-11-comics-sales_N.htm; Lucas Siegel, 'Diamond Announces Full Year-End Data', *Newsarama*, 12 January 2010, http://www.newsarama.com/comics/Diamond-2009-Year-Sales-100112.html.

151. Similar to the Marvel and DC universes, the 'Whoniverse' attracts a highly dedicated audience invested in charting its continuity.

152. Matt Hills, 'Absent Epic, Implied Story Arcs, and Variation on a Narrative Theme: *Doctor Who* (2005–2008) as Cult/Mainstream Television', in *Third Person*, ed. Harrigan and Wardrip-Fruin, 336–338.

153. Ibid., 336.

154. Ibid., 337.

155. In this particular way, the plotting of *Ultimate Spider-Man* emulates that of *Amazing Spider-Man* in the 1960s.

156. Steve Ekstrom, 'An Uncanny Update with Matt Fraction', *Newsarama*, 3 March 2009, http://www.newsarama.com/comics/030903-Fraction-UXM.html.
157. This annual marks Simon Trask's first appearance within Marvel continuity.
158. Bolivar Trask's first appearance was in *Uncanny X-Men* #14 (1965).
159. Ekstrom, 'An Uncanny Update with Matt Fraction'.
160. Vaneta Rogers, 'New Avengers 3: Brian Bendis—The Flagship Captain', *Newsarama*, 14 December 2009, http://www.newsarama.com/comics/091214-brian-bendis-avengers-reassembled.html.
161. Karen Lury, *Interpreting Television* (London: Hodder Arnold, 2005), 14.
162. Regarding the plotting of storylines within this series, Morrison segmented his run into successive three-issue arcs, thus permitting DC to compile two arcs per six-issue collected edition.
163. Morrison, 'Morrison Manifesto'.
164. Allen, 'Speaking of Soap Operas', 69.
165. Ibid., 69–71.
166. Grant Morrison, Cameron Stewart and Andy Clarke, *Batman & Robin: Batman vs. Robin* (New York: DC Comics, 2010), 154.
167. Admin1, 'CBR TV @NYCC: Scott Snyder on "Batman," "Severed" and Bat Continuity', *Comic Book Resources*, 16 October 2011, http://video.comicbookresources.com/cbrtv/2011/cbr-tv-nycc-scott-snyder-on-batman-severed-and-bat-continuity/.
168. Ibid.
169. Vaneta Rogers, 'Scott Snyder on BATMAN #10 & You-Know-Who [SPOILERS]', *Newsarama*, 14 June 2012, http://www.newsarama.com/9671-spoiler-sport-scott-snyder-on-batman-10-you-know-who.html.

CHAPTER 5

Technological Specificity in Narrative Design: Story-Driven Videogame Series in an Upgrade Culture

Introduction

While many attributes of DC and Marvel's ongoing storyworlds were reconfigured in the twenty-first century so as to complement shifts in audience specificity, the following example of change within the serial storyworld of the *Red Faction* videogame series reflects, instead, transition in technological specificity. The four instalments of the *Red Faction* series, developed by Volition, and published by THQ, comprise a science-fiction narrative concerning the tribulations of a human colony of miners on Mars. As part of the original *Red Faction* game (2001), which was released on the Sony PlayStation 2, the player takes charge of the miner Parker, whose role is to lead a rebellion against his draconian employers, the Ultor Corporation. As part of its moment-to-moment game play, the first *Red Faction* typically presents event sequences that recall the traditions of its 'first-person shooter' (FPS) predecessors, such as *Doom* (1993) and *Half-Life* (1998); to aid the rebellion, the player is required to navigate Parker through the corridors and enclosed combat spaces of various interior environments including mine networks and Ultor facilities while eliminating via firearms the enemy non-playing characters (NPCs). The game's first sequel, *Red Faction II* (2002), which was also released on PlayStation 2, along with Microsoft Xbox and Nintendo GameCube, picks up the miners' struggle decades later within story time. The sequences of combat-related events that emerge through its game play are broadly similar to those of its predecessor.

© The Author(s) 2018
A. N. Smith, *Storytelling Industries*,
https://doi.org/10.1007/978-3-319-70597-2_5

The overarching narrative premise of the series' third instalment, *Red Faction: Guerrilla* (2009), which was developed for PlayStation 3 and Xbox 360, doesn't hint at any great adjustment to the storyworld's ingredients; the player takes control of mining engineer Alec Mason, who must lead a further rebellion, one hundred years after the first, this time against the Earth Defence Force (EDF), which in the first game had supported the workers' revolution, but has since evolved into a tyrannical overlord of the planet's mining operation. The type of event sequences that manifest through game play, however, represent a departure from storyworld precedent within the series, a shift underpinned by altered technology. The greater processing speeds and memory capabilities of the later console-hardware generation enabled Volition to engineer within *Guerrilla* an entirely destructible environment and to also incorporate improved real-time physics and collision-detection systems. So as to complement the change in the storyworld setting's affordances, Volition opted to make the destruction central to the events that arise through game play. In *Guerrilla*, the player is tasked, for example, with ensuring that Mason uses the explosives and sledgehammer at his disposal so as to raze EDF buildings before swiftly retreating from direct confrontation with the game's overpowering enemy NPC force.

The event sequences that such game play presents contrast greatly with the typical combat narratives of earlier *Red Faction*s. The first game presents the point-of-view of a player-character that (if under the guidance of a skilled gamer who wishes to progress) advances to and engages with one set of enemy NPCs and moves on to the next. In contrast, the storyworld events that emerge through *Guerrilla*'s game play concern a more asymmetrical form of combat that is more in keeping with the series' central storyworld theme of a small rebel resistance rising up against a conventional military power. While these three games all contribute to the same ongoing storyworld, the home console upgrade of the mid-2000s facilitated a transition in storyworld event types, from the conventional 'run and gun' action of the first two *Red Faction*s to *Guerrilla*'s distinctive 'hit and run' event sequences.

Hardware memory and processor upgrades within the development of the *Red Faction* series ultimately contributed to this clear shift in narrative design. This process whereby changing technological specificities of video-game hardware influenced a new type of storyworld action within the *Red Faction* series therefore indicates both the potential for technological variability within a given medium and the relevance of such variability to narrative.

This chapter investigates further this relationship between narrative and the variability of videogame technologies; in so doing, it gauges the significance of the sub-dimension of technological specificity within a given medium's narrative design conditions and processes. The videogame medium serves as a useful test subject for this investigation due to its high degree of techno-logical instability, with the console hardware transition that occurred during the narrative design process of the *Red Faction* series proving indicative of the videogame industry more generally. Since the industry's inception in the 1970s, the technological contexts of videogame development have consis-tently altered at a great pace, leading to: (1) the ever-increasing sophistica-tion of graphical presentation in videogames; (2) the integration of new forms of screen technologies, such as handheld consoles and virtual reality head-sets; and (3) new types of player input, such as touch-screen and motion control technologies. Due to this 'permanent upgrade culture', observe Jon Dovey and Helen W. Kennedy, videogame development studios operate 'within a system where technology is never stable'.[1]

The topic of narrative in videogames has proved a highly contentious one in the past two decades, generating much scholarly debate regarding the role of storytelling within the medium (an issue I go on to clarify).[2] Yet despite intense focus on this issue, the connection between videogame narrative and the medium's technological inconstancy is one that has been consistently overlooked. While Marie-Laure Ryan, Angela Ndalianis, Geoff King, Andrew Darley and Andrew Mactavish, for example, all observe the industry's upgrade culture, they each focus in particular on how successive generations of videogames invite players to admire the technical mastery of their graphical spectacle (relative to prior games).[3] Through their increases in surface texture detail, environmental complex-ity and 'naturalism' of character movement, the videogames of a new hardware cycle typically provide players with, notes Ryan, a 'spectacle of technology', or as Mactavish puts it, 'a virtuoso performance of techno-logical expertise'.[4]

Many of these discourses concerning technological virtuosity have come to echo those within film studies, observed in Chap. 2, that regard the spectacle of grand-scale action set pieces and computer-generated spe-cial effects within Hollywood blockbusters as having marginalised narra-tive.[5] Darley, for example, suggests that narrative is 'subordinated' to the pleasures of spectacle that a videogame provides, while Mactavish argues that 'the widespread appeal of computer games is based less upon internal narrative meaning' and more on 'our astonishment at visual and auditory technology'.[6] Putting to one side the issue of whether such interpretations of game-play experience speak for all or even the majority of players, this discursive opposition of, on the one hand, narrative, and, on the other, the capacity for graphical presentation, has served to elide their shared relationship; the implications that the latter holds for the former are neglected. By testing the relevance to narrative of the sub-dimension of technological specificity within a single medium, this chapter supports this book's broad objective. By examining the connections between narrative and videogame technology in particular, however, it simultaneously serves as a necessary intervention within videogame scholarship.

Those media artefacts that are culturally labelled videogames represent a remarkably diverse set, but so as to trace the influence that variable technological contexts impose upon narrative design conditions and processes, I focus in particular on a loose category that I refer to here as the *story-driven videogame* series (or SDV series). This category unites games that:

- provide, through their metaphorical representations of game play, elaborately defined characters embroiled in clearly articulated events within defined storyworld settings;
- contextualise the events that emerge through game play, via text or such devices as cut-scenes (non-interactive animated sequences), as part of a broader storyworld, which is plotted serially over multiple games of a series.

Twenty-first century examples of videogame series that fall within this category include many first- and third-person shooter game series, such as *Halo* (2001–present), *Dead Space* (2008–2013), *Red Faction* and *Gears of War* (2006–present); action-adventure game series, such as *Uncharted* (2007–present), *Assassin's Creed* (2007–present) and the *Batman: Arkham* games (2009–present); and RPG/exploration/'open world adventure' game series, such as *Mass Effect* (2007–present), *Elder Scrolls* (1994–present), *Dark Souls* (2011–2016), *Grand Theft Auto* (1997–present) and *The Legend of Zelda* (1986–present).[7] While SDVs are rich in fictional narrative, and are thus appropriate for focus here, they should not be considered as indicative of the medium more generally; a great array of videogames are not configured so as to present coherent fictional storyworlds as part of play.

The development processes of many such game series have spanned multiple technological contexts (as with those of *Red Faction*), yet the reliance on a single storyworld within a given series nonetheless bonds the instalments to form a coherent narrative (as with *Red Faction*). Because the storyworld continuity they share invites comparisons to be made between separate instalments, the SDV series proves a highly useful form of case study with which to highlight the influence of technology on narrative. Due to the continuation of the characters, storylines and/or settings within a given series, those clear discrepancies in narrative that do emerge between series instalments—as a consequence of variable technology—are made clearly apparent.

SDV series are developed for a variety of hardware platforms (such as computers, consoles, tablets and smartphones) and published for a range of distinct videogame markets. These include: (1) the PC market, that is, the market for games intended for home computer and laptop platforms, which are largely distributed via the digital online platform Steam; (2) the app market, that is, the market for games intended for tablets and smartphones, which are largely distributed via (Apple's) App Store and Google Play; and (3) the videogame console market, that is, the market for games intended for the home and portable console hardware devices currently manufactured by the oligopoly of Sony, Microsoft and Nintendo, which are distributed physically via retail stores and digitally via these hardware manufacturers' online stores. This study focuses exclusively on the latter market.[8] This is appropriate as the two distinct ways in which technology is utilised in the home and portable console business serve to complement my methodological approach here. Firstly, due to the hardware cycle that typifies the industry, whereby one console is succeeded every five to ten years by a new, technologically advanced model, I am able to easily identify and compare over time the distinct technological phases of this industrial sector. The upgrading processes of the PC and smartphone/tablet platforms' technological capacities are, in contrast, far more regular, but they typically only occur in slight increments; due to this subtle process, it is more difficult to make clear distinctions between technological contexts with regards to the PC and smartphone/tablet platforms. Secondly, due to console manufacturers' efforts to differentiate their hardware from those of their competitors, technological conditions in the console space are not only variable across time, but simultaneously also. For example, in the late 2000s, the motion control player-input device of Nintendo's home console, the Wii, distinguished the platform from those of Nintendo's rivals at the time. By focusing on the console market the chapter is therefore able to clearly identify and consider variable technological contexts of narrative design over time and at a given moment.

For my case study narratives, I centre upon three US-published SDV series in particular, namely *Halo, Red Faction* and *Grand Theft Auto* (*GTA*). These series are appropriate as, due to the development of each having traversed at least one console upgrade, they invite comparison between the narrative design processes of distinct technological contexts that have altered over time. These series are all representative of a subsection of the console games market that we might refer to as 'full-price boxed retail' games; that is, games that are released at premium price points and as physical copies (alongside digital versions). Typically featuring intricately detailed three-dimensional characters and settings, games within this particular sector are typically the most expensive to develop, as the chapter goes on to discuss. This sector of the market is therefore distinct from that of the console 'indie' game sector that developed in the late 2000s. While a number of intriguing and innovative SDV games have emerged from this sector, developers of these games, which are less costly to produce and purchase, have so far tended not to pursue the construction of SDV series, and so this sector is not explored here.

As part of the study, I focus mainly on the influence of one particular twenty-first century transition in technological contexts upon these series' narratives; that is, the mid-to-late 2000s hardware transition between what are known in videogame culture as the 6th home console generation (which includes the Xbox and the PS2) and the 7th generation (which includes the Xbox 360 and the PS3). The *GTA* series, due to the simultaneous developments of *GTA IV* (for PlayStation 3 and Xbox 360 [2008]) and *GTA: Chinatown Wars* (for the Nintendo DS [2009]), additionally permits analysis of the implications for narrative of simultaneously variable technological conditions, which I provide here. While each of these series represents a single coherent ongoing storyworld, the chapter considers how technological changes during these series' development have influenced narrative designers' approaches to plot, style and storyworld from one instalment to the next. In the following three sections, however, I provide necessary theoretical, academic and industrial contexts for these case studies, firstly by elucidating the unique relationship that narrative and videogames share, and identifying how this relationship informs narrative design processes.

NARRATIVE AND VIDEOGAMES

It is important to stress a key distinction that separates SDV narratives from those of other entertainment media. Previous chapters conceive of film, comics and television texts as permanent narrative objects. This approach is appropriate for these forms, as film, comics and television narratives are generally invariable and determined at the point of production. But this paradigm is insufficient here, because SDVs are, at the level of textual artefact, not narrative objects per se, but rather interactive systems that facilitate the emergence of fictional narrative through the playing of games. As Astrid Ensslin puts it, videogames 'don't tell pre-conceived ... stories in the same way as novels and movies do', instead 'stories come into being as players experience [fictional] gameworlds'.[9]

To explain this process, it is first necessary to define 'games' and the connection they share with videogame narrative. According to Jesper Juul, a game 'generally constitutes a rule-based system with a variable and quantifiable outcome, where outcomes are assigned different values'.[10] A game as structure, then, usually provides a player with goals (the most valued outcomes) and the parameters by which the goal can be obtained (the rules). During a (real-world/non-digital) game of soccer, for example, a player taking a penalty kick has a most-valued outcome (that is, the ball breaching the opposing team's goal) and there are rules by which this most-valued outcome can be achieved (the player must attempt to score the goal with a single kick from the penalty spot). While scholars such as Gonzalo Frasca and Markku Eskilinen have argued that the two distinct cultural phenomena of games and narratives are incompatible, with regard to SDVs, the two are mutually dependent; the pursuit of goals via the adherence to rules in such games leads to the presentation of characters and events within settings—that is, narrative.[11] As Juul suggests, a 'player's real-world actions [that is, their pursuit of goals via button presses and thumb-stick movements] have a metaphorical relation to ... fictional in-game action'.[12] As Gordon Calleja puts it, a player's interaction with a game's rules 'generates' storyworld material.[13]

The example of *Batman: Arkham Asylum* (2009) demonstrates this process. The game's goals, which include having the 'player-character' (Batman) both rescue Jim Gordon from the maniacal Harley Quinn and defeat Poison Ivy within the asylum's botanical gardens, for example, are to be achieved *within* a coherent storyworld of characters and settings. For the player to achieve these goals they must, then, have Batman perform actions and effect change within the storyworld. The game's rules structure this pursuit of goals by imposing limits on player-character events. In a non-digital game of soccer a rulebook establishes the rules and a referee enforces them; but, notes Calleja, the rules of SDVs usually constitute the possible actions that a player-character is able to take within the storyworld.[14] Thus the rules in *Arkham Asylum* represent the range of onscreen character actions—the storyworld events—that the player is permitted to instigate as a means to achieve the assigned goals. The player is, for example, able to have Batman walk, run, crouch, punch and kick, while, consistent with fictional precedent, the player can also have the Dark Knight utilise his many gadgets, such as batarangs (which will stun enemy NPCs) and the grapple gun, which allows the hero to ascend to elevated points within the environment.

With SDVs such as *Arkham Asylum* the playing of the game (which requires the guiding of a player-character) instigates the onscreen presentation of storyworld action. Such instances of storyworld activity, which I will refer to here as *player-generated events*, are an integral part of the experience of playing SDVs. As Ryan observes, without such conveyed actions, 'players would have no idea of the consequences of their actions, and they would not be able to play the game intelligently'; players, as a result, become 'not only agents but also spectators of their own pretended actions'.[15] According to Ryan, 'The game experience is therefore halfway between living life and watching a movie.'[16] Juul similarly regards game play as a dichotomous process between the real (the player's engagement with the rules) and unreal (the onscreen narrative), suggesting that the videogame player operates 'in the half-real zone between the fiction and the rules'.[17]

Due to its dependence on a given player's choice of input, much of a given SDV narrative is (in contrast to the pre-established narratives of most other media) highly variable; that is, the emergent narrative of one player's play-through is likely to vary, as least to some small degree, from the next. To consider the player-generated storyworld events that emerge from game play, I must move beyond the structuralist narratological paradigm that underpins much of this book, and detail my own unique game-play experiences. As Dovey and Kennedy suggest, 'In order to study a computer game we cannot have recourse solely to its textual characteristics; we have to pay particular attention to the moment of its enactment as it is *played*.'[18] I do not, however, consider a given player-generated sequence of events born from my own playing experience to be in any way definitive, but rather just one possible narrative outcome for which a given SDV lays down conditions.

The more important implication of the SDVs' potential for narrative variability is that, just as I am unable to *identify* a particular fixed sequence of storyworld events within a given SDV, developers have no means with which to *establish* a fixed sequence of storyworld events. But if developers do not, indeed cannot, determine precisely 'what happens' within the onscreen presentation of a given SDV play-through, then in what ways do they design narratives? To consider how technology shapes narrative design processes, it is necessary for me to engage here with this question and explain the various practices that constitute the narrative design process within SDV development. I therefore detail below the various aspects of SDV development that shape player-character action and/or situate it within a wider storyworld.

The SDV Narrative Design Process

Settings

Despite the role of player agency in the forming of a given SDV narrative, the storyworld environments that developers 'sculpt', notes Jenkins, strongly influence the narrative possibilities that a game affords.[19] With regard to first- and third-person shooters specifically, videogame designer Manveer Heir echoes Jenkins' point. He suggests that the particular nature of a contested area of environment offers players with a particular set of 'micro choices' by determining: (a) if and where points of cover (from enemy NPCs) are provided; (b) the different angles of attack towards enemy NPCs that are permitted; and (c) whether or not there is the provision to flank enemy NPCs undetected.[20] For instance, during a mission in the Western open-world game *Red Dead Redemption* (2010), outlaws ambush the bounty hunter (and player-character) John Marston within the ghost town of Tumbleweed, with this location providing the basis for a range of possible player-generated events. The setting, for example, is heavily peppered with potential cover, in the form of crates, outhouses, stone walls, derelict buildings and upturned horse carriages. During my own play-through, this environment facilitated a narrative of cautious combat, whereby I guided a crouching Marston from cover to cover, dispatching enemies one by one.

Developers not only design settings in such ways that lay down conditions for particular player-generated activity, they also often make reference within environments to prior storyworld events (often unrelated to a player-character's actions). Jenkins refers to this mode of storytelling, whereby the setting evokes a fictional historical context, as *embedded narrative*. 'One can imagine', says Jenkins, 'the game designer as developing two kinds of narratives—one relatively unstructured and controlled by the player … the other prestructured but embedded within the mise-en-scène'.[21] Techniques of embedded narrative are well evidenced within the *Portal* series (2007–2011), for example. The games' setting, the Aperture Science laboratories, incorporates many visual clues (such as graffiti) that imply prior events that have occurred there; as *Edge* magazine observes, the *Portal* setting represents an 'architectural CV: a company history written in strata'.[22]

Player-Characters

While storyworld geographies impose parameters on the possibilities for player-generated narrative, so too do the affordances of a given player-character. As Ensslin observes, a player-character's actions 'are contingent upon game makers' decisions regarding … the ways they can and cannot interact with the gameworld'.[23] Thus while a player of *Arkham Asylum* can, as noted, have Batman perform various physical actions and utilise various props (his gadgets), there are certain actions that the developer Rocksteady prohibited. For example, while the asylum's escaped inmates can (and do) fire rifles at Batman, a player would not be permitted to have the hero utilise these weapons himself; and, while a player can (in accordance with the game's goals) have Batman fight and subdue these inmates, he or she would be unable to have the hero deliver similar beatings to the asylum guards that are situated within the environment. In both cases, the game's coding will not allow such events to occur. By determining the actions that a player-character can (and cannot) take, developers install parameters for the possible characterisation of a given player-character. As noted in Chap. 2, a character's actions, along with their speech and external appearance, indirectly define the network of traits that establish a particular characterisation.[24] But, as actions help to establish a network of character traits, a given characterisation, notes Margolin, is 'constrained by what is possible in the storyworld'.[25] Rocksteady, by ensuring that Batman cannot harm innocent bystanders or kill (as opposed to subdue) villains, makes certain that the characterisation of the Caped Crusader that emerges in *Arkham Asylum* does not contradict the pre-existing characterisation of Batman (within films, comic books, etc.) as having a strict moral code. Developers further indirectly define a network of character traits via their design of player-characters' physical appearances. In the *Gears of War* series, for example, player-character Marcus Fenix is conceived as a tough ex-con-turned-military-campaigner; his typical visage—scarred cheek, jutted jaw and narrowed, deep-set eyes—complements the characterisation.

Non-Playing Characters
While, at least within the boundaries that developers set, a player will determine player-character actions in any given play-through, it is the developer that shapes the ways in which NPCs respond to such actions. Developers achieve this through their establishing of a game's AI (artificial intelligence) system. For example, as Chris Opdahl, character designer on the (FPS) *Halo* series, observes, enemy NPCs have been configured to 'react in many situations based on how the player is choosing to interact with the encounter'.[26] As Damián Isla, AI programmer for the first three *Halo*s, notes, the actions of enemy NPCs in *Halo 2* (2004) are derived from three categories of behaviour; they 'fight' (that is, shoot, fire gre-nades or melee attack), 'hide' (find cover) or 'search' (pursue or 'uncover' the player-character).[27] From which category of action an NPC draws, however, is dependent on player-character action. So if, in a given play-through, the player-character retreats to the periphery of combat space, at least some NPCs will have been programmed to pursue.

The motivation to craft optimal adversaries has traditionally guided the application of videogame AI.[28] However, the aim driving the AI-programming process in *Halo* games is not, notes Isla, solely to design enemy NPCs that are difficult to play against, but also to convey an 'illu-sion of strategic intelligence'.[29] NPC design in the *Halo* series is, then, as it is in many other SDVs, at least partly geared to facilitate NPC actions that contribute towards coherent fictional characterisations. A further example of the *Halo* AI implementation process indicates this. As Earth's war with an alien species alliance—dubbed the 'Covenant'—is a central and enduring tenet of *Halo* fiction, the player-character in a given *Halo* game is typically pitted against enemy NPCs of contrasting species. *Halo* developers support this fiction by attributing each species with a distinct set of behaviours, and which speak to political dynamics within this alien league. In *Halo 3* (2007), for example, the 'grunt' species are designed to fan out around the 'brutes', protecting them from attack, an AI imple-mentation that reflects a fictional hierarchy within which the grunts are the lowest. Further indicating the grunts' subservience, should a player-character fell a brute, a surviving grunt will, as per its programming, 'break'; this process will lead the grunt to either launch itself kamikaze-style towards the player-character with a live-grenade in hand or to aimlessly wander the environment, quietly babbling.[30] As with player-characters, the physical appearances of NPCs can complement the process of indirect character definition that occurs through NPC actions. The grunts' squat and hunched bodies, for example, reflect their deference to the muscular and towering brutes.

Scripted Events

While the player-generated event sequences that emerge from player-character actions and subsequent NPC actions are at the core of the SDV experience, these games also rely heavily on fictional events that require little to no player input, which, following Calleja, I will refer to here as *scripted*.[31] As Calleja notes, these elements, which typically take the form of cut-scenes, 'quick-time events' and NPC dialogue delivered during game play, usually assign goals and provide particular narrative meanings to those goals.[32] I refer to those game goals assigned within the storyworld as *narrative goals*.

Scripted storyworld events in the *Halo* series demonstrate this process. At an abstract level, *Halo* games each represent a succession of distinct FPS combat encounters between the player-character and enemy NPCs. Scripted events, however, convert this succession of player-generated event sequences into a coherent storyworld that is plotted through a single game and serially across multiple games, and which concerns the ongoing battle between the Covenant and the United Nations Space Command (UNSC).

Halo: Reach (2010), the fifth FPS in the *Halo* series, provides an example of this practice. During the game, which functions narratively as a prequel to the first game (*Halo: Combat Evolved* [2001]), the player controls a Spartan (cyborg soldier) dubbed Noble Six, who, together with his Noble Team comrades, supports the UNSC's attempts to defend Reach (a human-colony planet) from Covenant attack.

Nearing the game's end, Six is tasked by ally NPC Captain Keyes, via a snippet of scripted narrative, with utilising a 'mass driver' (mounted laser cannon) to clear Reach's skies of Covenant spacecraft, as doing so will allow Keyes' UNSC Pillar of Autumn cruiser to launch out of Reach's atmosphere. The task provides a simple ludic challenge for the player (have

Six point the cannon at the Covenant spacecraft, then shoot). Scripted material, however, situates within a broader pre-plotted narrative the player-generated events that emerge from the player's engagement. Following the player's achievement of the goal, a cut-scene depicts the Pillar of Autumn taking off as Six looks on, which is a sequence that narratively connects with the initial cut-scene of the first *Halo* game; in this latter scripted event sequence, Keyes is depicted on the bridge of the Pillar of Autumn following the cruiser's departure from the embattled Reach.

The scripted storyworld events contextualise the player's achievement of narrative goals and the player-generated events it instigates (Six destroying the Covenant craft) within the serial plotting of the *Halo* series. It is the use of scripted narrative techniques, in particular, that thus enables SDV developers to establish, if not the precise micro details, then at least the rough shape of a storyline, which can be plotted so as to span many hours of single-player game play and serially across multiple games (as with the *Halo* series).

These discussions with regard to both scripted and player-generated narrative indicate that, in the development of SDVs, the design processes of game and narrative are often two sides of the same coin. The developer's establishing of rules manifests as the determining of character and setting affordances, while the goals they set are shrouded in narrative meaning. For a player also, both the consumption of narrative and the abstract engagement with a game system are closely related; to pursue and achieve goals within the boundaries of the rules is, in an SDV, to simultaneously advance and experience narrative. In keeping with the book's narrative focus, and to avoid confusion, I will avoid the term 'game design' within my case studies. My investigations into the possibilities for narrative that an SDV affords and the narrative goals it assigns nevertheless speak by implication to issues relating to the design of games systems also.

Style
Similar to scripted narrative, aspects of SDV narrative style are also usually predetermined at the point of development. For example, developers opt for a particular point of view via their choice of 'camera placement' on player-generated action. Such perspectives in SDVs include first person (whereby the perspective is that of the player-character), third person (whereby the perspective is positioned a small way behind the player-character) and 'isometric projection' (whereby the perspective is positioned at a high, steep angle, overlooking the action). For many schol-

ars, the distinction between these narrative styles holds important implications for the narrative experience. Jo Bryce and Jason Rutter, for example, suggest that the first-person perspective offers an intimacy between player and player-character, while Ensslin argues that, in contrast, elevated views of character action, such as the isometric projection perspective, are psychologically distancing.[33]

A given technological context clearly has an influence on many aspects of the narrative design processes that I have discussed here. The particular capacities of a given hardware platform's central processing unit (CPU), graphics processing unit (GPU) and random-access memory (RAM) ultimately set limits regarding, for example, the nature of the events, characters and setting that might be graphically rendered in real-time response to player input. By imposing constraints upon that which can be presented on screen, technology is thus intrinsic to the facilitation of videogame narrative. Yet, despite the centrality of technology in videogame development, scholarly analysis, as noted, tends to consider the topic of technology in isolation from that of storyworlds and their presentations. The following section accordingly explores the underlying presumptions that have led to technology becoming theoretically marginalised from issues relating to narrative design.

PARADIGMS OF NARRATIVE AND TECHNOLOGY IN VIDEOGAME SCHOLARSHIP

The prevalence of a particular assumption within videogame discourses at least partly explains the dearth of interest in the manner by which a specific technological context, such as the available means of graphical presentation, informs narrative; this assumption, which Bob Rehak identifies, is that '*games are conceptually separable from their technologies*' (emphasis in original). According to this paradigm, observes Rehak, the 'graphical shells' of videogames are variable according to available technology, but game designs remain 'eternally fixed, like Platonic ideals'.[34] Espen Aarseth, who regards games as 'medium-independent', strongly reflects this position. A given game, he argues 'can be translated from board and dice, to a live role-play out in the woods, to numbers and letters on a screen, to a three dimensional virtual world', while continuing as 'basically the same game' throughout.[35]

The common impression that the priority placed on graphical enhancement within videogame development stalls innovation in narrative design has proved a corollary of this perceived disconnect between narrative and technology. Geoff King and Tanya Krzywinska, for example, suggest that developers' investment of time and money in the construction of three-dimensional settings 'often appears to be privileged over dimensions such as narrative and game play'.[36] Identifying that which he regards as the redundancy of innovation in SDVs, Aarseth shares this interpretation: 'What keeps the genre alive is increasingly more photorealistic, detailed three-dimensional graphical environments, but apart from that, it is mostly the same story-game over and over again', he argues.[37] Ryan too echoes this view; she writes:

> [Developers] so far have had little incentive to vary the narrative design of games, because sufficient novelty could be achieved in the domain of technology to sell their new products: better graphics, larger worlds, faster action [and] more realistic game physics.[38]

There are, however, analyses that challenge the dominant paradigm whereby technologies are disassociated from aspects of narrative. Andrew Hutchinson, for example, provides a detailed account of the various ways in which the modes of narrative style within the landmark PC games *Doom* and *Myst* (1993) reflect the technical limitations of each of their production contexts. Hutchinson's research shows that the techniques used to convey storyworld information in these titles were born from the pragmatic choices that development teams were required to make due to their respective technological constraints.[39] Nick Montfort and Ian Bogost demonstrate ways in which the specificities of display technologies have determined narrative design processes. They show how the natures of basic fictional components of games during their development in the late 1970s and early 1980s were sometimes influenced by whether a game was intended for raster- or random-scan display screens.[40] This chapter expands on such lines of inquiry into the influence of technology upon narrative.

It is, however, important to first situate technology within the broader dynamics of the videogame industry so as to avoid the pitfall of technological determinist theory. The philosophy of technological determinism, popularised by Marshall McLuhan in the 1960s, and adhered to by technophiles to this day, perceives technology as an inevitable cultural force that conditions our existence.[41] On the one hand, McLuhan's perception of technology as an influence that shapes cultural practice is useful, and one that this chapter echoes; but, on the other hand, as Williams observes as part of his critique of McLuhan, theories of technological determinism neglect the way in which social and industrial forces shape the development and utilisation of technologies.[42] In their respective studies of the role of technology in videogame culture, Dovey and Kennedy, and Stephen Kline, Nick Dyer-Witheford and Grieg De Peuter, wisely share Williams' broader perspective. Dovey and Kennedy, for example, stress that research into videogame technology should consider the 'economic and cultural drivers' that shape a given technological context.[43] Kline et al. similarly suggest that the videogame medium should be understood as 'an interplay of technologies, culture and economics'.[44] Reflecting these scholars' holistic approaches, the following section acknowledges the ways in which economic imperatives within the industry power that which Kline et al. term 'perpetual technological innovation'.[45]

Industrial Contexts of Videogame Technologies

The three key institutional categories that comprise the console industry are the developers (those development studios that create a videogame in code form), publishers (the companies that often finance games development, manufacture and distribute physical copies of games, and also promote games), and hardware manufacturers (those companies who build, market and distribute videogame platforms). As Dovey and Kennedy observe, it is the oligopoly of hardware manufacturers (presently Sony, Microsoft and Nintendo) that control the 'technological system' of the console industry and thus drive its upgrade culture.[46] Console manufacturers' reliance on technological advances as a means to differentiate their products has proved the key motivating factor for this pattern. The distinct economic model prevalent within the industry, whereby a given console manufacturer receives royalties from publishers for the games sold for its platform, has further stimulated this process. Since Nintendo's introduction of this model in the mid-1980s, console manufacturers have, as Dovey and Kennedy note, regarded this sustained revenue of publishing royalties as having a greater potential for profit than that of hardware sales.[47] This logic has led to a landscape in which console manufacturers have invested heavily in the development of technologically advanced hardware so as to attract the widest possible user base, even at the cost of a loss on each console sold.[48] It is this industrial practice that has ultimately led to a cycle whereby home consoles are upgraded every five to ten years, and has thus instigated the continuing shift in technological parameters within which developers operate.

In their development of a new hardware technology, console manufacturers usually place a particular emphasis on the improvement of graphical capacities. The resultant graphical upgrades will often then go on to become a central component of the manufacturers' marketing strategies. This is evidenced by Sony's introduction of the PlayStation in 1994. The Japanese firm's first home console was built to facilitate the development of 3D gaming environments, and was distinguished from the popular Sega and Nintendo hardware of the time, which specialised in 2D-scrolling games.[49] Sony stressed this point of differentiation within its promotional material; one television ad, for example, sees PlayStation mascot Crash Bandicoot standing defiantly outside Nintendo's US headquarters, bragging through a megaphone about the 3D graphics that his game provides.[50]

Microsoft's discourse surrounding the development of the Xbox 360 provides a mid-2000s example of hardware manufacturers' dependence on enhanced visuals as a promotional tool. The former Microsoft corporate Vice-President J. Allard promised, prior to the hardware's launch, that the new console would mark the introduction of the 'HD era' of gaming due to its capacity to provide a 'high definition' display (and thus a greater number of pixels on screen than previous consoles).[51] Promotional discourse concerning Sony's PS4 Pro console, which launched in 2016 (and which is an advanced model of the PS4, which was released in 2013), serves as a more recent example of hardware manufacturers relying on a console's graphical capacity as a means to market it to consumers; according to the playstation.com website, the PS4 Pro enables 'super-charged graphics … vivid textures … extraordinary realism' and 'stunningly vibrant colours'.[52]

There are exceptions to this marketing rule. Nintendo, for example, enjoyed phenomenal sales success in the 2000s marketing its Wii home console and handheld DS hardware on the basis of unorthodox input devices (the Wii's motion control and the DS' touch-screen), rather than with regards to their graphical power (which, in each case, was lower than that of their respective rivals).[53] With the marketing of its more recent Switch console (launched in 2017), which can innovatively serve as both a home and portable handheld console, Nintendo again avoided emphasising graphical capabilities, and instead promoted the device on the basis of its unique functionality. Nintendo's twenty-first century manufacturing and marketing practices aside, however, hardware manufacturers have more generally placed a strong emphasis on improved graphics as part of console development and marketing activities. As James Newman argues, this has been a logical approach, as it is particularly convenient for companies to market a videogame or videogame console through television adverts, publicity screenshots and the like, on the basis of the 'visual richness' they provide.[54]

The particular nature of this hardware upgrade culture has greatly influenced the practices of videogame development and publishing. As the technology of home consoles has advanced, developers have been obliged to produce games that maximise the potential of new hardware so as to ensure their games' marketability. To support the marketing requirements of publishers, developers have, similar to hardware manufacturers, traditionally placed a strong emphasis on delivering enhanced graphics. Reflecting a common sentiment within broader gaming culture, Dovey and Kennedy contend that the console industry's configuration, wherein there is an imperative on developers to ensure their games deliver 'visual richness', greatly inhibits innovation and experimentation within the narrative design processes of videogames.[55]

Underpinning this circumstance, they argue, are the videogame development budgets required to meet this imperative, which have greatly escalated over the previous three decades. In 1993, the era in which the Sega Megadrive and Super Nintendo competed, average videogame development costs were approximately $300,000.[56] By the early 2000s, the time of the Sony PlayStation 2, Microsoft Xbox and Nintendo GameCube, average development costs for home console games had grown to $3–5 million.[57] By the decade's end, in the era of the Xbox 360, the PlayStation 3 and the Nintendo Wii, average costs of development had soared to $18–28 million.[58] Contrasting with this trend, the emergence of digital distribution within the home console market in the latter part of the 2000s and 2010s has served to make low-cost home console game development more viable than it was in the first part of the twenty-first century. Online platforms such as PlayStation Store and Nintendo eShop have enabled independent studios to bypass the market for full-price boxed-retail videogames and make smaller-scale, less labour-intensive 'indie' games sold at lower prices.[59] These games, which include *Limbo* (2010), *Gone Home* (2013) and *Hyper Light Drifter* (2016), typically prioritise innovative game design and highly stylised, and relatively simplistic, visuals over the achievement of intricately detailed and photo-realistic imagery. Despite this significant shift within the industry, the production of full-price boxed-retail games has remained extremely costly. Rockstar Games' development costs for *Max Payne 3* (2012), for example, were reported as $105 million, while the development costs for the publishers' subsequent release, *Grand Theft Auto V* (2013), reportedly surpassed $137 million.[60]

Largely contributing to these recent high costs of full-price boxed-retail games has been, observes Newman, the necessity for developers of such titles to grow team sizes so as to take advantage of increased console performance.[61] Whereas, in the 1970s and 1980s, a single coder could develop a retail game in its entirety, many contemporary console videogames need a workforce of hundreds to see them through to completion. Developers of contemporary full-price boxed-retail games, for example, require labour to construct complex cut-scenes, to design vast 3D geographies, to model and apply detailed textures to a multitude of characters, objects and settings, and to generate the great quantities of voice acting, motion-capture, character animations and orchestral music required for the tens of hours of game play that such games often provide. The developer is also charged with programming the 'game engine' technology; that is, the multitudes of code that control the presentation of the game as process. The game engine's tasks include the supervision of the AI system, the graphical rendering of characters, objects and environments in real-time response to a player's input, and the simulation of real-time, real-world physics (thus ensuring, for example, that the presentations of collisions between characters and objects achieve verisimilitude).[62] The game engine is built or modified so as to utilise the particular capabilities of a specific hardware for which a given game is intended. As Dovey and Kennedy observe, many developers reduce their workloads by procuring prefabricated engines or separate engine components (such as physics simulation systems). Epic Games, for example, widely licenses its Unreal Engine tech to the professional development community.[63]

Dovey and Kennedy argue that these dramatic rises in development costs that labour increases and/or game-engine procurement entail have driven two related trends within the industry's recent history that have combined to restrict innovation within development of full-price boxed-retail games. Firstly, they observe, rising budgets have contributed to a process of industrial consolidation. Development studios have traditionally been able to operate as entities separate from publishers but, with development costs having risen so sharply, such studio autonomy has proved increasingly difficult. Contemporary developers thus 'look to publishers to bear the risk of production investment', resulting in the acquisition or part-ownership of development studios by large publishers, including console manufacturers.[64] The publisher Activision, for example, owns Treyarch, Infinity Ward and Sledgehammer Games, the three studios behind the majority of the *Call of Duty* (2003–present) games, while Naughty Dog, developers of the *Uncharted* and *Last of Us* (2015–present) series, are a Sony subsidiary. This consolidation process has led to a small group of publishers, comprising the likes of Sony, Ubisoft, Activision, Nintendo, Square Enix, Electronic Arts and Take-Two Interactive, bankrolling and controlling a considerable portion of videogame development within the console sector.[65]

The second, related trend that Dovey and Kennedy identify as having arisen as a consequence of spiralling costs is the reliance by the aforementioned publishers on videogame series. Whereas new intellectual properties represent risky publishing endeavours, sequels provide 'publishers with guaranteed sales on the basis of previous marketing effort', and thus 'defray ever-increasing production costs'.[66] Former Activision CEO Bobby Kotick confirms the high importance to publishers' economic models of pre-sold properties. He observes that Activision seeks to publish titles that have the 'potential to be exploited every year on every platform with clear sequel potential to become $100 million dollar franchises'.[67] This process has led to a marketplace dominated by ongoing series, with instalments of such series as *Call of Duty*, Ubisoft's *Assassin's Creed* and Electronic Arts' various long-running sports titles being released year on year.[68]

For Dovey and Kennedy, this contemporary industrial/technological context in which development costs have become increasingly prohibitive, and in which publishers are looking to invest in 'safe bets', has restricted creativity within development. They perceive that developers' industrially mandated reliance on established game series contracts the 'space for innovation' within the creative process.[69] They observe that developers' often economically enforced dependence on 'off the shelf' game-engine tech has a 'determining effect upon the choices available to a software studio', leading to a predominance of particular game-design genres (such as the FPS).[70]

As a broad assessment of contemporary console-game development, this appears a reasonable one. It is true that the economically driven upgrade culture limits, through the sequel reliance that it induces, the range of storyworlds that the full-price boxed-retail games can convey. The pressure it places on developers to procure prefab game engines restricts creative options also. But, notwithstanding Dovey and Kennedy's conclusions, this very same cultural-industrial pattern consistently affords potential for innovation and experimentation within narrative design processes. While technological upgrade culture might lead to the restriction of certain choices due to the high development costs it necessitates, it nevertheless frequently alters and/or increases the technological possibilities of narrative. The following case studies explore the ways in which narrative designers' exploitation of such altered conditions has led to change and innovation within the narrative design processes of SDV series instalments.

To again refute the paradigm of technological determinism, however, it is important that the role of technology should not be considered a wholly defining force upon development. Rather, as with other sub-dimensions of specificity, the available technology establishes the parameters within which creative human agents operate. As I will show in the following case studies, the way in which developers negotiate these parameters is a complex activity, with individuals' creative visions, aesthetic preferences and assumptions regarding potential player experience filtering into decisions. To unpack this process it is helpful to break down into two categories the influence that technology brings to bear on narrative design processes. The first category of influence is the *essential influence*. Via this category, the particular affordances of a given technological context permit certain narrative design choices that would not otherwise be feasible. The second category is the *persuasive influence*. Via this category, creative decisions are not necessarily dependent upon the reconfigured technological context but are nonetheless informed by it. In such instances, developers, working with their own particular assumptions, adjust approaches so as to complement the introduction of new technologies in the way they deem best. The first case study, which compares the narrative design processes of the fifth game of the *Halo* series, *Halo: Reach*, with those of earlier instalments, focuses exclusively on the essential influence that a specific technology-set brings to bear on narrative.

'It's a Dark Story to Tell': Depicting the Fall in *Halo: Reach*

Halo: Combat Evolved, developed by Bungie, and published by Microsoft, served as the 'killer app' launch title for the Xbox, Microsoft's hardware entry into the home console market (in 2001). The game spawned an epic science fiction transmedia narrative concerning the human race's war with the Covenant that has been plotted serially across videogame sequels as well as literary and comic-book tie-ins. The example of *Halo: Reach*, Bungie's swansong for the franchise it birthed, demonstrates how technological upgrades during the series' life span influenced modifications to the narrative design process.[71] The game, the over-arching narrative of which charts the fall of the human colony of Reach, represents a significant technological advance for the series. This advance was due to an evolutionary hardware-facilitated leap in game-engine technology. Each *Halo* game operates via a proprietary game engine, which was initially engineered so as to complement the technological specification of the first generation of Xbox hardware (for which not only *Combat Evolved* but also *Halo 2* was developed). Despite developing *Halo 3* and *Halo 3: ODST* (2009) for the Xbox 360, Bungie's former creative director Marcus Lehto acknowledged that the *Halo* engine was, nine years on, 'showing its age'. It was in need of 'a major overhaul with particular regards to graphics', so that the developer could take greater advantage of the hardware upgrade (which occurred with the transition from Xbox to Xbox 360).[72] With *Halo: Reach*, Bungie rebuilt the *Halo* engine to maximise the 360's improved GPU and CPU and its superior memory. 'We're bending the Xbox as far as it'll bend', stressed Lehto.[73]

As part of Bungie's engine redesign, the developer incorporated, for the first time, an automated LOD (level of detail) optimisation system.[74] Via the LOD system, the amount of graphical detail that a character, or object, or area of setting possesses is determined by the distance of the first-person perspective from it. Thus a character viewed from far away is rudimentarily detailed, yet is positioned at such a distance that the paucity of detail is imperceptible. But as the first-person perspective nears said character, the detail enhances. This system provides a highly economical approach to the task of graphical rendering, as those characters and settings that are depicted at a great distance require far less processing capacity than they otherwise might. *Reach*'s LOD-supported engine permits graphically upgraded depictions of character and setting that markedly improve on even those of (the same hardware-utilising) *Halo 3*.[75] But Bungie's motivation for the engine overhaul was not merely to *enhance* appearances of character and setting, but also to significantly *expand* the scope of settings and *increase* the number of characters within settings at a given time. As Lehto explains, the developer was driven to transform its engine and thus fully exploit the Xbox 360 hardware so as to 'open up battlefields, push combat distances out and pack it full of twice as many things as [we've] ever managed to put into an environment'.[76]

The increased setting size that the upgraded game engine facilitated in *Halo: Reach* expanded the possible types of player-generated event sequences relative to earlier series instalments. In the development of game space, the scale of environment is influenced by the degree of graphical resolution that a developer intends to achieve. The higher the resolution, the greater the burden on the hardware's processing capacity. A developer keeps this burden at a sustainable level by limiting the size of the environment. As King and Krzywinska suggest, a developer faces a trade-off 'between detail and extensiveness'.[77] While *Combat Evolved* contained some memorably expansive combat spaces, the game environments in *Halo*s 2 and 3 contracted in size so as to permit more visually-complex depictions of characters, objects and setting.[78] This prioritisation of intricacy of detail over expanse of setting is reflective of an industry in which increased graphical resolution is often so central to the marketing of games. But, with *Reach*, the combination of LOD system and improved graphics-processing capacity permitted Bungie to construct larger environments than it had previously while still meeting the market requirement for enhanced graphical detail.[79] In a game such as *Halo 3*, many of the missions contain relatively narrow combat spaces that often lead to players being 'corridored' along specific routes, thus limiting the scope of potential player-generated event sequences.[80] In contrast, the expansive environments of *Reach* increase narrative possibilities. In the game, players are almost always presented with relatively wide, deep geographies that permit direct assaults from a variety of angles and routes, along with multiple opportunities to discreetly flank.

This expansion of setting, however, not only opens up the range of possibilities for player-character action, but for NPC action and characterisation also. In *Halo 3*, the Covenant brute species proves a perennial feature of combat encounters; their AI programming reflects not only their burly, angry appearance but the game's environments also. The brute, for example, charges directly if the player-character is in close proximity. As there are, in many situations, few other possible options available to the brute in the game's relatively restricted environments, this programming makes good sense. In *Halo: Reach*, however, rather than the brutes, it is the Covenant's 'elite' species that serves as an ever-present adversary. Bungie conceived the elites (which first appeared in *Combat Evolved*) to be, in contrast to the brutes, 'agile and cunning'.[81] The elite's appearance—long, relatively slender limbs and looking as if poised to pounce—certainly complements this intended characterisation. But, as noted, a given character's network of traits is indirectly defined not only by appearance, but also by a character's actions as depicted via narrative. To evoke agility and cunning, then, the elites require the capacity to demonstrate agility and cunning, which is something the game's environment provides. For example, during my play-throughs, elites (as per their programming) often exploited the width of the environments by executing subtle flanking manoeuvres so as to catch player-character Noble Six unawares. Many of these encounters indeed evolved into twisty 'hide and seek' event sequences between player-character and foe, with the elites able to frequently exhibit the sneaky personality programmed within them. The increase in environment size thus led to possibilities for player-generated events in *Reach* that are rarely present in *Halo 3*.

While its reconfigured game engine permitted Bungie to expand its settings, it similarly enabled the developer to elevate the number of characters and vehicles within a given environment. In *Halo 3*, for example, Bungie had to limit the number of active NPCs within a given combat space to approximately 20; in *Halo: Reach*, the developer could incorporate up to 40 active NPCs, plus a further 20 vehicles.[82] This facility for greater character numbers in *Reach* added complexity to player-generated action. With Noble Six having to face a greater number of enemies in a single encounter than at any point previous in the *Halo* series, the player-generated event sequences often unfold as chaotic, bewildering battles.

The facility for an increased number of NPCs has, however, also laid conditions for player-generated event sequences to emerge that are unusually idiosyncratic for the series. For example, as part of the 'Nightfall' mission, Noble Team arrives at a pump station under Covenant siege. A Reach militia force is already penned in at the location, under fire from a Covenant phantom ship that is offloading a division of grunts, elites and other species. Noble Team's objective, the player is informed by a UNSC communication, is to aid the militia in their fight. Rounding out this already relatively complicated cast is a flock of moaa (harmless ostrich-type creatures) that inhabit the environment, and which Noble Six will likely happen upon during the mission. The inclusion of the moaa adds a layer of fictional complexity often absent from FPS player-generated narratives. These nervous birds scamper around the battlefield, searching for cover while emitting pitched shrieks that pierce the sound of incessant artillery. During my second play-through of the pump-station siege, Noble Six fell through a trapdoor to a basement in which the moaa were cowering from the firefight. Taking a few seconds to absorb the oddness of the view, I slowly weaved Noble Six through the shivering, murmuring birds and guided him back to the fray. In the context of the tradition of first-person shoot-outs, such a strange, offbeat event sequence is unusual. By affording such action, the game fleshes out the storyworld, adding variety and complexity; but this is an affordance that is born from the increased NPC numbers that Bungie was able to incorporate within the setting due to the specificities of the technological conditions of narrative design.

With its game engine built to maximise the graphical capabilities of the Xbox 360, Bungie facilitated the type of player-generated event sequences that, due to their requirement of an increase in setting and cast size, are not feasible within prior *Halo* instalments. As a result of the distinctive nature of some its player-generated action, the *Halo* storyworld presented in *Reach* thus contrasts with that conveyed in prior games. But the *Reach* engine, with its LOD system freeing up hardware capacity, in addition permitted Bungie to incorporate multiple scripted events within the backdrop settings (beyond the boundaries of playable areas), which unfold onscreen simultaneous to player-generated event sequences. This storytelling practice, which serves to richly contextualise the player-generated storyworld material within *Halo*'s wider serial narrative, represents an important departure in plotting technique.

This approach to narrative design grew out of a trend within development processes to achieve ever-lengthier draw-distances (that is, the visible distance from a player's perspective to the horizon) that the late 2000s home console generation facilitated. As part of those discourses regarding the lure of spectacle, scholars observe that the detail drawn into the distance of 3D environments can provide pleasures unconnected to narrative. Barry Atkins, for example, notes that rich backdrops to an environment allow players to experience 'touristic moments of restful admiration'.[83] The first *Halo* game, however, while generally celebrated for its graphical prowess, contains background landscapes that were regarded as unremarkable, even at the time of release.[84] But the technological advance of the subsequent high-definition console generation permitted the series drawdistances far greater in length, enabling developers to present deeper and more detailed background environments. *Halo 3*, with its inclusion of an array of remarkable vistas of vast deserts and mountain ranges, was roundly regarded as having achieved some of the most impressive feats of drawdistance within gaming.[85]

Supported by its overhauled game engine, *Reach* incorporates draw-distances not only greater than *Halo 3* but more detailed also.[86] Throughout the game, however, a player who accepts the invitation to gaze into the backdrop scenery is not necessarily disconnected from the game's story-telling. This is because Bungie specifically engineered many of the back-grounds in *Reach* to support the game's broader fiction. The draw-distances in *Reach* thus represent not only feats in technical virtuosity; they also function as an added dimension to *Halo* narrative. Bungie, utilising a tech-nique that I will refer to here as *draw-distance storytelling*, crafted scripted event sequences to play out within the environment's non-playable back-drop spaces. This practice, which is also evident in SDV series such as *Gears of War* and *God of War* (2005–present), relates to the broader tradi-tion of embedded narratives, but is distinguished by its utilisation of set-ting, not to speak to a fictional history (as in *Portal*), but so as to incorporate distinct scripted storyworld action that advances concurrent with player-generated events.

Certain instances of this storytelling were introduced into the extended backdrops of *Halo 3*, but equipped with the LOD system Bungie were able to significantly expand upon this technique within *Reach* so as to convey the great scope of the Covenant's planet-wide attack. The devel-oper's implementation of larger scale battlefields and increased numbers of enemy combatants certainly contribute towards providing the depiction of 'full scale planetary invasion' that the description on the *Reach* game-case promises. But Bungie in addition utilised its distances, along with its sky-boxes (which contain the graphical presentation of the storyworld's sky), to portray the wider conflict beyond those clashes within which Noble Six is directly engaged. As Lehto observes, the *Reach* engine allowed Bungie 'not only to draw further distances than ever before in any *Halo* game, but [also to] cram [these distances] full of objects'. These objects most nota-bly include all manner of background vehicles and aircraft—'hundreds of little units out there fighting one another'—that comprise 'huge battles raging in the distance'.[87] By allowing 'us to not only see the localized battles we're engaged in, but the battles that are out and around us as well', suggests Lehto, 'we really get the sense that Reach is under siege'.[88]

By having this scripted backdrop storyworld action occur parallel to the player-generated combat sequences, Bungie disrupts plotting patterns tra-ditional to the *Halo* series and SDVs more generally. Via a more conven-tional approach to plotting, the cut-scenes that intervene in game-play segments would provide a perspective on the storyworld action of the wider Reach conflict, while the game-play sections would focus on the player-generated action exclusively. This type of plotting whereby a game alternates between scripted events and player-generated events is one typical of SDVs. Yet the structure is often regarded as a jarring one, with the relationship between cut-scenes and game-play sections sometimes considered tenuous.[89] *Reach* continues this reliance on traditional cut-scenes as a means of storyworld exposition; but, crucially, by exploiting the particular affordances of its upgraded game engine and intended hardware platform, Bungie aligns scripted and player-generated event sequences to appear onscreen simultaneously as parallel plot strands. This narrative design strategy engineers further coherence between player-generated elements and the broader scripted storyworld that is presented within the game and serially across multiple instalments.

The game's 'Tip of the Spear' mission, which includes complex, faraway battles within its distances, shows how Bungie has utilised this system of parallel plotting so as to forge a tighter narrative unity between player-generated action and the broader storyworld. The menu description for 'Tip of the Spear' reads, 'Two massive armies clash. Time to go to war against the Covenant.' The cut-scene prior to the mission start emphasises this theme; a high-angled shot reveals a vast UNSC force comprised largely of warthogs (armoured ground vehicles) and falcon helicopters heading fast across a craggy desert setting to face a similar-sized mass of Covenant aircraft and land vehicles. But, so as to evade Covenant mortar rounds, a warthog containing Noble Six navigates away from the army's course, crossing a canyon bridge. The cut-scene ends as a mortar round destroys the bridge, with the impact simultaneously putting Noble Six's warthog out of commission. At this point, game play recommences and Noble Six finds himself within a combat zone surrounded by enemy NPCs. The events within the foreground of the camera perspective concern the player-generated actions that transpire between Noble Six and the enemy NPCs within his proximity; but Bungie, due to specific technological affordances, is able to layer a secondary plot strand of scripted events within the distance that pertain to the larger UNSC force from which Noble Six's Warthog has become detached.

For example, one of the mission's narrative goals requires Noble Six to neutralise an anti-aircraft gun overlooking a valley, within, above and beyond which a battle rages. Upon the valley floor, the warthog convoy from which Noble Six departed is shown heading towards three imposing scarabs (towering four-legged Covenant vehicles). Above, dogfights between falcons and banshees (Covenant air-fighters) populate the sky-box. In the distance, red lights flicker and black smoke plumes, implying further large-scale combat and/or destruction. This draw-distance story-world action, which picks up a loose plot strand from the prior cut-scene, serves to strengthen association between player-generated events and the wider conflict of the 'Tip of the Spear' mission.

Bungie enriches this fictional context for game play by establishing fur-ther connections between these dual plot strands of backdrop scripted events and foregrounded player-generated action. One such connection occurs if and when Noble Six destroys the aforementioned anti-aircraft gun. By completing the narrative goal, Noble Six frees the skies, permitting two UNSC heavy frigates to descend upon the background and rain heavy fire upon the scarabs, destroying them in the process and consequently freeing up the path for the warthog convoy.

It is a winning moment for Noble Six; gratitude rings from a commu-nications device lauding the Spartan soldier for his efforts. But as the game progresses, as the Covenant gain the upper hand, the tone darkens, and such triumphalism dissipates. As Lehto remarks, 'Reach is going to fall and 700 million people are going to perish as a result. It's a very dark story to tell.'[90] In later missions, distant action contributes to this narrative theme of despair via its contextualisation of player-generated events within the general storyline of the planet's destruction. So, whereas the draw-distance storytelling in 'Tip of the Spear' indicates the positive effect Noble Six's input has upon the wider storyworld, the backdrop scripted action that appears later within the game emphasises the *lack* of influence a player has over the planet's decline. By detailing the collapse of Reach, a storyworld incident that serves as catalyst for future UNSC/Covenant battles, these instances of distant scripted action function as foundations to the serial narrative of the entire *Halo* franchise.

Halo: Reach's 'New Alexandria' mission, within which Noble Six pilots a falcon above the city of New Alexandria as it perishes from Covenant attack, provides a useful example of this practice. Noble Six's mission requires the Spartan to fly to multiple city locations so as to provide air support to the UNSC's evacuation of citizens. During this player-generated event sequence, Bungie conveys the full scale of a city under siege within the background. The setting, as depicted at the commencement of the mis-sion, consists of rows behind rows of skyscrapers, seemingly tens of miles deep. Isolated infernos can be seen littering the cityscape, with black smoke flowing up into a purple dusk. As the mission progresses, the condition of the city visibly worsens. In the backdrop, as a night sky descends, torched towers stand as twisted silhouettes between the player and a fiery skyline. The precise cause of the destruction is indicated when two Covenant battle-cruisers are depicted descending upon the city to dispatch further carnage. The two craft deliver sustained plasma blasts to various sections of the city, a process known within *Halo* fiction as 'glassing'. Such scripted narrative subverts that which Ryan identifies as the 'archetypal narrative pattern' common within SDVs whereby 'a hero receives a mission, and fulfils it by performing various tasks, and gets rewarded in the end'.[91] While this 'hero-quest' storyworld model is typical of prior *Halo* games, the draw-distance storytelling within the 'New Alexandria' mission undermines this convention. The player can ensure that Noble Six completes his narrative goal via his support of the evacuation of some New Alexandria citizens, and thus gain a small victory. But the orbiting scripted events consistently emphasise that the wider, crushing conflict is beyond both the player and player-character's scope of control.

The specific capabilities of the Xbox 360 hardware, and the affordances of a game engine configured so as to fully exploit these capabilities, permitted Bungie to elaborate significantly on the *Halo* series' trademark epic storytelling. As part of its narrative design process, the developer ensured that player-generated storyworld event sequences, due to increased setting size and character numbers, marked an elevation in complexity. It furthermore reinforced, via its draw-distance storytelling device, the association between player-generated event sequences and the broader scripted plotting that serves to cohere the various instalments of the series. Yet, despite these clear innovations, the console upgrade of the mid-2000s facilitated in *Red Faction: Guerrilla* a more drastic transformation in narrative design process. Utilising advanced physics and geometry modification game-engine systems in order to make setting destruction central to player-generated events, the developer Volition ensured that *Guerrilla* represents a major narrative departure for the series.

'DIRECT ASSAULTS ARE SUICIDE': *RED FACTION: GUERRILLA*'S NARRATIVE OF DESTRUCTION

The first *Red Faction* game's unique selling point on release was the degree of destruction within the Martian setting that the developers' geometry modification (Geo-Mod) game-engine tech permits.[92] Within the game, players are able to have the player-character use weapons to deform and/or destroy the terrain of the planet's mine network. The capabilities of this Geo-Mod system afford certain possibilities for player-generated action that would otherwise be unavailable. For example, rather than approach Ultor security personnel through existing paths, you can have the player-character use explosives to blow through cave walls and then reach enemy NPCs via the alternative routes that the tunnelling creates. While innovative for the time, the environmental destruction in *Red Faction*, and its sequel *Red Faction II*, was, as contemporary reviewers lamented, still limited, and an often-peripheral component to the player-generated narrative experience.[93] Only certain stages incorporate destructible environments within the games, and usually only certain elements of a given environment are destructible. In these games, geometry modification is generally a novel supplement to the conventional player-generated action typical of FPS games.

The comparison between the first two games of the series and the third, *Red Faction: Guerrilla*, demonstrates the all-encompassing influence on development that a generational leap in hardware can bring. For *Guerrilla*, Volition was able to build the Geo-Mod 2.0 system, which utilises the increased processing capacity of the newer console generation, with this updated engine permitting the player a far greater range of destruction. Set above ground within a vast Martian settlement, comprising homes, skyscrapers, administrative halls and industrial plants (among many other building types), every single man-made structure within *Guerrilla* is completely destructible. As the game's senior associate producer Sean Kennedy observes, Volition had to wait for 'technology to catch up' so as to realise its vision of a 'completely destructive environment'.[94]

Not only does the range of setting destruction that *Guerrilla* affords represent a departure from the earlier two *Red Faction*s, so too does its game engine's incorporation of upgraded real-time physics systems. This tech contributes to simulations of destruction that achieve a far greater sophistication than those of previous *Red Faction* games, and which facilitate entirely new kinds of player-generated storyworld events. The game's physics are well evident in the environmental structures' 'stress system'. Following the player-character Mason's partial destruction of a tower's foundations via explosives, for example, the structure might begin to slowly collapse from the pressure of its own weight, with parts of the building crumbling. As a result of the developer's design, the process of complete collapse might continue for minutes after Mason's initial action.[95]

Due to the physics system's sophisticated collision detection component there are often meaningful consequences to such destruction, as the game simulates realistic outcomes of storyworld elements colliding. As one of the game's producers Rick White puts it, the fall-out of destruction often 'hurts you, and it hurts the people around you'.[96] The delayed collapse of said tower, for example, could (depending on where explosive charges have been placed) result in parts of the structure falling upon, and killing, Mason, or enemy EDF troops, or even the fellow colonists that Mason is tasked with protecting. Instead, maybe, the tower will only fall upon and destroy Mason's vehicle, and thus his means of escape from his guerrilla-warfare excursion. Or maybe the tower will only subside harmlessly into the red dust, without any knock-on storyworld events. The engine's process of simulating real-world, real-time physical consequences of the player's input, then, often results in highly variable and unpredictable player-generated event sequences that can surprise, entertain, even horrify (as at least was the case in my own play-through).

Via the facilitation of these new possibilities for player-generated storyworld action, the essential influence of increased memory and processing capacity upon the series' narrative is clear. But the presence of this advanced technology also performed a persuasive influence within development, with wider aspects of the narrative design process altered so as to complement the narratives of destruction that the game permits. For example, *Guerrilla* marks a departure in the series from a traditional fixed linear plot. In the first two games, players are often given little choice but to conform to a predetermined sequence of narrative goals. But for Volition, a tightly controlled linear plot pattern, supported by a corridor-heavy environment, was deemed to be practically and philosophically at odds with the game engine's affordances. Volition had little incentive to tightly hem in a player with impenetrable barriers simultaneous to its implementation of a completely destructible setting. The developer opted instead for an open-world, variable plot structure, thus facilitating a far greater freedom of movement, and providing players with a great deal of choice regarding the sequence in which missions are undertaken. As Sean Kennedy recalled during development, 'With that level of destruction and that freedom it [Geo-Mod 2.0] gives you, it only makes sense to take it and move it into an open world.'[97] To progress within the game, the player is still obliged to have Mason engage in particular player-generated event sequences so as to achieve certain narrative goals, but, via this approach to plotting, the order in which these batches of action occur is flexible.

Changes in the nature of setting from earlier games reflect this shift to an open environment and non-linear plot structure. In the first two *Red*

*Faction*s the closed interiors within which the player-character generally operates (inside buildings or subterranean caverns) complements their relatively constraining level designs. As Fig. 5.1 indicates, so as to complement a design approach that metaphorically 'corridors' the player-character, Volition sometimes chose to restrict player-characters to long corridors within the game's fiction. In contrast, *Guerrilla*'s open, exterior Martian setting is appropriate to the greater freedom of movement that the game provides. As Fig. 5.2 illustrates, the player is presented with open, expansive exterior spaces, offering players a wider range of options concerning the path the player-character will take.

Volition's strong motivation to encourage players to utilise *Guerrilla*'s distinct affordances led to further changes in narrative design from the first two *Red Factions*. The developer, for example, ensured that narrative goals in *Guerrilla* made geometry modification a more central component to player-generated events than it had proved in previous games. As White notes, Volition's desire was to 'make the destruction meaningful to the game play, make it part of the game play'.[98] The 'high' and 'low' narrative goals that *Guerrilla* assigns reflect this, as they are more closely linked to the game engine's destruction-based tech than in previous games. An

Fig. 5.1 'Corridored' setting in the original *Red Faction* (2001)

Fig. 5.2 Open, exterior Martian setting in *Red Faction: Guerrilla* (2009)

example of a low-level goal would be an individual mission that tasks Mason with destroying the structures of an EDF industrial works or army barracks, say. But such missions also contribute to the higher-order goal of 'liberating' the settlement, an objective that is ultimately achieved, not by killing members of the occupying force, but by destroying the many buildings and structures under EDF control within the setting.

Along with the privileging of destruction via the assignation of narrative goals, Volition made further efforts to have players engage with the game's particular environmental affordances by deterring players from the first two games' 'trigger-happy' FPS play style. While, in *Guerrilla*, the EDF often protects its buildings (Mason's targets) with armed guards that require negotiation or elimination, the game punishes a conventional attack. The game's scripted tutorial elements indeed warn the player of this, mandating instead a guerrilla warfare 'hit and run' approach. The 'Guerrilla Handbook' (which comprises a collection of tutorial videos), for example, grounds such guidance within the overriding storyworld fiction of a rebel outfit taking on a military force:

> The EDF is a professional military organisation. They've got the money, the training, and the firepower to take us down. Direct assaults are suicide, we need to hit their weak points, attack them when they least expect it, destroy their high value targets ... and then get the hell out of there.

If a player, however, opts not to heed this warning and have Mason take on EDF personnel in a protracted shoot-out, enemy troops are configured to overpower in their numbers. White observes that the futility of a direct approach within the game was intentional on behalf of Volition. 'If you just "run and gun" straight in there, you're going to lose. We wanted that', he says.[99] Volition, instead, intended for players 'to use the destruction to be able to overcome the EDF [troops]', thus making it 'part of [the player's] tactics'.[100] The weapons that Mason is provided throughout the game further reflect Volition's mandate that players generate event sequences within which destruction is central. Mason begins the game, not with a firearm (as per generic convention), but with explosive charges and a sledgehammer, weapons that are inappropriate for direct confrontation with enemy NPCs. A more traditional pistol and assault rifle are made available later in the game, but so too are further weapons intended to exploit the setting's destructible nature, such as: the nano rifle, which allows Mason to shoot a liquid that triggers the fast deterioration of a wall's integrity; the rail driver, which permits Mason to identify and shoot EDF troops through walls; and the thermo barrack rocket launcher, which has the capacity to bring down entire buildings.

Through the narrative goals it assigns, its incorporation within the storyworld of an enemy force resistant to direct assault, and its inclusion of a weapon set more useful for demolition than for directly eliminating NPCs, Volition has encouraged players to tactically utilise the destructible setting. While, in the first two *Red Factions*, a player looking to progress within the game is required to directly engage with enemy NPCs, *Guerrilla*, in contrast, rewards engagement via oblique means. Tasked with destroying a heavily guarded EDF facility, for example, a player might have Mason strap explosives to his truck and speed towards the target, timing his leap from the vehicle just before impact. Or, having had Mason place explosives within a structure, the player, alerted to the approach of an EDF force, might have Mason lure the NPCs within the structure before triggering the explosives, thus collapsing the building down upon them. Or, in an effort to ensure escape after destroying a target, the player might have Mason bring down a smokestack so that its rubble impedes the path of the oncoming EDF. By urging and affording such tactics, *Guerrilla* lays the conditions for an array of player-generated events that would not be possible in earlier *Red Factions*.

The ramifications of the destruction-based technology also persuaded Volition to considerably alter its approach to the narrative style of *Guerrilla*, with the developer departing from the first-person view of the first two *Red Factions*. The shift in style came about during the game's development process as the implications of the real-time physics and collision detection systems became apparent. As Sean Kennedy recalls,

> At the beginning of [the development process] we actually had it in first-person ... and what we found was that it wasn't any fun ... There's all this stuff blowing up around you, and you can't see it. Suddenly you die and you don't know why, but it's because some piece fell on you, whereas if the camera had been further back you'd have seen the aircraft shooting that block off a building ... If you have a game built around destruction, where you're forced to really use it, you need to be able to see it.[101]

In response to the problems they encountered, the developers opted, recalls Sean Kennedy, to 'pull the camera back', switching the series' previous first-person perspective to a wider third-person style, with Mason in full view.[102] The change permits players a greater awareness of the sequences of events that occur within this dynamically shifting environment, and then have Mason act accordingly. Mason might still die as the result of the fall-out from his destructive acts, but at least with a third-person perspective the player will understand *why* Mason has died in a particular instance. This insight thus gives an indication regarding how technological specificity can factor into a developer's decisions regarding the designation of 'point of view'.

While the key distinction between *Guerrilla* and earlier games in the series relates to the different modes of player-generated action it facilitates, the hardware upgrade that separates *GTA IV* (2008) from its predecessors did not influence a similarly significant shift. Broadly speaking, the narrative goals and affordances for player-generated storyworld events established in *GTA III* (2001) are indeed akin to those of *GTA IV*. In both games, the player guides a player-character around the three-dimensional setting of Liberty City so as to undertake missions typically entailing some variation on car-theft, the shooting of rival hoodlums and the evasion of police capture (via car chases). Yet *GTA IV* does provide an important example of the way in which enhanced technologies influence different approaches to the development of the key storyworld components of character and setting. The following section charts this process, demonstrating how technology informed the formulation of *GTA IV*'s distinct urban landscape and its enigmatic player-character, the troubled East European immigrant Niko Belic.

'MISERABLE BASTARD': GETTING 'REAL' IN *GTA IV*

Whereas distinct unbroken storylines run through each of the *Halo* and *Red Faction* series—the ongoing war between the UNSC and the Covenant in the former, and the miners' continuing fight against dictatorial oppression in the latter, the seriality of the *GTA* games is far subtler. The storytelling of the series, developed by Rockstar North, and published by Rockstar Games (a subsidiary of Take-Two Interactive), is indeed analogous to the implied continuity of contemporary comics (see Chap. 4). Each sequel features a new player-character and a distinct storyline that plays out via a combination of scripted events and the player-character's pursuit of narrative goals, while references to an ongoing storyworld remain at the periphery. For example, *GTA IV* sees the return of Lazlow, a radio presenter who appears in prior *GTA* games; the broadcaster can be heard through car stereos speaking wistfully regarding a previous rock-DJ stint (which occurs in the earlier *Grand Theft Auto: Vice City* [2002]). The most consistently implied continuity relates, however, to the games' fictional settings. The original *GTA* game, for example, introduced the location of Liberty City, an analogue of New York City, and a setting that features in many *GTA* games, including *III* and *IV*. The city sometimes bears the marks of its history; graffiti within an apartment block in *IV*, for instance, name checks a roster of previous *GTA* player-characters.

Despite this storyworld consistency, however, the nature of the city as presented in *GTA IV* marks a departure from previous articulations of the location. The hardware upgrade from Xbox and PlayStation 2 (the host platforms for *GTA III*) to Xbox 360 and PlayStation 3 (the host platforms for *GTA IV*) afforded this change, permitting a great increase in the degree of detail with which Rockstar North was able to infuse the metropolis and its citizens. As Rockstar Games co-founder and creative vice-president Dan Houser claimed during the development of *GTA IV*, the later generation of hardware enabled a 'low-def to hi-def' transition in the developer's depiction of Liberty City.[103] As this section shows, the upgraded graphical technology permitted Rockstar North to achieve its objective of providing a more realistic and complex environment than in previous *GTA* games; as the section also shows, this process, in turn, ultimately exerted a persuasive influence upon Niko's characterisation.

Reflective of an industry that seeks to gain cultural legitimacy while simultaneously demonstrating its technical mastery, the production culture of videogames has long aspired to photorealistic visuals. As Darley suggests,

'The dominant visual aesthetic of verisimilitude is now viewed as the main sign of success and progress within the [videogame] form.'[104] Symptomatic of this cultural preference, developers have, as scholars observe, often utilised upgraded technologies with the express aim of generating graphics that edge ever closer to a 'real' ideal.[105] This goal proved central to the development of *GTA IV*. As Rockstar Games president and co-founder Sam Houser recalls regarding the direction the project took during the conception phase, 'A more realistic Liberty City very quickly became the favourite option.'[106] This led to the developer heavily mining its reference point, New York City, for realistic detail. A research group, for example, stationed within the city, filmed hours of traffic flow and sky movement, took hundreds of thousands of photos of structures and pedestrians, and broke down the ethnic make-up of particular inner-city locations.[107]

Equipped with such research, Rockstar North utilised the intended hardware's advanced graphical technology to create a storyworld setting that not only edges closer to photorealism but that also provides a truer representation of the dichotomies of urban space. The Liberty City of *GTA III*, with its relatively rudimentary surface textures, had merely been, notes Rockstar North art director Aaron Garbut, 'a generic American city with a Manhattan-esque skyline in the middle'.[108] But as Rockstar Games' Hamish Brown suggests, *GTA IV* captures 'not just the beauty, but also the oppressive, stifling and gritty urban environment of New York'. This setting dichotomy is evident, for example, in the contrasting surface textures of different locations. The brash neon artifice beaming down upon a grimy sidewalk; the glistening riverbank sand, and the grim detritus collected upon it; the stark, white sterility of a sports-car showroom and its contrast to the squalid tenement building stairwell, the graffiti and flaking paint plain to see on its grubby, yellowing walls.

During the narrative design process of *The Wire*, as Chap. 3 shows, the specificity of HBO's economic model was an important factor in Simon and his collaborators being able to foreground the diverse Baltimore environment; the subscription service's model facilitated the extensive location shooting and lingering wide shots that this storytelling approach entailed. During the narrative design process of *GTA IV*, however, it was the specificity of technology (in the form of console hardware) that provided Rockstar with the means to build and present a highly detailed, multi-faceted Liberty City.

The more naturalistic actions of NPCs complement Liberty City's greater degree of realism within the game. The integration of the Euphoria physics system, as part of the *GTA IV* game engine, for example, enables the console to process simulations of NPCs' nervous systems, thus leading to subtle physical responses to player-character actions.[109] For instance, in *GTA III* a pedestrian will remain oblivious to their close proximity to its player-character Claude; but in *GTA IV*, if Niko walks carelessly close to another citizen, the NPC might stumble a step back, raising their hand, whilst emitting a line of dialogue that suggests they are affronted to have their personal space invaded so. By permitting Rockstar North to increase the verisimilitude of its characters and setting, this technological context exerted both an essential and persuasive influence upon the developer with regard to the design of Niko Belic. This influence ultimately resulted in *GTA IV*'s player-character attaining a degree of complexity that was unprecedented for the series at that time, and which is evoked through physical appearance and cut-scene material.

Protagonists from prior *GTA* games are generally basic personalities. *GTA III*'s Claude, for example, remains a shallow, nondescript figure throughout the scripted cut-scene sequences. He carries out errands for Liberty City's crime bosses without question, and reveals little within scripted events regarding the emotions or motivations that drive his player-generated felonies. *GTA: San Andreas'* (2004) CJ proves a richer persona; following the gang-related deaths of his mother and brother, he endeavours to rise above the street life of his youth. But, in comparison to *GTA IV*'s Niko, the unreflective CJ appears rather a simple, uncomplicated construct—a 'likeable chump', as *Edge* magazine remarked.[110] Niko, a veteran soldier of the Balkan Conflict is revealed, via conversations in cut-scenes, to possess an intricate and contradictory personality (much like *GTA IV*'s Liberty City). He is, for example, at times sweetly naive while at others, jaded, cynical, nihilistic even. As Dan Houser puts it, 'On the one hand he's an innocent, on the other hand he's battle hardened and world weary.'[111] He arrives at Liberty City believing in his cousin Roman's false promises of wealth and opportunity, but he also responds with the driest sarcasm to people and the world around him. He is disdainful of the values and capricious consumerism of the capitalist West, though he simultaneously deplores the former Communist ideals of his homeland. He often cuts a morose figure, too, haunted by the atrocities he witnessed and participated in during conflict, details of which are divulged or alluded to within scripted storyworld material throughout the game. An off-hand remark by Roman emphasises the distinct, unusually complicated nature of Niko's character within the context of the *GTA* series. During one cut-scene, subsequent to Niko making yet another oblique reference to his dark past, Roman declares, 'You know, for a sociopathic killer, you're really a miserable bastard.'

The specific graphical affordances of the game's intended platforms exerted an essential influence on this characterisation, as it permitted the developer to design a physical appearance for Niko that corresponds with the character traits that are evoked through cut-scene dialogue. As Dan Houser confirms, Rockstar North has tended to ensure that *GTA* characters are written in accordance with the degree of characterisation that game-engine and hardware can visually articulate and thus indirectly define.[112] In developing *GTA III* and *GTA: San Andreas*, Rockstar North did not operate within a technical context that would permit characters to express a wide range of facial expressions. Claude and CJ's faces are instead often vacant and do little to help convey any particular emotion. The simplistic nature of their characters as imparted via dialogue was intended to complement the technological specificity of these games' development processes. With *GTA IV*, Rockstar North, utilising the enhanced capabilities of the intended console platforms, integrated the Image Metrics animation system into its game engine, which afforded improved facial detail and movement. 'We can have some degree of emotion now because we can go in close on the characters and their faces look great', Dan Houser remarked.[113] As a consequence of the technological upgrade, Niko's visage often contrasts with the blank expressions found in previous *GTA* games, and complements the characterisation that emerges through the scripted-narrative dialogue. For example, shadowy eyes and furrowed brow complement the jaded aspect of his character, while his wide, goggle-eyed responses to certain events contribute to the defining of his innocent side.

If technology proved an essential influence due to its permission of more highly complex facial animations, however, the heightened verisimilitude that the technological context more generally provided the game was the persuasive influence that informed the particularly dark, morose nature of Niko's personality. According to King and Krzywinska, 'Graphics that offer more closely grained or photorealistic impressions of the world on-screen can increase—at least relatively—the resonance of the experience.'[114] One might question whether this claim is applicable to the universality of gaming experiences, but the assumption is certainly one that Rockstar North shared. The developer perceived that the enhanced graphical presentation of Liberty City and its inhabitants (in *GTA IV*) brought with it a greater resonance with reality.[115] Working with the assumption that the trademark *GTA* experience would feel more 'real' than ever before, Rockstar North concluded that the implementation of a bleaker narrative tone was required. This would, the developer surmised, provide the appropriate context for the game's more realistic presentations of murder, mayhem and general violence that regularly punctuate player-generated action. As Sam Houser observes:

> The game as a whole definitely is darker, but that's because the resolution of the experience is greater. So if you think about playing *GTA III* or *San Andreas* in this resolution, we'd have to harden and toughen up the tone because the characters would look that much more real and the place would look that much more real.[116]

This creative mindset also led to the developer culling certain light-hearted storyworld components that feature in previous games. The clothes available to Niko are not nearly as ostentatious and outrageous as those available to player-characters in prior instalments, for example; other frivolous items, such as the fan-favourite jetpack from *GTA: San Andreas*, were also abandoned. But the character of Niko proves the key indicator to this transition in sensibility. The formulation of his dour, angst-ridden personality and the foregrounding of his horrific past within the scripted storyworld material was the strongest consequence of the persuasive influence of technology upon Rockstar North's vision.

The comparison between *GTA IV* and earlier games in the series demonstrates the complex ways in which the upgrading of graphical capacity can factor into the formulation of storyworld elements. But the final case study, which compares *GTA IV* to *GTA: Chinatown Wars*, reveals not only how the particular degree of graphical capacity within a given hardware device influences development, but also how other specific hardware components inform narrative design processes. *Chinatown Wars*, developed by Rockstar Leeds simultaneous to Rockstar North's development of *GTA IV*, was built initially for the Nintendo DS handheld console, and released mere months following the *GTA IV* home console release. By considering how the availability of contrasting hardware at a single given time informs narrative design processes within the same SDV series, this case study, unlike those earlier in this chapter, tests the relevance not of diachronic variability in technology but synchronic variability instead.

'THOSE LITTLE DETAILS': DS SPECIFICITY IN *GTA: CHINATOWN WARS*

According to Rockstar Leeds president Gordon Hall, 'All the design ideas [for *GTA: Chinatown Wars*] were tailored from their inception for the [DS] platform.'[117] Nevertheless, much of the storyworld that the game presents is firmly within the fictional tradition of *GTA*. In the game, the player guides the player-character of Huang Lee, who is tasked with ensuring the Lee family's consolidation of Liberty City's Triad gangs. As with *GTA IV*, much of the player-generated events that emerge from the game's missions, which are contextualised by this higher-order narrative goal, concern car chases and shoot-outs. But despite the thematic similarities of storyworld actions and locations, the specificities of the DS hardware technology exerted a persuasive influence on Rockstar Leeds, leading to approaches to narrative design that were new to the series. In some instances, the limitations of Nintendo's handheld device, relative to the more powerful home consoles, factored into these fresh approaches; but in other instances the unique capabilities of the hardware, specifically regarding its touch-screen input, also proved an important influence. Looking first at the relative limitations, I show how the graphical capacity, audio capabilities and screen size of the handheld console proved key to influencing *Chinatown Wars'* narrative style, which is unique to the series.

The most obvious point of distinction with regards to style in *Chinatown Wars* relates to the game's 'camera' angle. During game play, the positioning of the perspective on Huang represents a compromise between the home console *GTAs* of the 1990s and those of the twenty-first century. Despite the 3D capabilities of the host PlayStation platform, Rockstar North (then DMA Design) utilised a top-down, 2D view of Liberty City for the original *GTA* (1997). This economical mode of presentation enabled the developer to permit the player a degree of freedom to explore Liberty City that was remarkable for an action game at the time.[118] Only by exploiting the superior graphical capacity of the Xbox and PlayStation 2 had Rockstar North been able to present the vast geography of Liberty City in a 3D third-person perspective in *GTA III*. Rockstar Leeds maintained the three-dimensional perspective of the latter games with *Chinatown Wars*, but elected to position the view from a steep angle at a high placement (the isometric projection perspective). There were, observed Hall, two distinct hardware-related reasons for this choice. Firstly, the high-angled perspective permitted the developer to achieve a three-dimensional presentation while simultaneously conserving the graphical capacity required to draw far off into the distance. For *GTA IV*, Rockstar North, utilising the more powerful home console hardware, developed a game in which miles of Liberty City's complex skyline are depicted in intricate detail. But, notes Hall, Rockstar Leeds concluded that 'the overhead camera would enable us to spend the [relatively limited] polygon budget the DS has on cool game play visuals, not far away cityscapes'.[119]

The second reason concerns not the graphical capacity of the handheld console, but its small screen size (6 × 5 cm approx.). As noted in Chap. 2, producers of transmedia television content have sometimes aimed to develop visual styles deemed to complement the small displays of smartphone screens. The isometric projection in *Chinatown Wars* was similarly conceived as a style appropriate to the restricted screen size of the game's host hardware. As Hall explains, via the third-person perspective of *GTA III* and *IV*, it would be difficult to present, within the confines of the DS screen, the full array of relevant events that can occur within a given moment, such as the actions of police or rival-gang NPCs. But by elevating the view the player can more easily discern the full scope of the unfolding storyworld events. 'On a big screen, having a camera behind the player's head works perfectly', says Hall. 'However, on this machine, with its relatively small display, you get a much more appealing experience if you can see all of the crashes, chases, and combat [via isometric projection].'[120] Similar concerns to those that motivated Volition to bring the camera back to a third-person perspective in *Red Faction: Guerrilla* thus contributed to Rockstar Leeds' decision to lift the camera up sky high.

Further influencing the distinct narrative style in *Chinatown Wars*, the specificities of the DS hardware also motivated Rockstar Leeds' decision to opt for the game's unique cel-shaded look. Presenting Liberty City as a cartoon landscape, *Chinatown Wars*' art direction contrasts starkly with *GTA IV*'s realistic visuals. Whereas Rockstar North pursued a downbeat, carefully detailed aesthetic, Rockstar Leeds conversely sought a less refined, less serious style that not only complements the console's reduced capacity for graphical detail but also, suggests Hall, 'ensured the onscreen vehicles and characters really "popped"' on the DS' small screen.[121] The hardware limitations, however, influenced not only the visual presentation modes of *Chinatown Wars* but also its audio presentation, or at least the reduction in its use. Since the first *GTA*, home console entries in the series have incorporated spoken dialogue within cut-scenes. But, according to Hall, due to what the developer perceived as the poor quality of the handheld console's in-built speaker system, the decision was made to convey dialogue via subtitles only. 'We could have spoken audio', he said, 'but it didn't seem right for the DS ... [because of] the fact you will be playing this game on public transport and the speakers aren't the loudest.'[122] In this instance, assumptions regarding the hardware's limitations within an anticipated real-world context of game play, rather than technological constraints per se, informed creative decision-making.[123]

Thus far the distinctive elements of *Chinatown Wars* discussed stem from the DS' relative limitations. But the hardware's touch-screen capability, which distinguishes it from other home and portable dedicated game consoles of its generation, forms the basis of perhaps the game's most significant point of differentiation with home console *GTA*s. While the upper of the console's two screens usually displays the player-generated events, the lower screen (the touch-screen) usefully permits the player, through much of the game, to alternate Huang's weapons, access Huang's emails and view the Liberty City map. However, for certain game-play elements, Rockstar Leeds innovatively integrated the touch-screen in ways that mark a break in series convention. The developer utilised the input device to facilitate instances of player-generated events that in other *GTA* games either occur as scripted events or are elided altogether. As Hall suggests, the player uses 'the touch screen to fill in those little details left out of most console games'.[124]

The example of the process of car theft in *Chinatown Wars* illustrates this distinction. Likely the most frequently used means by which a player-character will navigate Liberty City in either *GTA IV* or *Chinatown Wars* is (as the series title hints) by stolen car. To heist a parked vehicle in *GTA IV* entails the player guiding Niko towards a desired car and then pressing a designated controller button. At this point, keeping within the standard third-person view, a scripted animation depicts, without any further player input, the act of car theft. Niko looks side-to-side, puts an elbow through the driver-side window pane, unlocks the door and sits within the vehicle; he can then be seen fiddling under the dash, an animation that presumably indicates the process of hot-wiring or some such activity. Subsequent to this fragment of scripted action, the car is running, and the player is able to have Niko take charge of the automobile.

In *Chinatown Wars*, to steal a parked car, the player similarly positions Huang close to a vehicle before pressing a designated button, which leads to Huang entering the car. At this point, however, Huang's first-person perspective from inside the car appears on the lower touch-screen, and the player is required to successfully complete one of either three 'mini-games' within a set time limit so as to start the car without activating its alarm. In one challenge, the player is required to have Huang insert a screwdriver into the car's ignition and then twist the tool in the designated directions. In another of the mini games, Huang must (via player guidance) hot wire the car by unscrewing the panel to the car's ignition and then twisting the correct wires together. A third game involves Huang installing an elec-tronic device into the car, cracking its immobiliser encryption, and then inputting the code. The incorporation of these brief games is entirely appropriate to the input of their intended hardware; making small circular motions with the DS stylus upon each of the screw heads as part of the hot-wiring task, for example, is simple and intuitive.[125]

Chinatown Wars incorporates many other mini-game sections that sim-ilarly result in events manifesting as player-generated action that would have been presented via scripted sequences in other *GTA* games (if they would have been presented at all). For example, while the use of sniper rifles, Molotov cocktails and road-toll booths have precedent within the series, in *Chinatown Wars*, the player can uniquely have Huang assemble the rifle, prepare the explosives and pay the road toll via touch-screen input. These sections within *Chinatown Wars* hold important implications for style, as they provide a hitherto never before witnessed close-up, first-person view on trademark *GTA* events. As Hall notes, the developer's motivation in using the touch-screen in such a way was to provide this new perspective on typical *GTA* storyworld action:

> [The] touch screen elements came from wanting to show more detail in the world than we could get from the standard camera. Even in a big console title, generally when the character is doing something, you just see their back while they play an animation. It seemed much nicer to let the player get in really close.[126]

In such instances, the specificities of the Nintendo handheld device thus influenced distinctive presentations of familiar events.

Conclusion

This chapter reveals myriad ways in which the inconstancy of technologi-cal hardware and software within videogames feeds into narrative, influ-encing the storyworld components of events, character and setting, their plotting, and also the style by which they are presented. It indicates, as a result, that considerations of the specificities of a medium and its narratives would do well to take into account the variability of production and consumption technologies over time and at a given moment. This is not to submit to a technological determinist philosophy, but rather to recognise that, due to the manner by which industrial systems tend to stimulate a fast pace of technological change, technology functions as a key subdimension of specificity within the narrative design conditions and processes of a given medium.

The chapter further signals the need to nuance two prevalent, related paradigms regarding technology within videogame scholarship and the broader gaming culture. It suggests that the perception of narrative and the industry's technological upgrade culture as oppositional components within the medium is a flawed one. The two components instead share a more complex relationship, with a given videogame narrative dependent on the unique affordances that a specific set of technologies provides. It also shows that publishers' reliance on the series format as a means to cope with the high development costs that the technological upgrade culture obligates does not, as is commonly assumed, prohibit narrative design innovation. Exploiting changes within technological conditions, narrative designers of games such as *GTA IV* and *Halo: Reach* did not merely reiterate previous instalments of these respective series but also successfully incorporated fresh elements within these storyworlds and developed new techniques by which to convey them. Upgraded hardware, then, can clearly open up new fictional possibilities for SDV series, which narrative designers sometimes aim to embrace.

Notes

1. Jon Dovey and Helen W. Kennedy, *Game Cultures: Computer Games as New Media* (Maidenhead: Open University Press, 2006), 52.
2. For key contributions to this debate, see Janet Murray, *Hamlet on the Holodeck: The Future of Narrative* (New York: Free Press, 1997); Gonzalo Frasca, 'Ludology Meets Narratology: Similitude and Difference between (Video)Games and Narrative', Ludology.org, 1999, http://www.ludology.org/articles/ludology.htm; Markku Eskilinen, 'Towards Computer Game Studies', in *First Person: New Media as Story, Performance and Game*, ed. Noah Wardrip-Fruin and Pat Harrigan (Cambridge, MA: MIT Press, 2004), 36–44; Espen Aarseth, 'Genre Trouble: Narrativism and the Art of Simulation', in *First Person*, ed. Wardrip-Fruin and Harrigan,

45–55; Jesper Juul, *Half Real: Video Games between Real Rules and Fictional Worlds* (Cambridge, MA: MIT Press, 2005); Ryan, *Avatars of Story*, 181–203; Gordon Calleja, *In-Game: From Immersion to Incorporation* (Cambridge, MA: MIT Press, 2011), 113–133.

3. Marie-Laure Ryan, 'Beyond *Ludus*: Narrative, Videogames and the Split Condition of Digital Textuality', in *Videogame, Player, Text*, ed. Barry Atkins and Tanya Krzywinska (Manchester: Manchester University Press, 2007), 14; Angela Ndalianis, *Neo Baroque Aesthetics in Contemporary Entertainment* (Cambridge, MA: MIT Press, 2004), 99–104; Geoff King, 'Die Hard/Try Harder: Narrative, Spectacle and Beyond, From Hollywood to Videogame', in *ScreenPlay: Cinema/Videogames/Interfaces*, ed. Geoff King and Tanya Krzywinska (London: Wallflower, 2002), 57–58; Andrew Darley, *Visual Digital Culture: Surface Play and Spectacle in New Media Genres* (London: Routledge, 2000), 149–151; Andrew Mactavish, 'Technological Pleasure: The Performance and Narrative of Technology in *Half-Life* and other High-Tech Computer Games', in *ScreenPlay*, ed. King and Krzywinska, 34.

4. Ryan, 'Beyond *Ludus*', 14; Mactavish, 'Technological Pleasure', 34.

5. Darley, *Visual Digital Culture*, 103, 106; Pierson, 'CGI Effects in Hollywood Science-Fiction Cinema'; Bukatman, 'Zooming Out'.

6. Darley, *Visual Digital Culture*, 155; Mactavish, 'Technological Pleasure', 34.

7. Prior examples of SDV include early text-based adventure games, such as *Zork I* (1980); the pioneering open-world games *Elite* (1984) and *Grand Theft Auto* (1997); id Software's trailblazing first-person shooters *Doom* and *Wolfenstein 3D* (1992); the first generation of 3D, third-person adventure games, notably *Tomb Raider* (1996) and *Super Mario 64* (1996); and the first wave of Japanese role-playing games (J-RPGs), which comprised *Dragon Quest* (1986), *Final Fantasy* (1987) and *The Legend of Zelda* (1986).

8. In contrast to the US television and comic-book markets, the videogame console industry is a far more globalised cultural market system (though publishers nevertheless often commission and target particular games for particular regional territories). Despite this distinction, I focus within this chapter on US published videogame series so as to maintain consistency with the other main case-study chapters.

9. Astrid Ensslin, *The Language of Gaming* (Basingstoke: Palgrave Macmillan, 2012), 143.

10. Juul, *Half Real*, 36.

11. Eskilinen, 'Towards Computer Game Studies'; Frasca, 'Ludology Meets Narratology'.
12. Juul, *Half Real*, 196.
13. Calleja, *In-Game*, 115.
14. Ibid., 148.
15. Ryan, *Avatars of Story*, 190.
16. Ibid., 190.
17. Juul, *Half Real*, 202.
18. Dovey and Kennedy, *Game Cultures*, 6.
19. Henry Jenkins, 'Game Design as Narrative Architecture', in *First Person*, ed. Wardrip-Fruin and Harrigan, 122–123.
20. Michael Abbot, '*Brainy Gamer* Podcast—Episode 35, pt. 1', *Brainy Gamer* podcast, 15 August 2011.
21. Jenkins, 'Game Design as Narrative Architecture', 126.
22. Edge Staff, 'Places: Aperture Science', *Edge*, 11 November 2011, http://media.nextgen.biz/features/places-aperture-science.
23. Ensslin, *The Language of Gaming*, 147.
24. See Rimmon-Kenan, *Narrative Fiction*, 61–70.
25. Margolin, 'Character', 73.
26. Anon., 'Tech Interview: *Halo: Reach*', *Eurogamer*, 11 December 2010, http://www.eurogamer.net/articles/digitalfoundry-halo-reach-tech-interview.
27. Damián Isla, 'Handling Complexity in *Halo 2* AI' (paper presented at Game Developer Conference, San Francisco, California, 11 March 2005).
28. David L. Roberts, Mark O. Reidl and Charles L. Isbell, 'Beyond Adversarial: The Case for Game AI as Storytelling', Proceedings of DiGRA 2009, http://www.digra.org/dl/db/09287.57257.pdf.
29. Damián Isla, 'Building a Better Battle: The *Halo 3* AI Objectives System' (paper presented at Game Developer Conference, San Francisco, California, 22 February 2008).
30. Ibid.
31. Calleja, *In-Game*, 120–122.
32. Ibid., 121. The quick time event, a device approximate to the cut-scene, is an animated sequence that requires a limited amount of player input (such as a button press at a designated instance).
33. Jo Bryce and Jason Rutter, 'Spectacle of the Deathmatch: Character and Narrative in First-Person Shooters', in *ScreenPlay*, ed. King and Krzywinska, 71; Ensslin, *The Language of Gaming*, 149.
34. Bob Rehak, 'Of Eye Candy and Id: The Terrors and Pleasures of *Doom 3*', in *Videogame, Player, Text*, ed. Atkins and Krzywinska, 151–152.
35. Aarseth, 'Genre Trouble', 50.

36. Geoff King and Tanya Krzywinska, introduction to *ScreenPlay*, ed. King and Krzywinska, 28.

37. Aarseth, 'Genre Trouble', 51.

38. Ryan, 'Beyond *Ludus*', 14.

39. Andrew Hutchinson, 'Making the Water Move: Techno-Historic Limits in the Game Aesthetics of *Myst* and *Doom*', *Game Studies* 8, No. 1 (September 2008), http://gamestudies.org/0801/articles/hutch.

40. Nick Montfort and Ian Bogost, 'Random and Raster: Display Technologies and the Development of Videogames', *Annals of the History of Computing* 31, No. 3 (2009), 34–43. Bogost and Montfort's interest in technological specificity is further evident in their 'Platform Studies' book series. As part of this series, which Montfort and Bogost co-edit, each book considers a particular videogame hardware platform's supports and constraints. Platforms considered within the series include the Atari VCS and the Nintendo Wii. Nick Montfort and Ian Bogost, *Racing the Beam: The Atari Video Computer System* (Cambridge, MA: MIT Press, 2009); Steven E. Jones and George K. Thiruvathukal, *Codename Revolution: The Nintendo Wii Platform* (Cambridge, MA: MIT Press, 2012).

41. For a review of McLuhan's theories on technological determinism, see Stephen Kline, Nick Dyer-Witheford and Greg De Peuter, *Digital Play: The Interaction of Technology, Culture and Marketing* (Montreal & Kingston: McGill-Queen's University Press, 2003), 33–37.

42. Williams, *Television, Technology and Cultural Form*, 14, 124, 130.

43. Dovey and Kennedy, *Game Cultures*, 43–52.

44. Kline et al., *Digital Play*, 46–59.

45. Ibid., 82–83.

46. Dovey and Kennedy, *Game Cultures*, 52.

47. Ibid., 50–51.

48. For example, analysts suggested prior to the launch of the PlayStation 3 that Sony would lose $307 on each of the 20-gigabyte versions it sold (at launch price). James Niccolai, 'Sony Losing Big Money on PS3 Hardware', *PC World*, 16 November 2006, http://www.pcworld.com/article/127906/sony_losing_big_money_on_ps3_hardware.html.

49. See Tristan Donovan, *Replay: The History of Video Games* (Lewes: Yellow Ant, 2010), 265–267.

50. Kline et al. describe this advert and other promotional strategies of the period in detail in Kline et al., *Digital Play*, 153–154.

51. Jesper Juul, *A Casual Revolution: Reinventing Video Games and their Players* (Cambridge, MA: MIT Press, 2010), 13.

52. 'PS4 Pro: Introducing the Super-Charged PS4', Playstation.com, https://www.playstation.com/en-gb/explore/ps4/ps4-pro/.

53. The Wii vastly outsold its home console contemporaries, the Xbox 360 and the PlayStation 3; the DS became in 2011 the largest selling console in the history of the US market. Brent Williams, '2010 Year on Year Sales and Market Share Update to June 26th', *VGChartz*, 2 July 2011, http:// www.vgchartz.com/article/80751/2010-year-on-year-sales-and-market-share-update-to-june-26th/; J. C. Fletcher, 'Nintendo is Now Best-Selling Console Ever in the US', *Joystiq*, 4 January 2011, http://www. joystiq.com/2011/01/04/nintendo-ds-is-now-best-selling-console-ever-in-us/.

54. James Newman, 'The Myth of the Ergodic Videogame: Some Thoughts on Player-Character Relationships in Videogames', *Game Studies* 2, No. 1 (July 2002), http://www.gamestudies.org/0102/newman/.

55. Dovey and Kennedy, *Game Cultures*, 47–69.

56. Amy Harmon, 'Disney Rubs the Video Lamp', *Los Angeles Times*, 5 June 1993, http://articles.latimes.com/1993-06-05/business/fi-43676_1_ video-game-development.

57. Ralph Edwards, 'The Economics of Game Publishing', *IGN*, 6 May 2006, http://uk.games.ign.com/articles/708/708972p1.html.

58. Rob Crossley, 'Study: Average Dev Costs as High as $28 m', *Develop*, 11 January 2010, http://www.develop-online.net/news/33625/Study-Average-dev-cost-as-high-as-28m.

59. Tristan Donovan provides a useful chapter on the emergence of this development scene. Donovan, *Replay*, 357–369.

60. Tony Ponce, '*Max Payne 3* Potentially Cost $105 Million to Develop', *Destructoid*, 10 September 2011, https://www.destructoid.com/max-payne-3-potentially-cost-105-million-to-develop-211058.phtml; Brendan Sinclair, '*GTA V* Dev Costs Over $137 Million, Says Analyst', gamesindustry.biz, http://www.gamesindustry.biz/articles/2013-02-01-gta-v-dev-costs-over-USD137-million-says-analyst.

61. James Newman, *Videogames* (London: Routledge, 2004), 37.

62. Dovey and Kennedy provide a more detailed consideration of the game engine's role. Dovey and Kennedy, *Game Cultures*, 57–59.

63. Ibid., 58–59.

64. Ibid., 47–49.

65. Separate to this process, the console market has also seen the emergence in the 2010s of an alternative mode of videogame financing, in the form of crowdfunding via sites such as Kickstarter, which enable online users to financially contribute to studios' projects. Due to the relatively low amount of money they typically generate, crowdfunding campaigns are more suited to the financing of smaller titles rather than projects intended for the full-price boxed-retail games sector. For analysis of how crowdfunding influences processes of videogame development, see Anthony

N. Smith, 'The Back-Developer Connection: Exploring Crowdfunding's Influence on Video Game Production', *New Media & Society* 17, No. 2 (2015), 198–214.

66. Dovey and Kennedy, *Game Cultures*, 49–50.

67. Stephen Totilo, 'Why Activision Let Go of *Ghostbusters* and 50 Cent games', *MTV Multiplayer*, 11 May 2008, http://multiplayerblog.mtv.com/2008/11/05/why-activision-let-go-of-ghostbusters-and-50-cent-games/Wire.

68. For example, with regard to full-priced boxed-retail games, 34 sequels to ongoing console game series were released in the last four months of 2011 (the industry's busiest period). In comparison, only seven non-sequel licensed games (based on multi-media franchises and sports/pop-culture personalities) were released, and only three were based on original intellectual properties.

69. Dovey and Kennedy, *Game Cultures*, 47.

70. Ibid., 59. Epic's Unreal Engine, for example, has proved particularly appropriate for first/third-person shooters and adventure games. This is demonstrated by its implementation in not only Epic's own *Unreal Tournament* and *Gears of War* franchises, but also the *Mass Effect*, *BioShock* (2007–2013) and *Batman: Arkham* series.

71. 343 Industries, a subsidiary of Microsoft Studios, took over the development reins of the Microsoft-owned *Halo* franchise subsequent to *Reach*.

72. Rob Taylor, '*Halo: Reach*: Creative Director on the Tech, AI and World of Reach', *Computer and Video Games*, 24 August 2010, http://www.computerandvideogames.com/261532/interviews/halo-reach/.

73. Tom Ivan, '*Halo: Reach* "Bending the Xbox as Far as it'll Bend"', *Edge*, 22 January 2010, http://www.next-gen.biz/news/halo-reach-ibending-xbox-far-itll-bendi.

74. Xi Wang, 'Automated Level of Detail Generation in *Halo: Reach*' (presentation given at Game Developers Conference, San Francisco, California, 4 March 2011).

75. Dan Ryckert, '*Halo: Reach* Developer Commentary', *Game Informer*, 25 January 2010, http://www.gameinformer.com/b/features/archive/2010/01/25/halo-reach-dev-commentary.aspx.

76. LikeTotallyAwesome, '*Halo: Reach* Interview', YouTube, 13 September 2010, http://www.youtube.com/watch?v=EeMVt0wLuIg.

77. Geoff King and Tanya Krzywinska, *Tomb Raiders and Space Invaders: Videogame Forms and Contexts* (London: I. B. Tauris, 2005), 87.

78. Mathew Kumar, 'Bungie on Eight Years of Halo AI', *Gamasutra*, 6 August 2008, http://www.gamasutra.com/php-bin/news_index.php?story=19653.

79. Anon., 'Tech Interview: *Halo: Reach*'.

80. The game's vehicular missions, however, are often exceptions to this rule.

81. Sketch, '*Halo: Reach*—3D Art Evolved', *Bungie*, 26 January 2010, http://www.bungie.net/news/content.aspx?type=topnews& cid=24541.

82. Matt Miller, '*Halo: Reach*', *Game Informer*, February 2010, 56.

83. Barry Atkins, *More than a Game: The Computer Game as Fictional Form* (Manchester: Manchester University Press, 2003), 63.

84. *IGN*'s review, for example, commented that the game lacked an 'outstanding depth of field'. Aaron Boulding, '*Halo* Review', *IGN*, 9 November 2001, http://uk.xbox.ign.com/articles/165/165922p1.

85. For example, one reviewer remarked, 'The single most impressive visual flair to *Halo 3* has to be the draw distance, the sense of scale is somewhat mind-numbingly beautiful.' Wayne Julian, '*Halo 3* Review', *MS Xbox World*, 24 September 2007, http://www.msxboxworld.com/xbox360/reviews/136/halo-3/review.html.

86. Digital Foundry, 'Tech Analysis: *Halo: Reach*', *Eurogamer*, 18 September 2010, http://www.eurogamer.net/articles/digitalfoundry-halo-reach-tech-analysis-article.

87. Taylor, '*Halo: Reach*: Creative Director on the Tech, AI and World of Reach'.

88. Miller, '*Halo: Reach*', 56.

89. The critic Steven Poole, for example, suggests, 'This alternation of cutscenes and playable action delivers a very traditional kind of storytelling yoked rather arbitrarily to essential videogame challenges of dexterity and spatial thought.' Steven Poole, *Trigger Happy: The Inner Life of Videogames* (London: Fourth Estate, 2000), 109.

90. Edge Staff, '*Halo: Reach*—Tales of the Fall', *Edge*, 21 January 2010, http://www.next-gen.biz/features/halo-reach-tales-fall.

91. Marie-Laure Ryan, 'From Narrative Games to Playable Stories', *Storyworlds* 1, No. 1 (2009), 50.

92. Games such as the PC FPS *Half-Life* had previously provided deformable environments, but the amounts of damage that these earlier games permit are more limited.

93. Joe Fielder, '*Red Faction* Review', *Gamespot*, 23 May 2001, http://uk.gamespot.com/ps2/action/redfaction/review.html; David Smith, '*Red Faction II*', *IGN*, 9 October 2002, http://uk.ps2.ign.com/articles/373/373878p1.html.

94. Gamesweasel, '*Red Faction: Guerilla* Interview with Sean Kennedy', YouTube, 22 May 2009, http://www.youtube.com/watch?v=ZhV-o_cH26w&.

95. 2.0, '*Red Faction: Guerrilla* Developer Interview: Smashy Smashy', *True Game Headz*, 1 June 2009, http://www.truegameheadz.com/blog-headz/red-faction-guerrilla-developer-interview-smashy-smashy/.

96. GamingOnly, 'Interview *Red Faction: Guerilla* with Producer Rick White', YouTube, 17 September 2008, http://www.youtube.com/watch?v=sip7dh2qC7U&.

97. Gamesweasel, '*Red Faction: Guerilla* Interview with Sean Kennedy'.

98. GamePro, '*Red Faction: Guerrilla*: Developer Interview', MetaCafe, 9 August 2009, http://www.metacafe.com/watch/3151591/red_faction_guerrilla_developer_interview/.

99. Anon., '*Red Faction: Guerilla* Interview 1', *Gamespot*, 23 March 2009, http://uk.gamespot.com/xbox360/action/redfactioniii/video/6206516.

100. Ibid.; GamePro, '*Red Faction: Guerrilla*: Developer Interview'.

101. Tom Orry, '*Red Faction: Guerilla* Preview', *VideoGamer.com*, 14 April 2009, http://www.videogamer.com/xbox360/red_faction_3/preview-1628.html.

102. Ibid.

103. Ben Fritz, 'Dan Houser's Very Extended Interview About Everything *GTA IV*', *Variety*, 19 April 2008, http://weblogs.variety.com/the_cut_scene/2008/04/dan-housers-ver.html.

104. Darley, *Visual Digital Culture*, 31.

105. Dovey and Kennedy, *Game Cultures*, 53–57; King and Krzywinska, *Tomb Raiders and Space Invaders*, 125–152.

106. Edge Staff, 'The Making of *Grand Theft Auto IV*', *Edge*, 18 March 2008, http://www.next-gen.biz/features/making-grand-theft-auto-iv.

107. Hilary Goldstein, '*GTA IV*: Building a Brave New World', *IGN*, 28 March 2008, http://uk.xbox.360.ign.com/articles/863/863028p1.html; Fritz, 'Dan Houser's Very Extended Interview About Everything *GTA IV*'.

108. Ibid.

109. Edge Staff, 'The Making of *Grand Theft Auto IV*'.

110. Edge Staff, '*Grand Theft Auto IV* Review', *Edge*, 13 May 2008, http://www.next-gen.biz/reviews/grand-theft-auto-iv-review.

111. Fritz, 'Dan Houser's Very Extended Interview About Everything *GTA IV*'.

112. Ibid.

113. Ibid.

114. King and Krzywinska, *Tomb Raiders and Space Invaders*, 129.

115. Adam Doree, 'Welcome to *Grand Theft Auto IV*', *VideoGamesDaily*, 25 May 2007, http://archive.videogamesdaily.com/news/200705/101_p2.asp.

116. Edge Staff, 'The Making of *Grand Theft Auto IV*'.

117. Craig Harris, 'Rockstar Leeds Talks *GTA* DS', *IGN*, 25 February 2009, http://uk.ds.ign.com/articles/957/957177p1.html.

118. The *Gamespot* review, for example, noted the unusualness of the freedom to roam that *GTA* provides. Ryan MacDonald, '*GTA: Grand Theft Auto*: European Version Review', *GameSpot*, 6 May 1998, http://uk.gamespot.com/ps/adventure/grandtheftauto/review.html.

119. Harris, 'Rockstar Leeds Talks *GTA* DS'.

120. Greg Ford, 'Exclusive *Grand Theft Auto: Chinatown Wars* Interview', *1up*, 5 December 2008, http://www.1up.com/previews/grand-theft-auto-chinatown-wars_2.

121. Ibid.

122. Harris, 'Rockstar Leeds Talks *GTA* DS'.

123. Elizabeth Evans observes that similar assumptions regarding portable media usage (as opposed to technological constraints) led to episodes of the *24* transmedia extension series *24: Conspiracy* being far shorter than those of the related television series. Evans, *Transmedia Television*, 123–124.

124. Ford, 'Exclusive *Grand Theft Auto: Chinatown Wars* Interview'.

125. In contrast, to replicate such game play with a traditional controller would require the manoeuvring of a cursor via analogue stick, a process that would likely be fiddly and tedious.

126. Harris, 'Rockstar Leeds Talks *GTA* DS'.

CHAPTER 6

Conclusion

Three related hypotheses drove the undertaking of this book:

1. Within our twenty-first century media convergence context, a given medium's set of industrial practices continues to uniquely condition narrative design processes.
2. Conditions of narrative design within a given medium are, due to the unfixed nature of various industrial factors, variable over time and at a given moment.
3. This variability in narrative design conditions can hold important implications for a given medium's narratives.

The book largely confirms these hypotheses. Via its comparative study of the *Star Wars* transmedia entertainment franchise it shows how the narrative design processes of *Star Wars* films and *Star Wars Rebels* were each uniquely informed by medium-specific industrial practices, leading to clear discrepancies between the film and television texts. Despite claims therefore that the perception of media as distinct entities is approaching redundancy within our contemporary era of media convergence, industrial practices continue to preserve conventional medium identities.

With specific regard to technological convergence, Chaps. 3 and 4 furthermore show how media institutions often utilise new media technologies as a means to complement and continue traditional medium-specific practices. For example, the licensing of broadcast network content to

© The Author(s) 2018
A. N. Smith, *Storytelling Industries*,
https://doi.org/10.1007/978-3-319-70597-2_6

streaming services such as Netflix has developed as a means to drive viewership of live network broadcasts. A further example: the mainstream comic-book industry appears to be primarily developing the digital comics market as a means to sell digitised versions of printed comic books. Rather than flatten traditional media boundaries, then, technological convergence has resulted in various interplays between internet-based technologies and conventional medium-specific practices.

The book also firmly establishes that the sets of possibilities made available to narrative designers within a given medium contrast across time and at a given moment due to the myriad distinct ways in which markets, audiences, institutions and technologies are configured. It further demonstrates the wide significance of such variability in narrative design conditions to narrative design processes, detailing the ways in which narratives come to reflect the specificities of their production contexts.

In revealing the connections between the instability of a given medium and its accumulation of disparate narrative design conditions and processes, the book makes an important intervention within transmedial narratology. As previously noted, studies into the particular ways in which a given medium informs a given narrative typically neglect to acknowledge and/or explore either the volatility of a given medium or the resulting implications for narrative. This book, however, suggests that such studies, due to their underlying perception of a given medium as a stable entity, fail to articulate the full complexities of the interrelation between narratives and a given medium's industrial contexts. Through the introduction of the dimensions of specificity model the book provides a means to unravel these complexities and account for the contrasting specificities within a given medium. Via its taxonomical breakdown of a medium's subordinate dimensions, the model enables scholars to trace the various factors and connections that prompt a medium's high variability of narrative design conditions and processes.

The book's application of this model within comics, television and videogames media has helped to demonstrate this use. Through focusing on the sub-dimensions of audience, economic and technological specificity, and considering each in relation to a single contemporary US media industry, the book tracks the various ways in which industrial variation within a medium fuels a plurality of distinct narrative design conditions. My accompanying analysis of narrative design processes from across contrasting conditions within contemporary US media industries indicates the wide reaching implications of medium inconstancy. As the main case study chapters suggest, the respective specificities of different audiences, technologies and economic models within the US have led to clear divergences in the construction of storyworlds, the plotting of storyworld events and the styles by which storyworlds are presented.

With regard to storyworld events, for example, the specificities of processing and memory capacity within late 2000s console hardware facilitated within *Red Faction: Guerrilla* player-generated action that contrasts with that of earlier games in the series. With regard to character, Marvel Comics' aims of attracting film-going audiences led to the alteration of superheroes' costumes, physical builds and the personas of their secret identities. With regards to setting, Netflix and HBO's subscription-based model permitted the assembly of the elaborate period spaces of *The Get Down* and *Boardwalk Empire*, environments that, due to their high costs, network and basic cable models would find difficult to countenance. With regard to plotting, comic-book publishers' imperative to appeal to wider audiences has seen writers arrange storyline lengths so as to complement their publication in the collected edition format, leading to plot durations distinct from those of the era of direct market dominance. With regard to style, the specificities of the Nintendo DS handheld console influenced Rockstar Leeds to institute a distant and elevated view on player-generated action in *GTA: Chinatown Wars*, a narrative perspective that serves as point of contrast with the standard third-person view deployed in the simultaneously developed *GTA IV*.

While the book establishes the high variability of a given medium it also indicates how a medium can be so internally inconsistent and yet retain a distinct identity. This is evident, for example, with regard to the widespread practice within television industries of commissioning and transmitting narratives as season units. As Chap. 3 makes plain, the contrasting season formats of network and cable drama series each hold implications for narrative that are distinct from those of the other. But, despite the important differences, each of the two formats still more generally represent a condition of narrative design unique to television; the way in which each of the formats ensures that a given grouping of episodes is commissioned, marketed and broadcast as a distinct narrative portion, and which is bordered by lengthy hiatuses in transmission, has no true analogue within other media.[1] So, while discrepancy in season formats is one particular example of contrast within television's narrative design conditions, this variation does little to undermine the perception of television as a distinct and meaningful medium category within the study of narrative and media. While a given medium's general inconsistency should be taken into account when assessing the connections that link narrative and media, the combination of a medium's diversity of conditions still, then, factors into its uniqueness.

A further conclusion to draw from the book's research findings concerns the various connections of influence that occur across contrasting conditions within a medium. While this volume clearly establishes that the heterogeneity of a given medium influences great narrative variation, it also often indicates that clear and highly particular narrative similarities are able to emerge within a given medium *despite* discrepancies in industrial contexts. Notwithstanding the plurality of economic models commissioning primetime drama series in the US over recent decades, the traditional network-derived act structure device, whereby episode running times are punctuated at regular intervals by narrative turning points, has largely transcended institutional categories. Despite the specificities of the US comic-book market, superhero narratives, such as *Runaways*, have come to incorporate storyworld elements clearly emulative of shojo manga, a loose genre developed within a different national market.

The explanation for the persistence of clear narrative similarities across multiple distinct production contexts can generally be put down to the flows of influence that circulate through and between contrasting conditions within a medium. As Chap. 3 observes with regard to the various narrative likenesses shared between premium and basic cable drama series, the many distinct industrial contexts that comprise a given medium do not each operate within a separate vacuum; instead commissioning institutions and narrative designers often absorb influences from outside of their particular industrial sphere.

The nexus of influences that evidently link the distinct narrative design conditions within a medium appear comparable to what scholars often refer to as the 'media ecology' that binds different media together as a connected system.[2] Scholars such as Jay David Bolter and Richard Grusin have shown how influence can flow through this quasi-ecological system, their theory of remediation accounting for the manner by which the representational techniques of one medium are translated within another.[3] (US comic-book writers and illustrators' practice of adapting Hollywood's cinematographic techniques, which Chap. 4 details, is one such example of this process.) Scholars within the field of transmedial narratology have certainly emphasised the need to consider the influences that circulate between different media within a wider network.[4] This book's research, however, suggests that a medium's array of distinct institutional contexts comprise their own ecological system, within which influences circulate between distinct conditions. The research suggests that, in understanding the connections between narrative and an individual medium, it is of potential use to consider the implications of not only a medium's array of contrasting narrative design conditions but also the influences that travel between them.

While the book permits important conclusions to be drawn regarding the links between narrative and media, further research via the application of the dimensions of specificity model has the potential to increase our understanding of these relationships. A full exploration of national specificity, the one sub-dimension of specificity that the book fails to consider in depth, would be of particular use. Building upon the three main case study chapters' consideration of narrative design conditions *within* twenty-first century US television, comic book and videogame marketplaces, future studies might, for example, compare each marketplace with others from within their respective media. While Chap. 4, for instance, considers shifts in publishers' intended readerships within the US comic-book marketplace, a further investigation might instead consider the specificities of this market system relative to those of the contemporary Japanese manga marketplace. Such a study might consider how the general industrial configurations of each market contrast, and also explore the implications to narrative design conditions and processes of any differences between the two.

As part of any potential studies into national specificity, it might be of use also to consider the significance of any interrelation between distinct national markets. As Chap. 4 makes clear, the circulation of Japanese manga within the US comic-book industry influenced narrative design conditions and processes in the US; but a study focused on both markets might consider if the presence this century of the sizeable overseas ancillary revenue source for manga (namely, the West) has in any way informed narrative design conditions and processes within Japan. As Christina Klein argues, global flows of culture are complex, multi-directional and can travel through multiple distinct industrial configurations.[5] Any examination of national specificity, particularly in regard to national markets within our highly fluid contemporary globalised economy, should bear in mind the manner by which distinct national market systems intersect.

However, while future studies into the connections that link a given narrative to its medium are most definitely required, this book serves as a necessary platform for the exploration of these deeper complexities. Through the introduction of the dimensions of specificity model it provides the apparatus to fathom the variable cultural forces that in part determine a given medium's identity. The clear understanding of a given medium's inconstancy that the model provides is, as the book's survey of narrative design conditions and processes within multiple media shows, a useful means with which to comprehend the complex relationship between narrative and media.

NOTES

1. In considering *Deadwood* in relation to nineteenth-century literary serial narrative, Sean O'Sullivan recognises television's practice of commissioning seasons of drama series as an important mark of distinction between the two media, and explores its implications. Sean O'Sullivan, 'Old, New Borrowed, Blue: *Deadwood* and Serial Fiction', in *Reading* Deadwood: *A Western to Swear By*, ed. David Lavery (London: I. B. Tauris, 2006), 121; Sean O' Sullivan, 'Reconnoitering the Rim: Thoughts on *Deadwood* and Third Seasons', in *Third Person: Authoring and Exploring Vast Narratives*, ed. Pat Harrigan and Noah Wardrip-Fruin (Cambridge, MA: MIT Press, 2009), 324–335.
2. For discussion of the 'media ecology' metaphor within media theory, see Ursula K. Heise, 'Unnatural Ecologies: The Metaphor of the Environment in Media Theory', *Configurations* 10, No. 1 (2002), 149–168.
3. Jay David Bolter and Richard Grusin, *Remediation: Understanding New Media* (Cambridge, MA: MIT Press, 1999).
4. See Ryan, *Avatars of Story*, 26.
5. Christina Klein, '*Kung Fu Hustle*: Transnational Production and the Global Chinese-Language Film', *Journal of Chinese Cinemas* 1, No. 3 (2007), 204–205.

INDEX[1]

---

[1] Note: Page numbers followed by 'n' refer to notes.

© The Author(s) 2018
A. N. Smith, *Storytelling Industries*,
https://doi.org/10.1007/978-3-319-70597-2

Printed in the United States
By Bookmasters